ACTIVE INTERVIEWING, BRANDING, SELLING AND PRESENTING YOURSELF TO WIN YOUR NEXT JOB

ERIC KRAMER

AXIOM
Business Book Awards
"SUCCESS THROUGH KNOWLEDGE"

2012 Gold Medal Winner - Career

Active Interviewing:
Branding, Selling, and Presenting
Yourself to Win Your Next Job

by Eric P. Kramer

Course Technology/Cengage Learning

Presented by Jenkins Group & IndependentPublisher.com

ABOUT THE AUTHOR

Eric Kramer is a "serial careerist" having held ten jobs in six distinctly different careers. Eric knows interviewing.

An accomplished career coach and consultant, Eric has used his clinical psychology background and extensive business experience to help thousands of individuals manage and advance their careers. Eric started his career as a clinical psychologist before becoming a thriving entrepreneur in software development and a sought-after career consultant. He has worked for both large and small companies, including serving as Senior Career Consultant and Career Center Manager for two of the country's largest career transition firms. As a Senior Consultant, Eric worked with hundreds of job searchers individually and in groups teaching them job search skills and coaching them through their interviews. Based on his background in psychology and through his work with transitioning professionals, Eric has become a career expert.

Eric has authored three books,

1. "Active Interviewing: Branding, Selling and Presenting Yourself to Win your Next Job"
2. "101 Successful Interview Strategies"
3. "101 Successful Networking Strategies"

Eric is the developer of the InterviewBest Interview Presentation- www.interviewbest.com – Tweets as InterviewBest and has numerous interview videos on YouTube at EricKramer

Eric earned a bachelor's degree in psychology from the University of Hartford and a Master's degree in Counseling Psychology from American University. He is trained in Positive Psychology Coaching and is licensed as a psychologist in the state of Pennsylvania.

DEDICATION

This book is dedicated to Zachary and Jake, the future and hope of the American workforce and terrific sons. Also, to Susanne, an entrepreneur who is courageously blazing a new career direction providing Well Being services to corporations and underserved communities as well as Covid 19 testing to essential companies.

I also dedicate this book to the thousands of job seekers whose wisdom, experience, and insights coalesced to guide the content of this book. Job search and interviewing is one of life's most challenging, frustrating, and disheartening undertakings. All job seekers, as the persevere day to day, searching for jobs to provide for their families and themselves are unrecognized heroes. I hope this book contributes to these heroes finding jobs they love and earning the money they deserve.

TABLE OF CONTENTS

Chapter 1 - The Job Interview is Broken

- Job Interviews are Broken
- Interviews Are Broken – Don't Make Them Worse
- Who is in Control Here?
- Interview Questions Are Not the Answer
- Job Interviews Are Broken, but You Can Repair Yours!
- Important Takeaways That Will Fix Your Interviews

The true nature of employment is hidden from us on a day-to-day basis. Employees go to work each day with the illusion of security and long-term stability—albeit less so today. However, the true nature of employment is that each day your employer makes a decision about whether to purchase your skills and experience, continuing your employment. As soon as your employer decides you no longer provide value, you are too expensive to maintain (financially or emotionally), or they simply cannot afford you, your employment is terminated.

Employment is a marketplace where your skills and experience are bought and sold daily. It sounds harsh, but here is the flip side: Each day you decide whether you are going to sell your skills and experience to your current employer. As soon as you determine that you are worth more than they are willing to pay, you have better opportunities elsewhere, or you can no longer abide by the culture or management, you take your skills and experience to the marketplace and find a better buyer. A recent LinkedIn.com survey found that as many as 78 percent of all workers are open to hearing about other jobs or are actively looking for other employment.

In any marketplace where products and services are bought and sold, salespeople and sales skills are critical to the process. Without salespeople, buyers would not have easy access to the products and services they require to do business. Large businesses have a sales force selling their products or services. In small businesses, the owner typically does the selling as well as the delivery of the product or service.

In addition, a marketplace may have "independent distributors" that represent or sell products and services of multiple companies. Independent distributors specialize in a market and have extensive expertise about the products or services in that market. For example, a distributor may represent several copy-machine manufacturers or software packages. In extremely crowded and complex markets, such as phone systems, customer relationship management (CRM) software, or manufacturing machines, companies may hire an independent consultant to help them select the best product or service to purchase.

In the job marketplace, you are a small business of one and an owner/salesperson. You are responsible for both selling and delivering your services. If you have been working at the same company for a while, you have sold a contract for your services that renews daily. Should that contract end, based on the company's decision or yours, you will be back in the marketplace in a sales role, selling your services. Depending on your level of skills, your experience, and your value in the marketplace, you may be contacted by an independent distributor to represent your services to a buyer. In the job marketplace, these distributors are known as *recruiters*.

Jobs are a marketplace, and you are an owner/salesperson who may find yourself having to, or wanting to, sell your services to a new buyer. What do you need to do to successfully sell your services in the job marketplace? Simply act like any good business would! Job searching works best when you approach it as a three-step, businesslike process.

*Step 1: Decide what services you are selling and to whom you are selling them. Then develop your marketing materials, including your resume, cover letter, biography, target-company list, positioning statement, references, and accomplishment stories.

*Step 1A: Develop your value-proposition statement, which should consist of four main parts:

*Capability. The services you can provide to an employer.

*Impact. The benefits your services provide to an employer. Benefits refer to time, money, quality, and efficiency that the employer will gain from using your services.

***Proof.** These are experiences, examples, and stories that support your capability and impact claims.

***Cost.** These are your compensation requirements and an assessment of the risks of hiring you. For example, if you are just out of school and have no success record, you are a greater risk. Likewise, if you are a career changer, you are a greater risk.

***Step 2:** Actively prospect for employers using a wide variety of marketing techniques, including live networking; responding to job listings; advertising yourself on job boards and social-media sites, such as LinkedIn; and working with recruiters.

***Step 2A:** Today's job search entails so many online resources, multiple job applications, and numerous contacts that managing information can get overwhelming quickly. Set up a job-search tracking system and record every interaction with a referral source and a potential employer in this system. Use this information to manage, measure, and track the progress of your job search.

***Step 3:** The interview is essentially a sales call. Prepare for your interview like any topnotch salesperson would by researching the company and the job and then developing an interview presentation.

Job Interviews Are Broken

You have followed the three-step process for your job search. You have a great set of marketing materials and a well-defined market, and you have networked and advertised yourself widely. As a result, you have been invited to interviews to sell yourself face to face with potential employers. Here is your challenge: More mistakes are made during the interview than in any other part of the job-search process, and the consequences of interview mistakes are catastrophic—no job offer. Here is the problem: The job-interview process is broken, and it has been for years!

Let's first define the employment interview. This is an interpersonal interaction between one or more interviewers and a job seeker to identify the interviewee's knowledge, skills, abilities, and behaviors that will be predictive of success on the job. The indicators of success in employment include prior job performance, training/education success, promotion(s), and tenure at prior jobs. In addition, the interview enables the organization and the job applicant to determine whether there are congruent values and interests—that is, a match between the individual's and the organization's values or a cultural fit. Overall, it's quite a task for an hour-long meeting where two or more people simply talk to—or at—each other. No wonder why it doesn't work.

There are numerous problems with today's job interviews. Some are due to the basic structure of the interview, others to the lack of the interviewer's skills, and still others to mistakes made by candidates. The following sections cover the leading problems.

Interviews Are Like a Coin Toss

According to a study done by Schmidt and Hunter, a structured interview based on a set of questions is only accurate at predicting job success 51 percent of the time. An unstructured interview with more of a free-flowing question-and-answer format, is only accurate at predicting job success 48 percent of the time.

According to a study by Leadership IQ, 46 percent of newly hired employees fail within 18 months (they're terminated, leave under pressure, receive significantly negative performance reviews, or receive disciplinary action), while only 19 percent achieve unequivocal success. This means only one in five people hired is a top performer, two will leave, and two will be just okay!

In other words, today's interviews could pretty much be replaced by a coin toss.

Subjectivity Is Rampant

"Intuition (n): an uncanny sixth sense which tells people that they are right, whether they are or not."

—Anonymous

Executives polled in a survey by Robert Half Finance & Accounting said it took them just 10 minutes to form an opinion of job seekers, despite meeting junior and intermediate candidates for an average of 55 minutes and management-level candidates for an average of 86 minutes. This finding reveals that an interviewer makes a subjective hiring decision in the first 10 minutes and then spends the rest of the interview narrowly focused on information that supports his or her initial decision.

Even companies with sophisticated selection software become subjective at the decision point. I recently spoke with a recruiter from a major pharmaceutical company about their selection process. Prior to interviewing candidates, the company feeds desired traits into an expensive interview-management system. The system generates a set of behavioral questions for interviewers to ask. The candidate is interviewed by three pairs of interviewers, all asking the designated questions and scoring the answers. At the end of the day, all the interviewers "huddle," the scores are presented, and the candidates are discussed. Then one member of the interview team will say something like, "That candidate Sally reminds me of Nancy, who works here, and Nancy does a good job." And voilà—Sally is hired!

Many hiring managers will talk about hiring candidates based on a gut feeling. The manager is unable to specify what the gut feeling consists of; however, he is convinced that he makes good hiring decisions. Many hiring managers fail to understand that hiring a person who works out is different from hiring a person who excels. Excellent candidates often lose out to simply adequate candidates based on a gut feeling.

Job Descriptions Are Poor

Any good purchasing decision, from canned soup to military aircraft, begins with a set of purchase criteria. These criteria specify the requirements the product or service must meet to be purchased. When you are reading a label in the grocery store, you are checking the product against your purchasing requirements.

In the employment marketplace, purchasing requirements are called *job descriptions*. Most companies spend more time deciding the requirements for purchasing stationery than they do determining and communicating the criteria for hiring employees. Poor job descriptions lack criteria and guidance for the hiring manager to make a good hiring decision and for the candidate to do her best sales presentation in the interview. How does a candidate know what to sell if the hiring manager is not sure what he is buying? Poor job descriptions are typically the result of a poorly defined job, which does not bode well for an employee's success in that position.

Interviewers Are Poorly Trained

Most hiring managers are poor interviewers. The vast majority of hiring managers receive no interview training, and they hire infrequently. Even hiring managers who have received training may not hire for months after interview training, and by then the training is forgotten.

One secret of job interviews is that hiring managers are often as nervous as the candidate—they're stressed about having to make a critical hiring decision. A bad hiring decision is one of the biggest mistakes a manager can make. Studies have shown that a bad hire can cost a company anywhere from two times a person's salary at lower employment levels to as much as 40 times a person's salary at higher levels. The financial ramifications of a bad hire include costs for recruiting, training, lost productivity, bad morale, and the manager's time spent trying to salvage the employee. At higher levels of employment, contract buyouts in the millions of dollars are not unusual. No wonder why the hiring manager is stressed when interviewing!

Many hiring managers compensate by spreading the decision-making around. They will have candidates go through multiple rounds of interviews with numerous interviewers. That way, if the employee does not work out, at least the hiring manager can say everyone was involved.

The problem with this approach is twofold. First, the other interviewers are typically no better at interviewing than the hiring manager is. Second, this burdens the candidate with numerous interviews conducted by poorly trained interviewers.

According to Development Dimensions International (DDI), candidates commonly complain about the following interviewer behavior:

*Withholding information about the position

*Turning the interview into a cross-examination

*Showing up late

*Appearing unprepared for the interview

*Asking questions unrelated to job skills

And a recent survey of interviewers by Monster.co.uk found that:

*Almost a third (30 percent) say they have forgotten a candidate's name.

*More than a quarter (28 percent) confess they have gone to interviews unprepared.

*Almost one in five (19 percent) admit they have forgotten an interview entirely.

*Fifty-four percent of employer respondents admit they have taken an instant dislike to a candidate.

Unconscious Biases Run Rampant

Like all of humanity, interviewers are vulnerable to unconscious biases that influence their decisions. Some biases that impact hiring include:

*Confirmation Bias – A tendency to search for or interpret information in the way that confirms one's preexisting beliefs. An example is the Hiring Manager that prefers hiring student athletes because they were a student athlete themself and they think athletes can take on multiple challenges at the same time such as studying and training. Is the student athlete candidate the best qualified – perhaps not.

*Decision Fatigue – Decision-making tasks drain people's mental resources; therefore, they tend to take the easiest choice. This may impact an interviewer after a long day of interviews. They become tired and hire the last person they interview. Is the last person interviewed thew best candidate – perhaps not.

*Dunning-Kruger Effect – This is an especially pernicious bias. This is a cognitive bias in which people who are ignorant or unskilled in a domain tend to believe they are much more competent than they are. In simple words, people who are too stupid to know how stupid they are. Many Hiring managers have no clue about how bad they are at interviewing but are convinced they can use their "gut" and hire the best candidate.

*In-group Bias – Refers to the unfair favoring of someone from one's own group. An interviewer might think they're unbiased, impartial, and fair, but succumb to this bias, having evolved to be this way. That is, from an evolutionary perspective, this bias can be considered an advantage – favoring and protecting those similar to oneself, particularly with respect to kinship and the promotion of one's own line. This results in prejudicial hiring and often overlooking the best candidate.

*Halo Effect – A cognitive bias in which an interviewer's overall impression of a person influences how they feel and think about his or her character. This comes into play when an attractive applicant is interviewed. Research shows attractive applicants are more likely to get hired. Conversely, applicants who don't make a positive appearance, don't get hired. This bias also comes into effect when an applicant's background is considered. If an applicant is from a prestigious school, they will be judged to be of better character.

Unconscious bias is a difficult obstacle to overcome in interviews. Because the bias is unconscious the interviewer will operate as if they don't exist. As a candidate you cannot confront biases head on however, being aware of possible biases will help you fix your interviews. Fix the interview by taking a more active role and making sure you communicate the information the interviewer needs to know that they may not ask about or focus on due to their biases.

Interviews Are Not Designed to Help Candidates Present Their Best

Think about a company buying a new accounting system. They do not call vendors and simply say, "We need a new system to do our books. What do you have?" They specify their requirements, establish a purchasing process to select potential systems, and then invite salespeople from multiple companies to present their products.

When a company is buying an expensive service, it behooves them to use a purchasing process that makes it as easy as possible for salespeople to make their best sales pitch. This includes a lot of upfront information about their requirements; access to company personnel to answer any questions; a well-defined purchasing process, including steps and a timeline, and a list of people involved in the purchasing decision.

Compare a purchasing process with the typical hiring process. A poorly defined set of requirements (job description); no access to the hiring manager to ask questions prior to the interview; an unknown timeline; and, other than perhaps the day of the interview, no list of people involved in the interview process. Similarly, to how they treat salespeople, companies should help candidates make their best interview presentation so that they, in turn, can make the best hiring decision.

Job Interviews Are Not the "Real World"

How often do employees go to a meeting with a supervisor where the agenda of the meeting is general, they do not know who will be in the meeting, they are not asked to prepare to present specific information, they are expected to answer questions on the fly for which they have not been able to prepare, and when the meeting is over, they simply get up and leave, hoping they did well? With any luck, not often!

Interviews are like this type of meeting. If interviews were structured more like real-world business meetings, candidates could prepare better, and interviewers would see candidates perform as if they were on the job. Observing the candidate performing in a realistic setting provides more accurate insight into the candidate's potential for excellent performance on the job.

Job Interviews Are Only Verbal

Only 20 percent of the population are auditory learners, thus only one in five interviewers will be able to retain more than 50 percent of the interview information they hear by listening to candidates. Couple this with the fact that interviewers pay selective attention to information that supports their initial impression (or bias) of the candidate, and this is a recipe for hiring mistakes. Forty percent of the population are visual learners, and forty percent are kinesthetic learners—they learn by doing or moving. So why is it that interviews consist of people talking to one another—the least successful form of learning? By adding a visual component, such as an interview presentation, interviewers' retention rates go up, they learn more about the candidate, and the candidate becomes more persuasive.

Interviews Are Broken—Please Don't Make Them Worse

Job interviews are broken, and many candidates take broken interviews and break them even further. According to Michael Neece, CEO of Interview Mastery, during a recession, the average applicant will interview for 17 jobs before getting one job offer. When job openings are plentiful and candidates are in high demand, the ratio drops to 6:1. So, candidates waste 6 to 17 job opportunities on broken interviews! The following sections will discuss how candidates make interviews worse.

Candidates Don't Think Like a Service Provider Competing in the Employment Marketplace

Most job seekers think of themselves as ex-employees, not as a business of one providing services that need to be sold. Employees are a part of a larger organization that provides a brand, infrastructure, sales support, training, career management, and a sense of being part of a team. Solo businesses operate independently, provide their own structure, develop their own brand, do their own sales and career management, and operate without the support of a team.

During a job search, if candidates maintain an ex-employee mentality, they become passive and hope that jobs will find them. They also believe that hiring companies will do a good job of finding talented people and interviewing them. With an ex-employee mentality, candidates are not active in guiding their interviews; they hope the interviewer does a good enough job without their intervention.

Taking on the attitude of a service provider competing in the employment marketplace is a powerful fix for the ex-employee mentality. Actively selling services to potential employers empowers candidates to guide their interviews and make sure they communicate the information the interviewer needs to know to make an informed hiring decision.

Candidates Fail to Communicate a Brand

A company brand is the personality of the company—what the public thinks and feels about it. Large companies spend millions of dollars managing their brand, with fanatical focus on even the smallest details, such as the color of flowers displayed at their meetings. They know their brand differentiates them, creates a unique selling positioning, and creates excitement in customers' minds.

Individuals have brands, although most people do not actively manage their brand. Consider the brands of those around you. Is the brand one of reliability, trustworthiness, and competence or of uncooperative and competitive behavior, pettiness, and unreliability? Are they always on time and prepared for meetings or often late and clueless? Are they "go-to" people in a crunch, or do you avoid them because they are easily flustered? And then, what is your brand?

When a company sends a salesperson on a sales call, the salesperson depends on the company's brand to help make the sale. If the brand is strong, the salesperson's credibility goes up, and the sale becomes easier. Imagine being a salesperson for highly esteemed companies such as Apple Computers, Amazon, or Google, as opposed to being a salesperson for disgraced BP or Goldman Sachs. Wouldn't your sale be easier if you worked for one of the first three companies? The same is true for a job candidate—the stronger your brand, the easier your "sale."

Job candidates do not have the luxury of spending millions of dollars to develop and advertise their brand. However, they do have the ability to define their brand and communicate it on their marketing materials and in their interview. For example, a candidate might brand himself as a strong leader, a good communicator, an analytical thinker, and a positive person with high energy. All these brand traits can and should be communicated to prospective employers.

Arriving sharply dressed, well prepared for the interview, and with a professional-level interview presentation communicates a positive brand. A brand has been well communicated when, after the interview, one interviewer turns to the other and asks, "So what did you think?" and the answer is, "That candidate seemed very well prepared and professional. I liked the way he approached problems analytically, he communicated well, and he seems to be a positive person with good energy." Determining your brand and communicating it in your interview is one of the interview-winning strategies you will learn in this book.

Candidates Sell Drills, Not Holes

Zig Ziglar, a well-known sales guru, said, "People don't buy drills, they buy holes." A customer will walk into a store and say, "I need a drill"; however, they really need a hole. Ziglar was commenting on the fact that the product being purchased, the drill, is only a tool to achieve the real desired result, the hole. The problem to be solved is the hole, not the item being purchased, the drill. Every person is hired to solve a problem, but many candidates don't focus on the real problem—they sell drills, not holes.

When a person is hired to unload a truck, what is the problem? Most people would say that the company is shorthanded and needs another person to unload the truck; the drill. However, the real problem is customer service. The truck has to be unloaded quickly enough to get the contents to customers, so they are satisfied with their delivery time. In an interview, potential employees could talk about how they will unload the truck, or they could address the issue of maintaining customer service, the hole, which they will do by unloading the truck quickly. Which is the more persuasive and powerful sales pitch?

As another example, consider a person interviewing for an accounting position. The candidate is told that the company needs someone to make sure the books are accurate because they have had trouble with the IRS in the past. Is the problem accurate books or avoiding the IRS? For this company, it is avoiding the IRS. The best "sales" approach in this case would be to communicate that, "I will keep the IRS from your door by making sure your books are accurate."

Candidates Focus Too Much on Interview Questions

> "Can a mortal ask questions which God finds unanswerable? Quite easily, I should think. All nonsense questions are unanswerable."
>
> —C. S. Lewis

Most interview books focus on how to answer the top 101 or the top 500 interview questions. And the most Googled topic for job interviews is "interview questions." Here's a news flash: There are more than 2,000 possible interview questions with more being thought up every day. They range all the way from the typical "What is your greatest strength/weakness?" to the unusual, such as:

*If you were a tree what kind of tree would you be?

*If you could be any part of a bike, which would it be and why?

*If John Lennon and Elvis Presley had to fight, who would win and why?

*If you were shrunk to the size of a pencil and put in a blender, how would you get out?

*How could you market ping-pong balls if ping-pong itself became obsolete?

*Rate how weird you are on a scale of 1 to 10.

*If you could be any superhero, who would it be?

*What would you do if you inherited a pizzeria from your uncle?

*What is the philosophy of martial arts?

*What is your fastball?

There is no way to prepare to answer all 2,000+ usual and bizarre questions, so why put so much emphasis on interview questions?

Like any good salesperson would, it does make sense to anticipate and prepare for questions. You can do this simply by asking yourself, "If I were hiring for this position, what questions would I ask?" After you have come up with a set of probable questions, prepare answers and then move on to preparing to sell yourself in the interview.

Candidates Ask Wimpy Questions

> "Judge a man by his questions rather than his answers."
>
> —Voltaire

One question asked in every interview is, "Do you have any questions for us?" However, most candidates don't have a good response to the question. Many candidates respond, "Not really" or "You answered all my questions." These are both weak responses that hurt your brand and indicate a lack of interest in or motivation for the job.

You should go into an interview with a set of powerful questions. A powerful question displays knowledge of the job, the company, or the industry. It indicates you have prepared for the interview and you have professional knowledge that enables you to ask good, insightful questions. I have had candidates hired in part due to the strength of their questions.

There also happens to be one all-time best interview question to ask an interviewer. I tell my clients that if they don't ask this question, they should kick themselves all the way to their car. This question is covered in Chapter 14, "Asking Powerful Questions."

Candidates Assume That Interviewers Know a Good Prospect When They Interview One

Imagine a person walking into a hardware store because he has a light on his front porch that isn't working. The person says to the clerk, "My front porch light doesn't work. What do you have for me?" The clerk knows the general problem but has no idea what to sell to solve it, as the cause could be anything from a burned-out light bulb to a broken switch. A good salesperson will ask questions of the customer to figure out the solution to the problem and then sell the solution.

Candidates go into interviews thinking that hiring managers have well-defined job descriptions and that they know the exact type of employee they want to hire. Not true! Often, the hiring manager knows the problem, but he doesn't know how to solve it or who can solve it for him. Hiring managers are on a fishing expedition, hoping to locate and catch the right person to hire.

This presents a great opportunity for candidates who are prepared to actively sell themselves into the job. The typical candidate will passively answer questions, and her answers may be good but not on target because the target is unknown. Candidates who are prepared to sell convince hiring managers of what they need to solve the problem and that they are the right solution. These candidates identify the problem and then sell themselves as the solution.

Candidates Sell Features Rather Than Benefits

Good salespeople sell on benefits; poor salespeople sell on features. A feature is a part of a product or service. It may relate to size, speed, parts, materials, power consumption, years in the marketplace, number of users, and so on. The benefit of the product or service is related to the problem it solves for the buyer. As discussed, buyers are focused on solving their problem. They care about features, but only to substantiate that the product or service will solve their problem and provide a benefit.

Most candidates try to impress hiring managers with their features. A candidate might say, "I have 10 years of experience running a project management office for a Fortune 500 company. I have a Project Management Professional certificate, and I'm a Six Sigma Black Belt. I have managed a staff of 200 people in five countries and have never gone over budget on a project." All that is great, but where is the benefit for the hiring company?

Most candidates stop short of saying "…and this is the benefit you will get from hiring me," and they let the hiring manager guess at the benefits. Your challenge is figuring out the problem to be solved, defining the benefit(s) derived from solving the problem, and then tying your features to the benefits. This challenge is addressed in Chapter 13, "Why Hiring You Is a Good Idea."

Candidates Follow the Herd

> "Be daring…assert integrity of purpose and imaginative vision against the play-it-safers."
>
> —Cecil Beaton, English photographer

Today, the competition for jobs is greater than ever. There are fewer openings, and companies are interviewing more candidates. During low unemployment, companies interview an average of eight candidates, hoping to find the best fit out of a small pool of candidates. In times of high unemployment, companies interview an average of 12 candidates, with the belief that they can find a perfect fit out of a large pool of candidates.

Most people tend to do what other people are doing, even when that behavior provides no advantage. Here is the question: What do you do to differentiate yourself in your interviews? Everyone being interviewed is qualified for the job; they all have good resumes, a good work history, and excellent references. All have read the typical interview information about dressing well, having a firm handshake, making eye contact, staying positive, considering body language, and so on.

Here is what they don't do: They don't use an Active Interview approach to differentiate themselves and sell themselves into the position. They do not go into the interview feeling confident, with a professional presentation that details how their background, skills, and experiences match the critical requirements of the position and with a clear sense of why they are the best candidate for the job. They have not identified their brand, and they do not communicate a distinctive brand to the interviewer. They have not learned presentation and persuasion skills and how to effectively answer any interview question.

When you have completed this book, you will be able to break away from the herd, brand yourself, differentiate yourself, and impress the interviewer. This book teaches a new and unique approach to job interviews with demonstrated dramatic success in winning interviews and landing jobs.

Who Is in Control Here?

Here is an interesting and pertinent question: Who is in control of a sales call? One might argue that the purchaser decides the time, place, format, participants in the sales call, and service requirements, and they make the final decision; thus, the purchaser is in control. This is all true; however, a skilled salesperson actively manages the sales process, influencing and guiding the sales decision. When you walk into a car dealership or an appliance store, the salesperson takes you through a sales process, hopefully leading up to a sale. You are in control of the purchase decision, and they are in control of the sales process. If they are good, then even if you spend more money than you intended, you end up feeling positive about the experience and your decision.

So, who is in control of the interview? Over the years, I have spoken with thousands of job seekers about their interview experiences. The most common complaint is that the interviewer spent the entire time speaking about himself or the company and didn't get to know the candidate. I often ask the job seeker, "Why did you let the interviewer get away with that?" Their typical response is, "What could I do? They control the interview." Well, what would a good salesperson do? A salesperson would take charge, guide the interview, and introduce the information she thinks the interviewer needs to know about her. In this book, you will learn exactly how a good salesperson would overcome this challenge in a job interview.

A very common misconception about interviews is that the interviewer likes being in control, and any effort to take control will doom any hiring chances. My clients' experience has been exactly the opposite: Hiring managers love to share control and be "sold" by candidates. Remember, typically you will have an unskilled interviewer stressed by making a critical hiring decision. When a candidate essentially says, "Sit back; let me take the lead and present the information you need to know to make a good decision," most interviewers are thrilled and relieved. Only once in hundreds of interviews has an interviewer *not* wanted to see and hear a candidate's interview presentation. That one time was a human resources representative doing a screening interview; the hiring manager loved the presentation.

This brings us to a related question: Who is to blame for a bad interview? The answer typically depends on whom you ask. The interviewer will blame the candidate for lack of preparation, lack of company knowledge, poor answers to questions, lack of good questions to ask, improper interview behavior, and so on. The candidate will blame the interviewer for lack of preparation, withholding information about the position, turning the interview into a cross-examination, showing up late, and/or asking questions unrelated to job skills. As you will read throughout this book, the blame for a bad interview is shared, although the problem of a bad interview is unfortunately yours. Good candidates are prepared with several interview strategies that will save the interview and win the job.

Interview Questions Are Not the Answer

Most interview books are compilations of answers to frequently asked interview questions. You will not find that in this book. As mentioned earlier, there are more than 2,000 possible questions, and you cannot prepare for them all. Too many candidates fixate on answering questions correctly and neglect to prepare to sell themselves. In addition, this missed focus has given rise to the number-one candidate interview concern—not answering questions correctly during an interview. Your number-one concern should be not selling yourself powerfully in your interview. How to change that is something you will learn about in this book.

Job Interviews Are Broken, but You Can Repair Yours!

As you have read, job interviews have a many chips and cracks. They don't do a good job of selection, but they are the gateway to your next job. Even though the interview process is broken, and you may have a lousy interviewer, you can fix your interviews. Yes, *you can fix your interview*. This is similar to a salesperson helping consumers be better buyers by taking them through a sales process that helps them understand what they need to ask, the information they need to know, and the right criteria for making their purchasing decision. The salesperson understands the purchaser's needs, establishes a trusted relationship, displays thorough knowledge of his and the competition's services, and clearly communicates why his services are the best choice.

You can fix your interviews by changing your attitude and approach to interviewing. Moving from a passive "answer questions" stance to a take-charge Active Interview approach will improve your confidence, interview preparation, interview behavior, and outcome.

You don't have to be a super salesperson to accomplish this; you just have to think differently and act differently. This book will give you all the information, strategies, and techniques you need to sell yourself into your next job. Will this book guarantee that you'll land your next job? No. But what this book *will* do is guarantee that by using the suggested techniques and strategies, you will leave your next interview confident that you did all you could to win the interview and land the job.

Important Takeaways That Will Fix Your Interview

*You are part of an employment marketplace where your services are bought and sold, just like any other service.

*Job interviews are broken, but you can fix yours and give yourself an advantage.

*You are more in control of your interview than you think, and interviewers are very open to sharing control.

*Interviewers are not always clear about the job requirements and the skills and experiences they are looking for in a candidate. You can help the interviewer clarify the requirements and be the candidate for which they are searching.

*Most candidates spend too much time figuring out how to answer questions and not enough time preparing to actively sell themselves in interviews.

*Doing the same things as every other candidate in the same ways will not help you win the interview. You have to break away from the herd and differentiate yourself.

* Asking good questions is critical to interview success.

*Hiring managers hire solutions to problems. Know the problem(s) and be the solution.

*List your features but sell your benefits.

Chapter 2 - The Job Search as a Sales Process

- The Top Six Customer Questions
- Selling Your Services
- A Job Search is Not the Same as Door-to-Door Sales
- Fear of Selling Is the Fear of Rejection
- Overcoming the Fear of Selling
- It Only Takes One
- Approaching the Job Search as a Sales Process Will Fix Your Interviews

"We are all salesmen every day of our lives. We are selling our ideas, our plans, our enthusiasm to those with whom we come into contact."

—Charles M. Schwab, founder and chairman of the Charles Schwab Corporation

Companies purchase talent as they purchase other services. In larger companies, there is a purchasing department responsible for managing the process of acquiring goods and services, and there is a human resources department responsible for managing the process of "talent acquisition." In smaller companies, a manager may be responsible for acquiring goods and services as well as for talent acquisition for his department. Regardless of company size, talent is purchased or acquired like all other services.

When purchasing services, a company goes through the following steps:

*Discovering a problem that requires a solution

*Documenting the specifics of the problem

*Determining that a service would solve the problem

*Developing a set of criteria and a process to evaluate available services

*Sending out a Request for Proposals (RFP) to service providers

*Evaluating and scoring the proposals

*Selecting a set of service providers as finalists

*Inviting the finalists to make face-to-face presentations

*Selecting one provider to offer a contract

*Negotiating the contract

*Signing the contract and receiving services

When hiring talent, a company goes through the following steps:

*Discovering a problem that requires a solution

*Documenting the specifics of the problem

*Determining that hiring the right talent would solve the problem

*Developing a set of criteria (a job description) and a process to evaluate available candidates

*Posting job description on job boards and, if required, contracting recruiters

*Evaluating and scoring cover letters and resumes

*Selecting a set of candidates as finalists

*Inviting the finalists for face-to-face interviews

*Selecting one candidate to offer a job

*Negotiating the compensation

*Signing the job offer and receiving services

As you can see, your talent is acquired by companies just like any other goods or services, so shouldn't you be selling your services the same way?

The Top Six Customer Questions

When customers purchase services, they typically ask six basic questions. These are the questions you will be answering as well in your interviews. The actual questions asked may differ in format or content; however, the underlying information remains the same.

***Who is [company]?** Customers are asking about industries or markets served, geographic presence, a layman's expression of the value created, time in business, and the size of the company.

***What do you do for customers?** Customers are asking about the value the company delivers and the top two- or three-ways customers benefit from it.

***Who are your top customers, and what do you do for them specifically?** Customers are asking for more specific proof or evidence that substantiates the company's claims of the value they deliver

***How are you different from other companies who do similar things?** The customer wants to learn the differences between the products or services the company provides and those offered by competitors. It is an attempt to clarify why selecting the company is the best choice.

***Others have made convincing promises about these things and then not delivered. How can we be sure that you will do what you say?** Customers have experience purchasing services that did not deliver the value promised, and they are concerned about being subjected to or persuaded by a clever sales pitch. They have been burned, and they are wary.

***How can we be sure that we would get the best value if we selected you?** Customers have multiple companies from which to choose. Asking this question forces a company to make comparisons with competitors and helps clarify the selection decision.

As you prepare for your interview, develop answers to these six customer questions. Then, in your interview, listen for these questions and use your prepared answers. In addition, develop examples and stories to support your answers. In Chapter 10, "Tell Stories That Engage and Persuade," you will learn how to develop powerful stories to support your claims of value.

Selling Your Services

In the employment marketplace, you are a vendor of services. All the rules of any marketplace, such as supply and demand, cost, profitability, advertising, and branding, apply to your services. In addition, like any vendor in a marketplace, you must actively sell your services to make a profit. The good news is that selling has been around for a long time, and there are tried-and-true strategies and techniques you can use to sell yourself into your next job.

The Three-Step Job-Search Sales Process

All businesses, regardless of size, go through a three-step process to begin building their business. Some businesses perform these steps formally, using a business plan, and others just wing it. However, most business experts agree that having a business plan is important to the success of a company.

As a job seeker, you are in the business of selling your services in the marketplace. Just as with any business, it is helpful to have a business plan. The typical pieces of a comprehensive job-search business plan include those covered in the following sections.

What Are You Selling?

Most job seekers can easily classify their professional identity and what their services generally include—for example, they may be an IT project manager, a banquet chef, a state representative legislative aide, a stockbroker selling energy stocks, a brand manager for consumer packaged goods, or an accountant. However, most job seekers do not sufficiently define the full range of services they provide, including intangibles that make them successful at the job. In addition to high-quality services, in a competitive marketplace intangible success factors differentiate you from your competition.

Services, Features, and Benefits

In defining your services, think like a business. What is the full range of features and benefits you offer? One business might differentiate itself by promising outstanding customer service, or it might offer a highly specialized component of the service that other companies do not have. One business might offer the base service but have ancillary services that add value and tip the buying decision in its favor. For example, a veterinarian might provide excellent pet care but may also have a mobile van for house calls.

What is the full range of base and add-on services you provide? For example, one of my clients was applying for a position as a manufacturing-plant manager. The position to which he was applying did not include reading blueprints or managing construction in the job description; however, during his interview he spoke about how he learned to read blueprints and manage construction contractors after having been involved in building a plant. The interviewer told him, "That's great! We're not currently building, but we anticipate that within 18 months, we will be expanding our current plant or building a new plant." My client was hired.

As another example, a client was applying for a staff accounting position. During his interview, he spoke about having been involved in evaluating, selecting, and implementing an accounting system. The posted job requirements did not include selection and implementation of accounting systems; however, coincidently, the company was beginning to consider purchasing an accounting system. My client was hired.

[4]**Personal Success Factors**

In both examples, the candidates evaluated the full range of services they provide, including ancillary services, and mentioned these related services in their interviews. It is equally important to identify your personal success factors. These are personal traits that make you successful on the job. Personal success factors can be classified into three categories:

*Interpersonal factors.** These pertain to interactions with others. Examples include ability to collaborate and facilitate, generosity, leadership, ability to convey feelings, ability to motivate, ability to sell.

*Personal factors.** These pertain to internal factors affecting only yourself. Examples include accuracy, adventurousness, good time-management skills, methodical nature, ability to take responsibility, ability to stay focused and productive, and optimism. In addition, an important and emerging personal factor is "learnability" this refers to your desire and motivation to learn new things. In an interview you may be asked, "What is the last thing you decided to learn on your own?" This question's goal is to evaluate your learnability.

*Information factors.** These pertain to how you think about things. Examples include analytic nature, ability to extract important information, ability to understand systems and identify underlying patterns, and ability to spot problems that matter.

In the terminology of the talent marketplace, personal success factors relate to the concept of a cultural fit. Companies select employees based on both basic services (experience, knowledge, skills) and how the candidate will fit into the company culture. A mismatch between the candidate and the culture will result in a bad hire. Presenting personal success factors as you actively sell your services in your interview will help the hiring manager get a feel for your fit within the organization's culture.

[4]Marketing Materials

Any business has a collection of marketing and sales materials. These include everything from business cards to websites, brochures, blogs, advertising, and sales presentations. Good marketing and sales materials clearly communicate the services provided, the brand, examples of successes, and the service's value to the marketplace.

After you have determined what you are selling—both skills and personal success factors—you are ready to develop your marketing and sales materials. These can include:

*Resume

*Cover letter

*Positioning statement (a brief "branding" statement about your services)

*Biography

*Target-market list (a list of companies for whom you want to work)

*Networking presentation (a printed presentation used when networking one on one)

*Interview presentation (a presentation used during an interview)

Developing these documents helps you think through your positioning in the marketplace and the message you want to communicate to prospective employers. Each document should contain a consistent message about your services, your brand, and your value to the marketplace. My colleague Ford Myers, a top career coach, does not let his clients even *begin* looking for a job until they have their marketing and sales documents developed and polished. He believes that without the documents, a job search is random and haphazard, which results in missed opportunities and numerous job-search mistakes.

To Whom Are You Selling?

The most successful businesses determine their ideal customer and only sell services to customers who match that ideal. For example, a business consultant that helps businesses grow may decide that her ideal customer has been in business for at least three years, has between $500,000 and $2 million in annual revenue, is privately held, has the CEO as an owner, and has at least 10 clients. This business consultant has determined that she is most effective with these clients, she can be successful selling to them, and she likes working with them. She has also learned that it is a mistake to take on non-ideal clients. The engagements don't go well, she dislikes the work, and the money she makes is not worth the stress.

Who is your ideal employer? The answer is not as simple as "any employer that will hire me and pay me enough," although this may become the criteria after a prolonged job search. Obviously, any definition of your ideal employer includes the requirement that the employer uses your type of services. However, what are your criteria beyond that? Think about size of company (revenue, employees), company culture, geographic location, company structure (private or public for-profit or not-for-profit), reputation, future growth, financial strength, flexible work hours, work from home, management style, and so on.

Well-defined ideal employer criteria can inform you about where to direct your prospecting and sales efforts. Of even greater help is a list of specific employers for whom you want to work. You can distribute this *target-market list* to individuals you meet during your job search. The goal is to get a referral to a contact within your target companies. As any salesperson knows, a warm contact beats a cold call any day.

Prospecting for Customers

After you have determined what you're selling and to whom you're selling it, and you have your sales and marketing documents finalized, you are ready to begin active prospecting.

Similar to sales, reaching potential employers is a fairly well defined, although challenging, process. A combination of the following works best: networking, advertising (posting your resume on job boards), public relations (maintaining a LinkedIn profile and/or a Facebook page, writing a blog), and personal selling (responding to job postings).

An underutilized job-search sales approach is a direct-mail campaign. This consists of sending three letters a day to various hiring managers at companies that employ people with your services. The letters are in direct-mail language, consisting of a grabber headline; a few brief, focused paragraphs highlighting accomplishments; a closing that says you will call to follow up; and a postscript. The PS is a brief statement of the benefits you will provide the hiring manager. It can reiterate benefits you have already stated, or it can make an offer. For example, "P.S. I would like to meet with you to tell you more specifically how I grew a company like yours from $2 million to $6 million in 36 months." (To learn more about this style of letter read up on information about copywriting. Copyblogger.com is an excellent source.) At the end of the first week, you will have sent out 15 letters. The second week you begin calling the people to whom you sent the letter the first week, and you send out 15 more letters. Within two to three weeks, you'll have a very active pipeline development process leading to interviews.

Prospects versus Sales Targets

During job search, you will have contact with a large number of people—some will be prospects, and others will be sales targets.

Prospects are individuals who work at companies that can hire you but that do not currently have any openings. These companies may have an opening in the next 60 to 120 days and are good prospects but not immediate "sales opportunities." It is important to maintain contact with these prospects on a regular basis, but they should not be the focus of your search. Put these individuals or organizations into a prospect file and touch base with them every four to six weeks.

Sales targets are individuals or organizations with which you have made contact and that have a job available now. You may have spoken directly with the hiring manager or submitted your resume. These are hot opportunities and should be the focus of your search.

It is important to maintain both a prospect pipeline and a sales pipeline, but it is equally important to differentiate between the two and spend your time appropriately.

Sales Is a Numbers Game

Salespeople understand that to close sales, they need a pipeline of prospects that they are continually replenishing. Each salesperson establishes a prospect-to-close ratio. For example, a salesperson selling office supplies knows that he must make 100 calls to prospects to have 10 conversations, get 5 face-to-face sales calls, and close 2 sales. His prospect-to-close ratio is 100 prospects to 2 sales. Good salespeople have trained themselves to be immune to rejection, knowing that each rejection gets them closer to a sale. As long as they keep making the 100 calls, they know they will make the 2 sales.

A job search is similar. Job seekers have a prospect-to-close ratio; they just are not aware of it. In good economic times, the prospect-to-sales ratio for a job search is approximately 30 or 40 to one. This means that a job seeker has to speak with 30 to 40 hiring managers (prospects) to land an interview. In a bad economy, this number goes up. Keep in mind that you don't have to talk to a hiring manager who has a job available; you just have to talk to a hiring manager who hires people with your services.

One of the challenges of a job search is constantly filling the pipeline with hiring managers with whom to speak. This becomes far easier if you don't limit yourself to hiring managers at companies advertising open jobs. You can access the hidden job market through prospective selling to companies in need of your services but not yet publicizing the need. In addition, depending on your consultative sales skills, you may be able to create a job for yourself at a company that was not aware they had a problem that would be solved using your services.

So how do you plan to sell your services once you get your face-to-face meeting? In a job search, this requires a powerful interview strategy, which is why you are reading this book.A Job Search Is Not the Same as Door-to-Door Sales

Many people have lowly opinions of selling and of salespeople. However, selling is a noble, challenging, and potentially very lucrative job. There are two types of sales: transactional sales and consultative sales.

Transactional sales evolved in the early history of selling (think of traveling peddlers); this is the simple matching of needs between buyer and seller. The main sales activities are finding prospects with a need and taking orders for the service at an acceptable price. Revenues increase when you make more sales calls and take more orders. In transactional sales, the customer generally is interested in the lowest price and chooses the low-cost supplier.

Transactional selling works where there is little differentiation of services, there is an ample supply of services, the services are simple, and there is ongoing demand for new service providers.

In the job marketplace, transactional sales techniques work well for lower-end entry-level positions with low wages and high turnover. These jobs are found by distributing large numbers of resumes, going into companies and filling out applications, and attending job fairs. However, even at the lower end of the employment marketplace, candidates still benefit from using a well-structured sales approach.

Consultative sales evolved in the mid-1980s and only came into full practice in the late 1990s. Consultative salespeople sell high-priced and complex services requiring longer-term relationships with customers. They sell in multiple calls over a lengthy time period and usually need to influence buying committees.

In consultative sales, salespeople add value through all stages of the buying process by developing an understanding of the challenges facing the customer and creating a vision of the potential solution. Critical sales activities involve having conversations about challenges or problems the customer faces. Questioning and listening are more important factors than communicating features and positioning statements. The purchase decision occurs through a proposal, contract negotiation, and solution delivery. The size of the transaction (cost) is managed by understanding the scope of the challenges faced by the customer and clarifying the value of overcoming these challenges.

Consultative selling is appropriate for businesses that offer a transformational service, such as consulting or specialized, rarely purchased items. Transformational services change the business processes of the client, producing a more productive organization or saving the client money. Suppliers of transformational services use consultative selling due to the customers' lack of understanding of the possibilities. Customers are aware of the challenges they face and are open to exploring alternative approaches, but they need to be sold on the service that solves these challenges.

The salesperson's responsibility is to clarify challenges and communicate a vision of a desirable solution. Most of the conversation will take place directly with key decision-makers and their influencers, while procurement officers play the role of a checkpoint at the end of the sales cycle. Quantification of the value of overcoming the challenge adds tremendous value to the sales process, both in facilitating the sale and managing the price.

Consultative selling is your best approach for a job search if you are at the professional level, from entry level to senior management. Savvy professionals position their services as enabling a more productive organization or saving money—why else would a company hire you? The critical skills of consultative sales include listening, clarifying problems, and communicating a vision of a desirable solution using the services you provide—in other words, why the company should hire you. As with all sales, the more substantially you can prove your value in solving the organization's problem, the easier the sale and the higher your salary.

Fear of Selling is the Fear of Rejection

Large outplacement companies that work with thousands of people in job searches never refer to the job search as a sales process. Their belief is that people are fearful of selling and referring to the job search as a sales process would overwhelm and immobilize them. Having worked with hundreds of job seekers and using the job search as a sales model, I have learned that this is not true. In fact, the opposite is true: Using the approach of a job search as a sales process helps job seekers feel more in control and more effective in their search.

So, what is the fear of selling? It's the fear of rejection. This fear becomes even greater when you are selling yourself rather than a product or service. Many very successful salespeople are bold, selling large, expensive items; however, when it comes to selling themselves, they become fearful and timid. Rejection of something impersonal, such as a product or service, is far less frightening than rejection of something highly personal, such as your skills and experience.

Fear of rejection is deep-seated in humans. Anthropologists believe that fear of rejection originated when primitive human beings lived in tribes and depended on the tribe for survival. Rejection by a tribe was essentially a death sentence. As the human brain evolved, the part of the brain that registers rejection combined with the part of the brain that registers pain. Thus, rejection is actually physically painful, and our fear of rejection is fear of pain!

Why is understanding the origin of rejection important? Because fear of rejection is one of the primary blocks for most people in becoming a good salesperson during their job search. This fear prevents people from going to networking meetings and connecting with others or making networking appointments. It prevents people from calling prospective hiring managers and pitching their services. And, it prevents people from being truly powerful in their interviews. Fear of rejection results in job seekers spending a lot of time on job boards, simply sending in resumes for job listings from which they get no response—but no direct, painful rejection, either.

To conquer the fear of rejection, start by asking yourself, "What am I actually scared of?" For example, "If I call this hiring manager to talk about a possible position, what am I scared of?" Or, "If I call this business acquaintance to meet me for a networking breakfast, what am I scared of?" Or "If I call the interviewer to follow up on my interview, what am I scared of?" Examine what you are scared of. Often job seekers are fearful that the person will not take their call, will not want to meet, will feel imposed upon, or will think less of the job seeker for asking. Is this the truth, or are you afraid of something that's probably all in your head?

Remember, the job search is a sales process. Think of situations in which you saw a commercial or read a brochure, or a salesperson contacted you about a service in which you were interested. Didn't you welcome the information and the salesperson's help? Now consider situations where you received information of no interest to you. Were you angry and annoyed, or did you just ignore it?

My guess is that you only get angry or annoyed if the information is pushed upon you in some aggressive or obnoxious way. The same is true in a job search. Companies and hiring managers like to learn about people who can contribute to the success of their company. Hiring managers are particularly thrilled to learn about people who will contribute to the success of their department. If you reach out to a company or a hiring manager and there is no current opening, typically they will politely ignore you.

I have often heard job seekers express concern that by calling or emailing a busy hiring manager, they are imposing and will anger or annoy the person: "I would call, but I don't want to impose upon him." Here is the reality: You can only impose on people who let you impose upon them. You have no power to impose on anyone without her permission. Busy people who do not want to talk to you will not let you impose upon them! On the other hand, if there is value in connecting with you, the busiest of people will find time in their already full schedule to meet you. Your challenge, like that of every good salesperson, is to convince the hiring manager that it is in her best interest to hear what you have to say.

Overcoming the Fear of Selling

Fear is a strong human emotion. Its grip is powerful. Taming your fears of selling yourself to prospective employers will make your job search briefer and more efficient.

You're a Salesperson Already, So What's the Fear?

Many of us don't think of ourselves as salespeople, but we are. We are selling our ideas and persuading people to do things all the time; we just don't think of it as selling. Want your kids to clean their room? Want your significant other to go to the movie of your choice? Trying to get a colleague to go along with your plan of action? In these situations, you are selling. We constantly use sales techniques to convince other people to go along with us. And what is the most effective sales technique? Showing the other person the benefits he derives from doing what you suggest.

Believe in Your Service

The best way to overcome fear of selling is to completely believe in the value of your services. Great salespeople love the service they are selling and believe the world would be a better place if more people used the service. They are on a mission to tell the world about the great benefits their service provides. If a person doesn't purchase, aside from being disappointed, great salespeople are genuinely concerned that the person is missing out on something important.

How much do you believe in your services as an employee? Are you completely convinced that an employer would lose a great opportunity if she doesn't hire you? If you are completely confident, then calling a hiring manager to inform her about your availability becomes far easier. Similarly, in your interview, if you come across as strong and certain, it is far easier to be persuasive about the wisdom of hiring you.

How does a salesperson become confident about his service? The first step is knowing the service inside and out. The salesperson must know all the details of what it does, its value in the marketplace, how it is delivered, the benefits it offers, how it's used, its strengths and weaknesses, and where it has had success.

Know Your Service's Value in the Marketplace

Consider all the various companies and people that sell the same services successfully. How do you choose which vendor to go with? Each service has a differentiator that separates it from the others and makes it more attractive to a particular purchaser. Each purchaser has different purchasing criteria; thus, many same-service vendors coexist.

If your knowledge, experience, and skills are in great demand and there is a shortage, you will have little difficulty finding potential employers. For many job seekers, their knowledge, experience, and skills are in demand, but there is no shortage of job seekers with similar knowledge, experience, and skills. Other job seekers find that their knowledge, experience, and skills are no longer in demand.

If the latter is the case for you, then you need to upgrade your skills through training or education. And if your knowledge, experience, and skills are in demand and you have a great deal of competition, you need to repackage yourself and highlight the qualities of your service that differentiate you and make you attractive to the right employer. Typically, this repackaging combines hard skills (knowledge, experience, and skills) and soft skills (interpersonal skills, emotional intelligence, reliability, flexibility, learnability and so on). This combination sets you apart from the competition, addresses how you deliver your service in the workplace, and helps you sell yourself to an employer looking for your specific set of skills and services.

The employment marketplace is crowded with many same-service vendors. So, how do you differentiate your services and prove your value in the marketplace? Do you have a special skill or a set of skills that makes you valuable? Do you have specialized knowledge? How do your personality and interpersonal skills contribute to your success on the job? For many job seekers, a set of skills or specialized knowledge does not differentiate them; rather, it is the combination of skills, knowledge, experience, and personal attributes that makes their services special.

To understand your value in the employment marketplace, first understand what the market values. Begin by assessing your specialized knowledge, experience, and skills and researching the marketplace for companies in need of those skills. I often hear from clients, "It's hard to describe what I do for my company; I wear so many hats." This is particularly true for employees working in small companies. But is there a common theme that runs through all those responsibilities? What personal success factors do you bring to each task? It might be that even though you are responsible for managing a doctor's office, you have outstanding project-management skills. Or, it may be that even though you do bookkeeping, you have terrific conflict-management skills. These are the skills that, when highlighted, will differentiate you in the employment marketplace.

When you have determined your value in the marketplace, you feel confident that employers will benefit from your services, and you can clearly communicate this value, you can attack the market with greater confidence and less fear.

Develop a Sales Attitude

Good salespeople work the sales process and don't focus too much on results. They know that if they are selling a good service using the right strategies with the right level of commitment and energy, they will be successful.

Good salespeople also have rewired their brain to see rejection as progress. They know they have a prospect-to-close ratio that holds true. Every time they speak with a prospect, even if the prospect doesn't purchase, the salesperson is one prospect closer to a sale. In your job search, focus on the process and measure your progress by the number of prospects with whom you connect.

My clients are always surprised when I tell them, "If you work this job-search sales process correctly, your biggest challenge will be how to manage multiple job offers at the same time." One of my greatest pleasures is telling my clients, "I told you so!" as they struggle to figure out which offer to accept.

Where Has Your Service Succeeded?

Salespeople take great pride in amassing positive reviews and recommendations of their services. One of the first things customers ask for is an evaluation or recommendation from a prior customer. How else can a buyer trust what the salesperson is saying? In addition, good salespeople have interesting and engaging success stories about how their services provided value to other customers.

Job seekers rely on their resume to tell the story of their services; however, most job seekers simply list the companies where they've worked and the services they've employed. Today's successful resumes include accomplishment statements that substantiate your ability to provide the services you advertise in your resume. For example, statements such as "Led a project team that implemented a $3 million enterprise software system for a Fortune 500 company. Installation was done on time and under budget" and "Received salesperson of the month three months running, exceeding sales quotas by 20 percent each month" show that the job seeker has proof of delivering the services he is selling.

Another way of substantiating your services is by getting endorsements. These can be in the form of written letters from prior employers, or they can be collected online on sites such as LinkedIn. Recent rule of thumb suggests that on LinkedIn you should have endorsements equaling 10 percent of your total number of contacts. In addition to putting a link to their LinkedIn profile on their resume, some job seekers are including brief endorsement quotes as well.

Know Your Strengths and Weaknesses

"What are your strengths and weaknesses?" Does this question sound familiar? Nearly every interview book written suggests that you should have a good answer to this question. If you Google the question, you will get more than 700,000 hits. However, interview books and websites that don't propose a sales approach are shortsighted in their suggestions about how to answer this question. They suggest knowing your own strengths and weaknesses that are typically related to soft skills—for example, "My strength is my ability to cut through confusion and establish a clear path forward," or, "My weakness is my tendency to be overly focused on details. I'm working on this by writing down and focusing on the major goals of a project."

Any good salesperson knows her service and knows her competition. Good salespeople sell around the weakness of their service, directly sell the strength of their service, and sell against the weaknesses and strengths of their competition. My suggestion is to know your strengths and weaknesses and the strengths and weaknesses of your competition.

Learning your own strengths and weaknesses is straightforward, but how do you learn the strengths and weaknesses of your competition? Typically, you will not know the other individuals competing for the job, so you'll have to make some educated guesses.

It is logical to assume that you are competing against other people with similar skills, experience, and knowledge as you have. So, what are your strengths and weaknesses relative to the skills, experience, and knowledge required for the job? What are your strengths and weaknesses relative to other people doing similar jobs either in companies where you have worked or in other companies? And what are your strengths and weaknesses relative to your co-workers and your bosses?

Understanding your strengths and weaknesses relative to your competition will enable you to position yourself to emphasize your strengths and sell around your weaknesses.

It Only Takes One

The nice thing about the job-search sale is that you only have to find one customer willing to purchase your services. Granted, it has to be a great customer, and it takes a lot of selling, but there are many great, qualified customers out there. Even in bad economies, there are customers for almost every service job seekers are offering. And as in every marketplace, the better salespeople make the sale.

Approaching the Job Search as a Sales Process Will Fix Your Interviews

Companies acquire talent the same way as they acquire any other service, and job seekers benefit by taking an active sales-oriented approach and using sales techniques in their job search. Using a sales approach will empower you to be more assertive, directed, and organized in your search. The more you use these skills, the more interviews you will be invited to. And the more interviews you have, the more interview practice you will get—and the more skilled you will become.

The benefits of using a sales approach include the following:

*You will have a well-defined service you are selling to the job marketplace and a strong set of marketing and sales documents.

*You will be more focused on establishing a good sales process and less focused on the outcome of landing a job. Focusing on the process rather than the outcome will improve your chances of landing a job.

*Companies know how to purchase services, and if you use a sales approach, it will be easier for them to purchase your services.

*Many candidates have a hard time "bragging" about themselves in an interview. Selling is not bragging, and it will empower you to present your most commanding reasons for why you should be selected for the position.

*You will have a better answer to questions regarding your strengths and weaknesses.

Chapter 3 - The Interview as a Sales Call

- The Basic Interview Tension
- The Interviewer is an Informed Buyer
- There is Only One Hiring Issue: Your Value to the Company
- There Are Only Three Questions
- A Sales Call Provides a Good Structure for Interviewing
- Sales Techniques Enhance Your Interviews
- Applying a Sales Process to an Interview Helps You Understand What is Going On
- Successful Salespeople Choose Their Customers
- Selling in an Interview Will Fix Your Interview

Now that you understand that a job search is a sales process, and hopefully you are over your fear of selling, it's time to focus on the most critical part of your job search: the job interview.

The definition of a sales call is clear: It is a face-to-face <u>meeting</u> between a <u>salesperson</u> and a <u>customer</u> or <u>prospect</u> for the purpose of generating a <u>sale</u>. Sounds exactly like an interview, doesn't it?

Let's just change a couple of words to make it clearer. A job interview is a face-to-face <u>meeting</u> between a <u>job</u> candidate and a hiring manager for the purpose of persuading the manager to hire the candidate. Like a sale, the hiring process typically includes a series of meetings with multiple decision-makers and influencers. The good news in a job search is that every interview is with a motivated buyer, so you don't have to worry about turning a prospect into a buyer.

The Basic Interview Tension

In any sales situation, the buyer is aware that the salesperson is trying to influence him to buy the product at the highest price. The salesperson's motivation is to sell his product, not to protect the buyer from purchasing the wrong product at the wrong price—this is where the phrase "Let the buyer beware" comes from. This dynamic creates a tension between the buyer and the salesperson, with the buyer wary of what the salesperson is saying and trying to find out where the salesperson may be misrepresenting, omitting information, or "positioning" his service. The buyer begins the purchase process from a position of distrust and skepticism. It is this distrust and skepticism that good salespeople can overcome using effective sales skills.

This same tension exists in a job interview. The hiring manager is aware that the candidate is motivated to sell herself into the position regardless of her exact fit or whether there is a better candidate for the job. The hiring manager knows the candidate won't willingly reveal her weaknesses, her lack of fit with the position, or a low level of a required skill. (This tension begins even before the interview—some experts say that 30 percent or more of people lie on their resumes, with most inflating their academic achievements.)

This basic tension is the primary reason why the interview is broken. The interview process is designed to reveal or expose how the candidate fits the requirements and how she falls short. This is why the interview is an adversarial process, with the interviewer asking tough questions to expose the candidate's weaknesses or misrepresentations. It is why a hiring manager is hesitant to help a candidate prepare for the interview, for fear of making it easier for the candidate to misrepresent herself. It is why the interview is a fearful experience filled with logical and nonsensical questions, where candidates struggle to be relaxed and present their best self.

The obvious solution to this tension is to make an interview more like a sales call, with the hiring manager becoming a helpful buyer and the candidate becoming a good salesperson. A helpful buyer is interested in getting a good sales presentation so he has the information he needs to make the best possible purchasing decision. He sets up the sales process to support the salesperson giving him the information he needs to present his services completely and consistently with the buyer's specific needs.

In an interview situation, this would include the hiring manager providing extensive information about the selection process, including the critical job requirements, interview participants, characteristics of successful employees, types of questions that will be asked, and selection criteria. The candidate approaches the interview as a sales call and uses proven sales strategies to present herself as the best candidate for the position. As in any sales situation, the seller-buyer tension would not be completely erased; however, it would be significantly reduced. Reducing the basic sales tension will improve the selection process for both the hiring manager and the candidate. The rest of this book goes into great depth about how you can reduce the tension and fix the interview process using an active sales approach.

The Interviewer Is an Informed Buyer

With the vast amount of information available online about potential candidates, hiring managers know more about available talent and their range of skills than they did years ago. This creates more competition for you. To beat your competition and win the mind and heart of the hiring manager, personal branding and selling become more critical. To win the job, you have to be highly credible and build the case during the interview that you meet the requirements of the position better than anyone else will. This requires a strong personal brand and an Active Interview approach using an interview presentation.

There Is Only One Hiring Issue: Your Value to the Company

When a company or person purchases any product or service, they are looking for value. Nothing is purchased without the prospect of getting value from the purchase. More expensive items have greater value expectations, and the same is true for hiring: The higher the salary, the greater the value expectation.

The hiring process is designed to determine one thing: Can you and will you deliver the expected value to the company? This is a two-sided issue. One side, based on your background skills and experience, is whether you can deliver value to the company. The other side is whether you are interested and motivated enough to deliver the value to this company.

During your interview, always think about value. What is your potential value to the company? How will you provide value? How will you provide more value than your competition? How will you provide value quickly? During the interview, there are only three basic questions interviewers want answered to determine your potential value. These are the three questions you should focus on during your preparation and during your interview. There Are Only Three Questions

A buyer making a purchasing choice has a few basic concerns:

*Can the service solve the problem for which the buyer is engaging the seller—and do it better than any other service provider available?

*Will the service provider be eager to help and motivated to provide quality work?

*Will the buyer get along with and like the service provider? (Customers prefer to do business with people they like.)

The higher the cost of the service and the greater the length of the engagement, the more critical and sensitive these questions become. Imagine hiring a building contractor who says, "Well, this is a smaller job than we typically take on, we usually get paid more, and this isn't exactly our area of expertise, but I think we can squeeze you in." Doesn't inspire much confidence, does it?

Even though interviewers ask dozens of questions and there are multiple rounds of interviews, ultimately interviewers are interested in the same three basic questions:

*Can you do the job better than any of the other candidates?

*Will you be motivated to do quality work?

*Will they enjoy working with you?

Convincing the interviewer that you are the best choice for the job is the basic goal of your interview. Like any good salesperson, you must proactively and assertively answer each of these three questions—don't leave it to the interviewer to ask you.

Can You Do the Job?

Based on your background, skills, education, and experience, is there sufficient evidence to prove that you can perform the job well? Typically, interviewers focus on basic skill sets and ask mostly objective questions about the job requirements. The question format is generally, "Here is something the job requires. Where have you done it before, how have you done it before, how well have you done it before, and how would you do it here?"

To convince the interviewer that you can do the job, you first must know the job—you need to have an in-depth understanding of it. See the upcoming "Fact Finding or Needs Analysis" section to understand how this question fits the sales-call process. Later in the book, you will find a series of questions you can ask to learn the critical job requirements.

Are You Motivated to Do the Job?

You may have a great technical background with all the required skills and experience, but will you actually *do* the job? Do you have the discipline, interest, and work ethic to do the job? Hiring managers are concerned about hiring people who are lazy, unmotivated, or simply spending time before finding a "better" job.

This is a difficult question for interviewers to answer based on an interview alone. They will attempt to guess the answer from your responses and actions during the interview. To do so, they will ask direct questions such as, "Why do you want this job?" They will also observe your actions, such as being on time and coming prepared with knowledge of the company and good questions; your level of energy and enthusiasm; and your freedom from distractions, such as cell phones.

When jobs are scarce, candidates often are willing to take lower-level positions and cuts in salary, just to have a job. They believe the company is getting a huge bargain—which it probably is—and they don't understand why they get classified as overqualified and don't receive a job offer. Hiring managers are concerned that once the economy improves, these candidates will quickly move on, so these "overqualified" candidates do not pass the "motivated to do the job" test.

Do You Fit Their Culture?

Companies realize that an individual with great skills who does not fit the culture will perform poorly and often leave quickly. Thus, likability is a critical hiring criterion. However, the impact of subjectivity is very high when determining cultural fit and likability. You might be the best candidate and even a good cultural fit, but one bad "gut reaction" or negative bias from any interviewer could end your chances of landing the job.

Your goal is to actively remove as much subjectivity as possible and replace it with objective data. The way to do this is to rely on good, solid sales skills and an interview presentation. These issues will be covered later in the book.A Sales Call Provides a Good Structure for Interviewing

There are several distinct advantages to approaching a job interview like a sales call. First, let's establish that a sales call is a well-defined format for a meeting. It consists of four distinct stages:

*Warming-up period

*Fact finding or needs analysis

*Sales presentation

*Close

These four stages will give you guidance for preparing and managing your interviews. During your interview, you will be able to identify which stage you are in, exhibit the appropriate behavior, and guide your interview successfully through each stage.

Warming-Up Period

The first stage is a warming-up period for building rapport. The salesperson wants to make the prospect feel comfortable—he doesn't walk into the prospect's office and immediately launch into a sales pitch. Good salespeople take time to observe the customer's environment and relax in the situation.

The first five or ten minutes are spent making small talk to build rapport. The goal is to find points of connection with the prospect. Points of connection are things you have in common with another person. They might include home cities, high schools or colleges, hobbies, sports teams, vacations to the same destinations, mutual friends or colleagues, and so on. Points of connection establish a commonality and a level of trust. To find a point of connection, a salesperson thinks about questions such as the following: Does the customer have family pictures? Sports teams they follow? Is the view from the office window spectacular? Are there signs of hobbies? The answers to these types of questions can help the salesperson start a friendly conversation with the prospect and build rapport.

Today with social media you may be able to find commonalities by researching an interviewer online. Do they have a LinkedIn profile, write a blog, have a website? It is becoming standard and accepted practice to research interviewers online. In fact, many interviewers are impressed you took the time to do the research to learn about them in preparation for the interview. This preparation contributes to communicating your interest and motivation for the job.

Well-prepared job candidates spend the first five to ten minutes of an interview establishing rapport with the interviewer. "Well-prepared" is a critical issue here, because the better prepared you are for the interview, the more relaxed you will be, and small talk and rapport-building become easier. If you go into the interview feeling nervous when you consider what to talk about, building rapport becomes a challenge.

Fact Finding or Needs Analysis

In a sales call, this stage is critical to understanding the customer's specific needs and wants. Good salespeople have done a lot of preparation, and they already know a great deal about the customer's needs and wants. However, they use this stage to confirm and delve deeper into what they already know.

Salespeople ask open-ended questions that lead the customer to discuss her business, her needs, and the problems she is looking to solve. The customer may also talk about problems she is having with current suppliers or vendors. Good salespeople—even highly experienced industry salespeople—do not assume they know what the customer needs and start selling to that need. They wait to hear the customer's perspective on the problem that needs solving, and only then do they begin to sell.

For a job candidate, establishing a needs-analysis stage may take some finesse. Often, once the warming-up stage has run its course, the interviewer will launch into asking questions. If this happens, you should politely redirect the interview to a needs-analysis conversation. You can do this by saying something like, "I'm eager to answer your questions, and I'd like you to get to know my background, skills, and experience. However, would it be okay if we talk about the job requirements first, so I can be more targeted with my answers?"

Most interviewers will hear this as a reasonable request and will begin talking about the job. Once they begin talking about the job, use probing, open-ended questions to get a far better understanding of the problem from the interviewer's perspective.

Also, consider that each person with whom you interview may have a different perspective on the problem and the job requirements. Don't assume that what was true in your first interview is true in your second or third interview.

Sales Presentation

The sales presentation is when the salesperson addresses the customer's needs by persuasively presenting the benefits of their service. Presentations can be informal, just part of the normal conversation, or a formal, prepared sales presentation. Formal sales presentations are prepared ahead of time and brought into the sales call. Keep in mind that *all* sales calls require a sales presentation, even if it's not a formal one.

For a job candidate, an interview presentation makes all the difference. Once you go through developing a presentation, you are fully prepared to powerfully sell yourself in your interview.

Like a sales presentation, an interview presentation can be either informal or formal. Some candidates prepare an interview presentation and introduce the information during the course of the interview conversation. Other candidates print and bind their interview presentation and give a copy to each interviewer. They then take the interviewer through the presentation page by page.

The interview presentation is covered at great length in later chapters of this book. Let me just mention that the interview presentation is a very powerful and effective interview tool that differentiates candidates and impresses interviewers. I have had a number of clients offered jobs solely on the strength of their interview presentation.

> "Yesterday, we finalized the offer, and I will be starting on Tuesday at a national sales meeting. FYI, the guy who hired me said that the interview presentation was the reason I was hired."
>
> —Jim, strategic accounts manager, technology

This makes sense, if you think about it—ask salespeople how often they have landed a sale based on a great sales presentation (or lost a sale based on blowing the presentation).

The Close

For salespeople, the close is the most important part of the sales call. If they don't close, what is the point of selling? There are literally hundreds of sales-closing techniques, including:

*__Daily-cost close.__ Reduce the cost to the daily amount.

*__Demonstration close.__ Show them the goods.

*__Embarrassment close.__ Make *not* buying embarrassing.

*__Emotion close.__ Trigger identified emotions.

*__Empathy close.__ Empathize with them and then sell to your new friend.

*__Exclusivity close.__ Suggest that not everyone can buy this product or service.

*__Handshake close.__ Offer a handshake to trigger automatic reciprocation.

*__IQ close.__ Express how this is for intelligent people.

*__Minor-points close.__ Close first on the small things.

*__Never-the-best-time close.__ For customers who are delaying.

*__No-hassle close.__ Make it as easy as possible.

*__Now-or-never close.__ To hurry things up.

*__Ownership close.__ Act as if they own what you are selling.

*__Quality close.__ Sell on quality, not on price.

*__Rational close.__ Use logic and reason.

*__Save-the-world close.__ Buy now and help save the world.

*__Selective-deafness close.__ Respond only to what you want to hear.

*__Similarity close.__ Bond them to a person in a story.

*__Standing-room-only close.__ Show how others are lining up to buy.

*__Summary close.__ Tell them all the things they are going to receive.

*__Ultimatum close.__ Show them the negative consequences of not buying.

Interview experts proposing a sales perspective and sales experts writing about job interviews suggest that a candidate close in the interview. They suggest asking a direct question, such as, "So, do I get the job?" or a less-direct question, such as, "So, do you see me as a member of your team?" I personally don't think a hard close in an interview works. Interviewers don't like to reject a candidate face to face or offer a job without talking it over with others. Typically, an interviewer avoids direct closing questions by saying, "We liked you, but we have other candidates to interview."

I suggest you never ask directly for the position. If you've managed the interview correctly, you and the hiring manager have come to a meeting of the minds, and the logical next step is that he will move you to the next round or hire you. Keep in mind that a success or a "close" in an interview is an invitation to the next round of interviews. The entire interview process isn't about convincing someone to hire you, it is about convincing each individual to approve you to advance to the next step until you get to the hire stage. In early rounds, if you are invited back, your interview was a success.

Sales Techniques Enhance Your Interviews

There is an entire industry dedicated to teaching the science of selling. Google "sales training," and you get literally millions of hits. Selling is a serious and well-researched discipline. Unfortunately, job interviews have not gotten the same level of research and training. Fortunately, many sales skills and techniques are applicable to job interviews.

The typical job candidate reads interview tips, many of which are standard, common suggestions. Using a sales approach opens a large inventory of strategies and techniques that elevate the interview. It gives you added dimensions and skill sets to prepare for your interview, manage the interview, and follow through after your interview.

Applying a Sales Process Helps You Understand What's Going On

As mentioned previously, the hiring process follows many of the same steps as a sales process. However, many companies have a haphazard hiring process that makes understanding the job-interview process confusing. Even companies with an organized process do not communicate well with their candidates. (It's interesting how many of these companies include good communication skills in their job descriptions!) In the face of confusion and lack of communication, candidates spend a great deal of time guessing about what's going on.

Using a sales model can help you understand the process and the stage of the hiring cycle. During the initial interview (typically a phone screening), it is important to ask about the selection process. Questions include:

*How many people are involved in the hiring decision?

*Who are the decision-makers?

*What is the general availability of the individuals involved in the selection process?

*Who are the influencers?

*How many rounds of interviews are there?

*What is the selection timeframe?

*Are there internal candidates?

*How urgent is it to fill the position?

*If this is a new position, is there a budget for it?

*Does hiring for this position depend on landing new business?

*Are there multiple positions being filled, and is there a more senior position that needs to be filled first?

*How will communication with candidates be maintained?

*How should candidates follow up, with whom, and when?

When you have these answers, you can gauge how far along the selection process is by comparing it to a sales process. Have they selected their final candidate (vendor) list or are they still accepting resumes and phone-screening candidates? Have they scheduled interviews with other candidates (vendors) yet? Have they been through a round of interviews but did not identify a suitable candidate (vendor)? Are there internal candidates (competitors) that may have a competitive advantage? What is the timeframe for making a hiring (purchasing) decision? As a candidate, you may not get answers to all these questions, but asking the questions is important and will position you as a knowledgeable, sophisticated, and motivated candidate.

While in the interview, use the stages of a sales call outlined above to understand the progress of the interview. Is the interview in the warming-up, fact-finding, sales-presentation, or closing stage? By identifying the stage, you can manage transitions or make sure you haven't missed or shortchanged a stage. For example, if the interviewer is asking you questions about your experience and has not given you enough information about the job, you may want to revisit the fact-finding stage. Also, there may be a good opening in the interview to move to the sales-presentation phase, at which point you can introduce your interview presentation. Identifying and labeling the stage of the interview will help orient you and provide a sense of where to guide the interview next. Even though the interviewer is ostensibly in control, by using the sales stages, you can influence the pace and direction of the interview.

Successful Salespeople Choose Their Customers

There are customers who companies just don't want to work with. They are demanding, difficult to please, inconsistent, and poor communicators; they want things at the last minute; and, worst of all, they don't pay their bills. And at times, a perfectly good customer simply does not fit the profile of a customer to whom the salesperson's company can deliver value. Desperate salespeople needing revenue may take on "toxic" customers or those who don't quite fit the desired profile and live to regret it. Regardless of how much business they have, successful salespeople choose not to work with these customers. Good salespeople discover these difficult qualities in customers during the sales process, don't contract the business, and avoid the headaches.

Job candidates have the same option. During an interview, you may find that the company is not a good fit for you. It may not be a good company to work for, or it may just not be a good fit for you.

Once you make the decision not to sell your services to a company, it is important to let the company down gently. Employees at companies have feelings related to the company, and they don't like rejection. I suggest you take the responsibility by saying something such as, "I appreciate you considering me for the position (or offering me the position); however, I don't think I can provide the value to your company that you are looking for." By positioning your rejection this way, you minimize the feelings of rejection, you don't burn any bridges, and you avoid any contentious discussions. In addition, you are telling the truth—if there isn't a good fit between you and the company regardless of the reason, you won't be able to provide value.

Selling in an Interview Will Fix Your Interview

Salespeople know that people love to buy; and they often need help making a buying decision. Hiring managers love to hire; they just don't like making hiring mistakes. As you have just read in this chapter and the preceding ones, approaching your interviews as sales calls provides a number of distinct advantages in your interview and over your competition. Selling yourself in an interview provides the following benefits:

*Using a sales structure will inform you of where you are in the interview process.

*There is a great deal of information about sales techniques and strategies (in this book alone) that you can use to improve your interview performance.

*Using a sales approach will keep you focused on the most important issue—your potential value to the company.

*You can use a sales presentation to powerfully communicate your fit with the job requirements and why you are a good candidate for the position.

*Using a sales approach will help you overcome the disadvantages of a bad interviewer.

Chapter 4 - Using Basic Sales Skills in Your Interviews

- You Don't Have to Be a Great salesperson to Sell Yourself in Interviews
- Selling is Mostly Listening
- Asking Good Questions Supports Good Listening
- Selling is a Fancy Word for Persuading
- Discovering the "Pain"
- Most Candidates Avoid Objections When They Should Embrace Them
- Handle Your Emotions
- Eliminate FUD (Fear, Uncertainty, and Doubt)
- Focus on the Buyer
- Keep it Simple
- Have a Successful Close
- Thank You, No Thanks – Follow Through, Yes Please
- No Doesn't Mean No Forever
- Using Sales Skills Will Fix Your Interviews

If you have 20 years of experience in sales and you know all the sales techniques, that's great—but you still have to bring your sales experience to the interview. And believe it or not, most salespeople do not!

You Don't Have to Be a Great Salesperson to Sell Yourself in Interviews

Even if you've never sold professionally, you can still bring a great deal of sales skill to your interview, dramatically improving your performance. Just approaching the interview as a sales call and developing an interview presentation will have significant positive results, and any additional sales techniques will provide incremental improvements. Let's begin with the most important sales skill: listening.

Selling Is Mostly Listening

This sounds counterintuitive, doesn't it? When we think of selling, we think of a salesperson actively telling us about his product or service and convincing us to buy it. Indeed, that is true for bad salespeople. However, good salespeople do a lot of listening first; then, they use what they have learned to guide you through making a purchasing decision.

There is a general lack of awareness that listening is the most critical interviewing skill, as well as the most important sales skill. This is another example of the type of misguided interview suggestions you may get. As noted earlier, most books emphasize answering questions—but that's talking rather than listening. Good answers depend on good listening.

There Are Two Parts to Listening

Listening is an active process that requires intense thought. As such, there are two parts to listening.

Empathetic Listening

Empathy is the ability to put yourself into the mental shoes of another person and understand his or her thoughts and feelings. There is a distinction between merely hearing words and really listening for the message. When you listen empathetically, you understand the other person's perspective about what he or she is thinking and/or feeling.

Understanding another person's perspective is a critical challenge. During interviews, candidates are so intent on being able to answer questions and talk about their skills, background, and experience that they often do very little empathetic listening. Their focus is on "Here is what I want to tell you," rather than on understanding the hiring manager's perspective on the challenges he is facing.

Experienced candidates often listen with a bias, based on their years of experience in an industry. They may ask, "What are your challenges?" but already have an answer based on what they know to be challenges in the industry. For example, a consumer-package-goods brand manager candidate might ask, "What are your greatest challenges in the supermarket?" It is well known that private-label brands are being challenged severely by supermarket store brands. The hiring manager might mention this challenge but also mention two or three more personal challenges, such as team coherence, internal support for her product, or crushing cost of ingredients. A candidate who is not listening empathetically will not register the hiring manager's greatest personal challenges and may just respond to the well-known industry challenge. In doing so, the candidate misses an opportunity to both bond with the hiring manager and address a more pressing problem.

Listening empathetically requires suspending your existing beliefs. You are developing an understanding from the interviewer's perspective; regardless of "rights and wrongs," it is the interviewer's perspective that counts. If you disagree, say to yourself (not out loud!), "I don't think that's true, but I understand that you see it that way." Then respond based on the interviewer's perception, not your knowledge.

Empathetic listening is easier when you connect with the other person. In an interview, being genuinely interested in the interviewer makes listening and interacting far easier. The interviewer has a personal and professional life he brings with him to the interview—keep that in mind. Too often, interviews are cold cross-examinations with no personal connection. It's important to remember that in addition to being interviewed, you are meeting another human being who is living on the same planet. It is no different from meeting a person at a social event and spending time getting to know him. In an interview, the focus obviously needs to stay on a professional level; however, being curious and asking questions about an interviewer's professional background and career goals is appropriate and a good way to connect personally.

At one point in my career, I was interviewing for a position as a senior career consultant. The interview did not go particularly well, and after 45 minutes, the hiring manager was wrapping up the interview. You know the signs: "Thanks for coming in. It was nice meeting you. We have other people to interview...." Just before standing up and escorting me out the door, she asked me whether I had any final questions. In an inspired moment, I asked her, "How did you get your position?" She settled back into her chair, and we spent the next 40 minutes discussing her career path, our common passion for working with people and helping them with their careers, and the joy of seeing people land jobs. She invited me back to do a training presentation to the staff, and I ended up being hired.

Information processing

In addition to practicing empathetic listening, listening requires information processing. This includes objectively collecting facts, categorizing the facts, and then prioritizing them.

Much of what you hear in an interview is factual: "We have this many accounts of this size. We have this many employees. We have this many deliveries a day. Our revenues are...." Some facts are interesting to know but not critical to your landing the job. Some facts are particularly important to the position and addressed as you answer questions. For example:

*Our major initiative next year is to expand our sales of plastic products by 30 percent by opening new markets in Asia.

*We are measuring success in this position by the reduction in parts defects and reduced production costs.

*A major challenge is shortening our time to market with new products by 10 percent during year one and an additional 5 percent during year two.

These facts are important and serve to focus your answers. Address how you would achieve the goals using the stated percentages. For example, "I would approach reducing time to market by 10 percent by doing the following...." Using the facts demonstrates that you are listening and that you heard the interviewer (and what hiring manager doesn't love being heard?). In turn, this gives your answers greater focus and credibility.

Most Candidates Are Hearing when They Should Be Listening

Hearing is passive, while listening is active. Let's use music as an example: Putting on headphones and relaxing is hearing. Paying attention to the beat, tempo, and various instruments and comparing that version of the song to other versions you may have heard is listening. Listening is actively engaging with the music and paying attention.

Listening in your interviews involves active engagement and an ongoing effort to understand and analyze what the interviewer is saying. Mostly, it is getting out of your own head and focusing on the interviewer's words and meaning.

There are five elements to listening:

*Pay attention. Give the speaker your undivided attention and acknowledge her message. Put aside distracting thoughts. Don't mentally prepare your response partway through an interviewer's comment or question.

*Demonstrate that you are listening. Look at the speaker directly with good eye contact and nod occasionally. Use body language and facial expressions to indicate that you are actively listening. Use small verbal comments, such as, "Yes" and "Uh huh" to encourage the speaker to continue. Maintain an open posture, facing the interviewer and demonstrating your receptivity.

*Provide feedback to clarify. Personal filters, assumptions, judgments, and beliefs can distort what you hear. As a listener, your role is to understand what is being communicated. Reflect on what you have heard by paraphrasing. "What I'm hearing is…" and "Sounds like you're saying…" are good reflecting statements. Ask questions to clarify certain points. "What do you mean when you say…?" "Is this what you mean?" Be open and receptive to corrections to your understanding. It's far better to be corrected than to continue based on a misunderstanding.

*Defer responding. Don't interrupt. Interrupting is a waste of time. It frustrates and insults the speaker and limits your full understanding of the message. If you are fully in listening mode and not formulating your answers, you will not interrupt. If you find yourself interrupting or resisting the impulse to interrupt, refocus on active listening. Not interrupting can be a challenge with an interviewer who drones on. However, even the droning conveys a message, and it's your job to determine what that message is.

*Respond appropriately. Active listening is based on respect and understanding. Remember, you are gaining information and learning the interviewer's perspective. You gain nothing by disagreeing with the interviewer or trying to get points by "being right" or seeming smarter than the interviewer. Be careful to assert your opinions respectfully. Interviewers are very sensitive to arrogant candidates who think they have the answers and act as if they should have the interviewer's job.

Listening the Flip Side

Interviewers are not good listeners, which creates a problem for you. Depending on the study quoted, people remember between 25 and 50 percent of what they hear. That means when you talk to your boss, colleagues, customers, spouse, or interviewer for 10 minutes, he or she pays attention to less than half of the conversation. You hope the important parts are retained in the 25 to 50 percent, but what if they're not?

Further along in the book, you will read about using an interview presentation to improve the interviewer's retention of important information. This is part of fixing your interview.

Listening Begins at the First Contact

Candidates have multiple contacts with employers during the hiring process, beginning with reviewing the job description and continuing through each round of interviewing. Most candidates take routine contacts, such as scheduling an interview, at face value and do not actively listen for information. By doing so, they may be missing a nugget of important information they can use in the interview. For example, while scheduling an interview, the administrative assistant might say, "Steve won't be available next week for interviewing; he's traveling in Asia." Hmmm…interesting. There is nothing on the company's website indicating that the company has any business in Asia—is this a new initiative? Do you have international experience? Have you traveled in Asia? If you have, bringing it up in the interview or including it in your interview presentation may tip the scales in your favor. Even a seemingly innocuous comment can provide useful information.

Listening Pitfalls

A number of listening pitfalls trip up candidates. These may include:

*Being so intent on what you have to say that you listen mainly to find an opening to make your point. You may be thinking that you have a very important point you want the interviewer to know, and if you don't say it now, the opportunity will be lost. In reality, you won't lose the opportunity, and this pitfall often results in an interruption— never a good thing during an interview.

*Formulating and focusing on your answers quickly, based on what the speaker is saying. Candidates often are so concerned about giving the "right" answer that they get nervous and stop listening. They also have the misconception that they have to answer a question immediately after it is asked. It is perfectly acceptable to say, "Let me think about that," and then take 30 to 40 seconds to formulate an answer. A thoughtful, considered answer is better than a quick, confused, or off-target response.

*Focusing on your own personal beliefs about what you're hearing. Your personal beliefs form a filter that may distort the interviewer's meaning. It is important to be aware of how your beliefs distort what you hear and adjust for the distortion. You can do this by paying attention to your beliefs. For example, the interviewer might be talking about the importance of offshoring certain functions in their department. Perhaps you are opposed to sending jobs overseas. Your opposition may impact how you listen to the interviewer's message. However, if you say to yourself, "This is an area of disagreement for me. I need to stay in active listening," you will be able to focus on the message and not your internal resistance and judgment.

*Evaluating and making judgments about the speaker or the message. While the interviewer is busy making subjective judgment about you, you are busy making subjective judgments about her. Judgments can distort how you hear things—both positively and negatively. If you have a positive impression of the interviewer, you might tend to believe what she is saying and not ask clarifying questions. If you judge the interviewer negatively, you might prematurely dismiss what she is saying and not listen fully. Be aware of your judgments, which can be as simple as whether you like or dislike the person, so that you don't lose the message.

*Not asking for clarification when you know you don't understand. Many candidates think that asking for clarification is a signal to the interviewer that they don't understand and that, as a result, they will appear stupid. A candidate of mine walked out of an interview sweating because the interviewer used an acronym he did not know, and he didn't ask what it meant. Throughout the interview, the candidate was hoping he wouldn't be caught; as a result, he was a nervous wreck and performed poorly. It turned out that the acronym was an obscure, little-known term that he couldn't have known anyway. The interviewer was either impressed the candidate knew or guessed that he was covering up—probably the latter, since there was no job offer.

Asking Good Questions Supports Good Listening

Good salespeople listen to hear important sales-related information. They also ask good questions to elicit the information they need to make a powerful sales presentation.

In interviews, you need to know important hiring decision, company, and position-related information. There are three domains of information for you to consider.

What You Know

This domain of information is clear. It is the information you know about the industry, the company, and the position.

What You Don't Know

This is information you want to know but don't. You get this information by asking questions that you know will elicit the information. For example, "When do you plan to make the hiring decision?" "What are the key success metrics for this position?" "Is this a new position or a replacement for someone who has left?"

What You Don't Know That You Don't Know

This is a tricky domain, but it usually has the most important information—information that your competition doesn't know how to get and that you can use. But if you don't know what you don't know, how can you formulate a question about it? You cannot.

To tap this domain of knowledge, start by asking for high-level information—for example, "Please tell me about working here." As opposed to asking, "What is the management style at this company?" this is an invitation for information that does not lead the interviewer in a narrow, specific direction. In response, the interviewer chooses what he wants to address and often provides information which you would not have thought to ask. When you get the new information, you can follow up with a series of questions. Other examples of information invitations include:

*Tell me about sales.

*Tell me about a day at work.

*What are your thoughts about the industry?

*Tell me about your competition.

*Tell me about challenges.

*Tell me about production.

An old quote goes, "It's what you *don't know* you don't know that will kill you." Fortunately, in interviewing this is not so extreme, but what you don't know you don't know could make landing the job more difficult and provide surprises if you do start working at the company.

Selling Is a Fancy Word for Persuading

Persuasion is the process of guiding another person toward the adoption of an idea, attitude, or action. In sales, the salesperson persuades the buyer to buy, and in interviewing, the candidate persuades the hiring manager to hire. The more persuasive the salesperson and the candidate, the more successful the outcome.

In sales, you can't force the buyer to purchase, and in interviewing, you can't force the hiring manager to hire. Thus, the art of persuasion is getting the other person to *want* to do what you desire. As you will note, the definition of "persuasion" includes the word "guiding." As mentioned in the Introduction to this book, the old concept of who controls the interview is outdated. As a salesperson for yourself, you are responsible for guiding your interview and persuading the hiring manager to hire you. You cannot depend on interviewers to persuade themselves.

Persuasion Stands on Three Legs

Persuasion is the attempt to convince someone of a set of beliefs or taking an action. A buyer or a hiring manager is open to being persuaded, it just has to be done in an effective way. Effective persuasion consists of the following elements:

Credibility and Trust

Hiring managers only hire people they believe in and trust. Establishing credibility and trust during the hiring process requires you to perform a number of both small and large actions. Making a mistake with any one of these actions can destroy or undermine your credibility and trust.

Candidates often wonder whether they should do one thing or another during job search and the interviewing process. Should you write a cover letter? Should you send a thank-you letter?" There are dozens of such questions. One way to answer these questions is to ask yourself, "Will doing this add to my credibility or trust?" If the action has a chance of adding to your credibility or trust, do it. Conversely, ask yourself, "Will not doing this detract from my credibility or trust?" If not doing it may detract from your credibility or trust, then do it.

The following is a representative list of actions that will increase your credibility and trust in interviews:

*Dress appropriately.

*Be on time.

*Have a good handshake and eye contact.

*Turn off your cell phone.

*Be well prepared for the interview.

*Listen well.

*Be positive.

*Have a professional interview presentation.

*Ask powerful questions.

*Have success stories that speak to your skills and expertise.

*Follow up after their interview.

Emotional Engagement

When a person's emotions engage, they are more focused and attentive, have better retention, and tend to believe what they are hearing. Typically, interviews are not considered situations that call for engaging emotions. But as you may have surmised, I am not suggesting typical interview approaches. I am suggesting that you go for the emotions. Candidates who engage emotions are far more memorable than factual, dry candidates.

You can engage your interviewer's emotions by telling stories. I coach clients to answer as many questions as possible beginning with the phrase, "Let me give you an example." Each example is a mini-story, no longer than two minutes, that engages the interviewer. Later in this book, you will read about success stories and how to format your stories for the greatest impact in your interview.

Persuasive Statements

Persuasive statements rely on good, solid facts that support the position you're taking, which is basically, "Hire me!" Persuasive candidates use solid facts to support their contention that they meet the critical requirements of the job and that they are the best candidate. These facts are a combination of prior jobs, education, experience, and, most important, examples of having performed the critical requirements previously.

In addition, telling stories of accomplishments related to the requirements makes the facts stronger and more memorable. For example, talking about having done software project management in a prior job establishes the fact that you can do software project management. However, telling a story about how you did project management for a particular type of software for a specific client and brought the project in under budget and against strong odds has more impact and is more persuasive.

Discovering the "Pain"

Many sales training programs instruct salespeople to look for the prospect's "pain" points. Their contention is that customers are motivated to purchase services only if the service relieves a pain or problem. In many sales situations, the prospect knows the pain and is looking for a solution—for example, "My computer is broken. It can't be repaired, and I need to purchase a new one." In other situations, a salesperson has to identify the pain for a prospect and then sell her the solution: "Are you aware that your computer isn't being backed up offsite to a secure location, and you could lose all your information? You need a backup service." The next time you are buying something, consider what pain you are hoping to relieve.

Candidates can do both—sell to the obvious pain and identify additional pain points. The obvious pain is the company's stated reasons for hiring—replacing a person who has left or staffing a new position. As discussed previously, there are typically more subtle issues beneath the obvious reasons for hiring someone. Your task is to discover the subtle issues beneath the obvious ones and include these in your interview.

You already have learned how to discover the pain points: Ask good questions and listen. When interviewing with the hiring manager, listen for subtle statements related to pain points. For example, suppose you're interviewing for a call-center supervisor position. In the interview, the hiring manager mentions that she spends so much of her time doing reports that she is not able to implement new money-saving programs (that would make her look good). The obvious pain point is supervising the staff, but the subtle pain is all the time-sucking reporting. The first step is to gather more information about the reporting pain by asking, "What kinds of reports are required and how often?" When you have this information, talk about things you have done in your past related to reporting and how your experience with reports can save her time. This could be just the differentiator you need to win the position.

Consider that a hiring manager's work pain may be related indirectly to personal issues. For example, a hiring manager might do a lot of traveling and thus sacrifice time with his family. If you can take some of the travel burden, he can spend time with his family, and you've addressed that pain. Once again, by asking good questions and listening, you can hear pain points that, if addressed, can be the pain reliever you can use to land the job.

The Best Pain of All

The best pain of all is the pain a hiring manager begins to feel when she thinks about working with someone other than you—another candidate who could be less than satisfactory, less efficient, less ethical, less timely, less friendly, less enthusiastic, and less able to solve her pain points. When you have done a great job of interviewing, the hiring manager will begin to experience this pain, and she will work hard to hire you. No one wants to hire number two, and she will negotiate with you to bring you onto her team. You are in your strongest negotiating position at this point, and later in this book we will discuss how to leverage this pain with regard to compensation negotiations.

Most Candidates Avoid Objections when They Should Embrace Them

A critical part of selling is handling objections. Salespeople get excited by objections, but candidates often fear them. Candidates hear objections as an expression of disapproval or opposition, meaning, "We are not going to hire you." Salespeople, on the other hand, hear objections as a sign of interest, a request for more information, or a prospect's concern or fear. When there are no objections voiced, it often means the buyer is not interested enough to state the objection and work through it with the salesperson.

So, think like a salesperson. Instead of fearing objections, embrace them. Every objection provides you with an opportunity to share persuasive information with an interviewer and move him to the next step of the selection process. One of your most important tasks in an interview is to raise all the objections you possibly can. Later in this book, you will learn the one best question for eliciting objections.

Handling objections skillfully is an important sales technique that you can learn quickly. The important first step is to consider the objection a positive and not get rattled. If the interviewer says to you, "I don't agree," or, "I see you don't have [*fill in the blank*] skill," or, "I am concerned about…," recognize it as an objection. But instead of tensing up, consider this an opportunity to address a concern that might disqualify you from the position. Rather than react to an objection with a defensive statement, which creates an adversarial posture between you and the interviewer, respond to the objection with a "leaning in" body posture and a question about the objection.

When you hear an objection, it is natural to get nervous and tense up, as well as to sit back and close up your body posture in a defensive position. This defensive posture quickly communicates that there is a problem and raises a red flag in the mind of the interviewer. So do the exact opposite: Lean in toward the interviewer and keep your body open. This communicates a willingness to hear the objection and a confidence about your response. Rather than suggesting a problem, you are communicating that there's no issue here that can't be addressed.

Asking a question or two about the objection accomplishes a couple of important goals. First, it gives you some time to regroup and prevents you from getting nervous and flustered. Second, it gives you important information about the objection. With more information, you can understand the exact content of the objection as well as its significance. Asking open-ended questions will give you greater insight into the objection. For example, "Can you tell me how my inexperience in financial services would impact my performance on the job?" or, "Please tell me why it is critical that the person you hire have experience working in a retail setting."

There are two kinds of objections: dead ends and detours. A dead end means that you're not going to get the job; a detour is simply something than needs to be overcome. If questioning the objection results in a dead end, it hurts, but at least you know where you stand. For example, the interviewer might state, "We're looking for someone who speaks Spanish fluently." You might question the objection and learn that speaking Spanish is critical to the position. Because you don't speak Spanish, you won't get the job, but at least you're not at home waiting for a phone call about the job.

Detours are an opportunity to overcome the objection. The interviewer might say, "We're really looking for someone who knows Excel." Perhaps you don't know Excel, but you know that you can learn it quickly. You can respond by saying, "I don't know Excel, but I have learned computer programs quickly in the past. When you hire me, I could do self-study and take a course. Within a week, I'll be able to use Excel, and within a month, I'll be an intermediate user. Would that be sufficient?" Notice that the ending "Would that be sufficient?" clarifies whether you have overcome the objection. Remember, the worst objection is the one you do not hear and that closes the door on the job without your having an opportunity to overcome it.

Handle Your Emotions

Many sales calls are high-stakes meetings with a "make it or break it" outcome. The same is true for interviews. High-stakes meetings cause anxiety and often result in poor performance. The more anxious you feel, the less you're able to think clearly, be flexible, and present a relaxed, open, receptive demeanor.

The following sections describe a few productive ways of handling anxiety about interviews.

Label Your Feelings Accurately

The definition of anxiety is free-floating fear. This means that when anxious, a person is feeling fear but has not attached the fear to a specific cause or issue. Once anchored, anxiety becomes fear of a specific thing and can be addressed. For example, suppose you have an interview scheduled and you realize you are feeling anxious. Replace the thought "I am feeling anxious" with the thought "I am feeling scared." Then ask yourself, "What am I scared of?" Identify your fears and deal with them. You can eliminate or reduce most interview fears with thorough preparation.

Preparation Means Confidence

> If you're not prepared, it's not pressure you feel, it's fear.
>
> —Bruce Bochy, San Francisco Giants manager

Feeling prepared results in feeling confidence and a decrease in fear. The number-one complaint of most interviewers is lack of knowledge of the company. Simply doing thorough research about the company will help you overcome your interviewer's primary concern. Being even further prepared with knowledge about the industry, a good list of questions, proper dress, selling skills, and an interview presentation will put you ahead of 98 percent of the other candidates. Walk into your interview thinking, "I am probably better prepared than almost anyone else they are interviewing," your fear will turn into confidence, and your performance will improve.

Focus on the Process, Not the Outcome

Salespeople know that they can't control the outcome of a sales call. All they can do is their best sales job and then leave it up to the buyer. Buyers make decisions based on such a wide and uncontrollable set of criteria that salespeople know it's a waste of time and emotions to worry about the outcome after they have made their best efforts. The same is true with interviews. Hiring managers make hiring decisions based on unpredictable criteria, from the logical to the highly subjective.

The most successful candidates prepare thoroughly, develop a great interview presentation, guide the interview, follow through carefully, and then let the interview go. Put the effort and emotion into the process of the interview; don't invest it in the outcome. If you have done your best possible sales job during your interview, feel great about your performance. And if you don't land the job, go into your next interview even more confident.

Have a Full Pipeline

Salespeople spend most of their time filling and managing their pipeline. A sales pipeline consists of a number of prospects at different places in the sales cycle. A salesperson is constantly adding new prospects to the beginning of the pipeline and moving other prospects from one stage to the next within the pipeline. If a salesperson's pipeline is empty or low, his number of sales decreases, and he tends to get panicky.

A full pipeline is important in a job search as well. I tell my clients that the best thing they can do to improve their interview is to have an interview scheduled with another company. With only one interview scheduled, all your eggs are in one basket, and that basket takes on huge importance. Every interview becomes a critical event with a great impact and high levels of fear. If you have multiple interviews scheduled, each one becomes more relaxed and less stressful because you'll place less importance on one single interview.

Eliminate FUD (Fear, Uncertainty, and Doubt)

All buyers are risk averse. They don't want to invest in any service or solution that may not generate value for the money spent. Good salespeople spend a lot of time and effort removing fear, uncertainty, and doubt (otherwise known as *FUD*) from the purchasing equation. Once FUD is removed, most sales objections are addressed, and the sale typically moves forward.

To remove FUD from your job interview, address what the typical hiring manger worries about most, including:

*Not delivering results.** You can't do the job.

*Cultural fit and compatibility.** You won't fit in, and they won't like you.

*Quality of your work.** You'll do the job, but not very well.

*Accuracy of your claims.** You misrepresent your skills and experience.

*Lack of caring about the job.** You would take the job but quickly leave for the next good opportunity.

In preparation for your interview, make sure you have a strategy to address each of these FUD factors. FUD-reduction strategies include the following:

*Leverage data.** The more data (and stories) you have that supports your ability to perform the job, the better. Letter of reference, examples, success stories, awards, case studies, and articles support your expertise. Also, recommendations on LinkedIn can be very helpful here.

*Be transparent.** Hiring managers want to know the truth. In this social-media age, there is a great deal of information available online. Make sure your online information is consistent with what you say in your interview. For example, is your LinkedIn profile and your information on Facebook completely consistent with your resume? It is a good strategy to assume that anything you say in an interview is verifiable either online or by checking references or records (school and criminal background). A good strategy is to research yourself online before the interview and see what comes up. If you find something negative, be prepared to speak about it.

*Manage expectations.** Be sure that there is clarity about the responsibilities, goals, and success factors of the job. Agreement about the critical responsibilities of the job builds trust and eliminates FUD, which reduces the perception of risk. A well-developed interview presentation will guide the interview and make sure that there is discussion of and agreement about the critical job requirements.

*Directly address areas of weakness and lack of job qualifications.** Regardless of the state of the job market, employers cannot find candidates who fit 100 percent of the written job requirements. Also, many job descriptions are a wish list and not necessarily a realistic list of requirements that any one individual can provide. Thus, you will have some but not all of the requirements—and the hiring manager knows this. Ignoring your shortcomings and hoping the hiring manager is not aware of them is a weak strategy and raises the FUD level. Directly addressing them and minimizing their importance is a far better strategy. Addressing, but not dwelling on, your weaknesses reduces risk. During your interview, use a statement such as the following, "Even though I don't have experience with [*fill in the blank here*], I make up for it by [*fill in the blank here*]."

Nobody wants to make a bad decision. People don't like the unknown; they fear it. If you ignore the hiring manager's fears, they don't go away—they simply get in the way of him making you a job offer. Remove the FUD, and the offer is more likely to be yours.

Focus on the Buyer

No one cares about products, services, or solutions. That's the hardest thing for sellers to realize. Buyers only care about the benefits the products, services, or solutions will provide to their organization. Similarly, buyers don't care about the profits a salesperson makes from a sale. Would you be motivated to buy if a salesperson said to you, "Buy this car, and I will make my quota for the month, I will get a bonus, and I can finally put that addition on my house!" Probably not.

If you mention to a hiring manager that the job is a good career move for you, it is a shorter commute, and it has a higher salary with better benefits, she won't be interested. Focus on the company; talk about the tangible outcomes they'd get from using your skills, and they will be interested. In interviewing, focus on your value to the organization. Avoid talking about how the job will benefit you.

For example, if asked where you want to be in five years, rather than talking about the progress of your own career, relate your answer to the organization: "In five years, I want to have taken on more responsibility in the organization and have increased the value I bring to the job." Similarly, if the interviewer asks, "Why should I hire you?" focus your answer on the benefits you will bring to the organization in general and to the hiring manager specifically.

Keep It Simple

Let your discourse with men of business be short and comprehensive.

—George Washington

Salespeople strive to make buying decisions as simple as possible. Buyers get confused and overwhelmed when presented with lots of facts, options, benefits, qualifications, and reasons to buy. Confusion results in FUD and no sale. Hiring an employee is a complex business decision. As a candidate, you want to make the decision to hire you as simple and non-confusing as possible, avoiding FUD.

Candidates—particularly those with extensive work experience—make the mistake of thinking that the more they add to their list of qualifications, skills, experience, and successes, the more likely they are to impress the interviewer. They are worried about leaving out the one small nugget of information that will convince the hiring manager to offer them the job. Indeed, they make the same mistake in their resumes.

Keeping it simple means choosing three or four reasons to hire and communicating these reasons clearly and repeatedly. Your reasons to hire are a combination of your match to the critical requirements of the job, the added value you will bring to the job, and your brand.

In preparation for your interview, write out your three to five reasons to hire. Start with the strongest fit you have with the critical job requirements. For example, if the job requires extensive expertise in mortgage loans, choose one or two facts that highlight your extensive experience and then repeatedly highlight your experience during the interview. For example, you might say, "Having worked in a high-volume mortgage lending operation, processing more than X loans, I...," or "Having processed more than $\$X$ in mortgage loans, I...." During the interview refer to your high-volume mortgage experience and the fact that you are a high-volume mortgage lender. The goal is to fix the idea of high-volume mortgage experience in the interviewer's mind.

Next, choose one or two value-adds you will bring to the job. It may be knowledge of information systems, an extensive social network in the mortgage field, or project management skills. When you determine which of your value-added skills will bring the most value to the position, mention the skills throughout your interview. Similarly, talk about your brand and how it contributes to your success on the job.

The strategy is to limit yourself to three to five powerful messages. This does not mean you should mention only these items in your interview, but these are the ones you emphasize. For example, Volvo dealers talk about gas mileage, leather seats, and reliability, but they focus relentlessly on safety, because people think of Volvo as the car to buy when you want a safe vehicle. At the end of your interview, you want the interviewer to think you can do the job well and have three to five strong thoughts about what you bring to the job that makes you the best choice for the position.

Have a Successful Close

Perhaps the most frequent criticism of salespeople relates to how they close. Some salespeople do not ask for the sale, whereas others are too aggressive, using "hard" close tactics. During interviews, most candidates do not think of a close; they simply shake hands and leave. But in reality, an interview requires a close as well.

For most of the interview process, a successful interview results in an invitation to the next round. Success is getting another interview, another opportunity to sell yourself. Salespeople also close a sales call by establishing the next sales call: "Based on today's conversation, I want to write up a proposal. Would next Wednesday be good to meet again and go over the proposal?"

Unless you are invited back during the interview, you will have to wait to be notified about the next round. There is no way around this; however, you can establish a timeframe and another point of contact. At the end of your interview, ask the question, "How and when should I follow up with you?" A good interviewer response is "We are interviewing through the end of the week and will notify you next Tuesday." An unacceptable answer is, "We have some more interviews, and we'll get back to you."

Regardless of the response, take control and establish a timeframe. You can do this by simply saying, "If I don't hear from you next Tuesday, would it be okay for me to call you next Wednesday?" Usually the interviewer will agree to be contacted.

This strategy accomplishes several important things. First, you have a timeframe (next Wednesday). Second, you have a method of contact (phone). Third, you can get on the phone and say, "Just as we agreed, I am calling you to follow up on our interview from last week." Because the interviewer agreed to the contact, she is obligated to take your call. Having established your next point of contact is a successful close for an interview.

Thank You, No Thanks—Follow Through, Yes Please!

When a sales meeting is over, a salesperson keeps the momentum alive by following through. A clever salesperson does more than send a thank-you note; he recaps the meeting, accentuates his service's strengths, mitigates the weaknesses, and suggests next steps. Sounds like a good strategy for an interview!

There is a great deal written about sending thank-you notes after an interview. Career coaches and human-resource professionals split evenly on the value of a thank-you note. Half think they have no impact on the outcome and are a waste of time, and half think they have value and may be the differentiator in close situations. This debate about thank-you notes takes up too much blog space, misses the point, and is a waste of time.

There should be no controversy about sending a follow-through letter—always send one! A follow-through letter continues the interview conversation, highlights your strengths, reinforces your interest in the job, provides an opportunity to address any objections once again, and supports your professional brand. It also reiterates the agreement about how and when you will follow up. In addition, should you get the position, your well-written follow-through letter reinforces the wisdom of their choice and establishes you as a polished professional with good communication skills—an excellent brand with which to start the job.

No Doesn't Mean No Forever

The candidate selected for the position has a 58 percent chance of being successful and lasting in the job for more than 18 months. If you were the number-two choice, you might become number one after 6 to 18 months. If you don't get the job, send a follow-through letter restating your interest in the job and expressing that you hope to hear from them should a position open up. Few (if any) candidates send this letter, and it could be a differentiator for you if the position becomes vacant. You can also follow up every four to six months to remind the hiring manager that you are still interested.

Using Sales Skills Fixes Your Interview

Actively selling yourself in your interview transforms you from a passive "hoping it goes well" candidate to an assertive "making sure it goes well" candidate. Sales techniques help you guide the interview, overcoming the interviewer's lack of skill and making sure the interviewer hears the information you think is important. Like any good salesperson, you will guide the interview, not control it, and make sure you are persuasive and memorable. Using sales skills in your interview provides the following benefits:

*It aids anticipation of hiring manager thinking and facilitates planning and preparation.

*It identifies the "pain" you need to alleviate to be hired.

*It eliminates fear, uncertainty, and doubt (FUD) in the hiring manager's mind.

*It maintains your focus on the needs of the hiring manager.

*It keeps your selling message simple and clear.

*It gives you an effective close strategy.

*It helps you write an effective and powerful follow-through letter.

Chapter 5 - The Interview Presentation: An Overview

- A Presentation in an Interview – Now that's Unusual
- Would You Go to a Gunfight Armed Only With a Knife?
- Isn't "Interview Presentation" Just Another Way of Saying PowerPoint?
- An Interview Presentation Is a Specialized Version of a Sales Presentation
- An Interview Presentation Goes Way Beyond a Resume
- Preparation is 90 Percent of the Value
- Presenting is a Basic Professional Skill
- The Eight Parts of a Powerful Interview Presentation
- A Presentation Will Fix Your Interview

This chapter introduces the interview presentation. Subsequent chapters will go into depth about each of the presentation sections, and then there will be a chapter about developing and effectively using a presentation in an interview.

> "[A]s soon as the hiring manager started to ask tough questions, I asked permission to give my interview presentation, and he said, 'By all means.' … He sat there and just took notes. He even asked me for an extra copy. He showed my presentation to several people, including an outside sales consultant. The next morning, I got an offer. I am convinced that the interview presentation made the difference and got me the job."

> Linda—Sales executive, global technology

A Presentation in an Interview—Now That's Unusual!

> Boldness in business is the first, second, and third thing.

> —Henry George Bohn, British publisher

The previous chapters of this book presented the interview as a sales call—that's also unusual! But it's effective. Salespeople know that most sales depend on a high-quality, persuasive presentation and that a sales presentation is the cornerstone of selling. Developing and delivering a quality sales presentation is a skill that salespeople work hard to develop. Great salespeople are great presenters. Even novice presenters vastly improve their interviews when they use a presentation approach.

As you probably know, most candidates and hiring managers approach an interview as a question-and-answer process, sometimes referred to as a *cross-examination* or an *interrogation*. However, the most effective interview consists of a combination of conversations, presentation, and questions. By using a presentation to guide the interview, candidates assertively communicate why they are a good match for the position, create job-winning conversations, and communicate the information they want the interviewer to know.

Would You Go to a Gunfight Armed Only with a Knife?

> If they bring a knife to the fight, we bring a gun.

> —Barack Obama

Most candidates go to an interview carrying a copy of their resume. Some bring a list of their references, and others may bring a few work samples. Compare this to a candidate who brings a customized spiral-bound presentation that clearly communicates her match to the critical requirements of the job and why she is the best candidate for the position. Would you want to be competing against such a well-prepared candidate? Shouldn't you be the best-armed candidate at the interview?

> "I used your interview presentation during the interview, and it went fabulous. It was over the top with this group. They asked me right on the spot for a second interview."

> Linda, HR recruiting executive, global oil company

End indented block quote

Isn't "Interview Presentation" Just another Way of Saying PowerPoint?

You may have heard the phrase "death by PowerPoint." This refers to the tens of thousands of boring PowerPoint presentations businesspeople suffer through every day. So why would a candidate want to subject a hiring manager to yet another one?

Although an interview presentation's format is indeed a presentation, the goal is to use it as a conversation starter, *not* as a presentation. For example, the candidate introduces the job requirements section of the presentation by saying, "These are the job requirements as I understand them. I would like to *discuss* them with you to make sure we both understand the requirements of the job." This initiates a productive conversation about the job requirements.

Interview presentations are not a stand-up form of presentation projected on a screen like a PowerPoint presentation. Interview presentations are typically printed, bound, and handed out to each interviewer or emailed to an interviewer prior to a video interview. Using this format, the candidate maintains eye contact with the interviewer and initiates a productive conversation, and the presentation makes an excellent leave behind.

An Interview Presentation Is a Specialized Version of a Sales Presentation

Unlike a sales presentation, which can be for selling unlimited services or products, every interview presentation has the exact same goal: landing a job. Because the goal is well defined, like a resume an interview presentation has a defined format, and the content is sharply focused.

As discussed earlier in this book, an interview attempts to answer three questions:

*Can you do the job?

*Are you motivated to do the job?

*Will you fit the culture of the company, and will they like you?

Using these three questions as the focus, the interview presentation includes all the information a hiring manager needs to answer these questions. Using a presentation, you will clearly communicate the information the hiring manager needs to know to make an informed hiring decision.

An effective interview presentation consists of a structure that frames the objective (presenting the reasons you are the best choice), covers all relevant material, transitions smoothly from topic to topic, and finishes strong. In addition, it should be well organized, short, focused, and relevant. A powerful interview presentation includes the following:

***A purpose.** This is the one thing you want the interviewer to remember when you leave the interview. Typically, this is the same for any interview: "Based on my background, experience, skills, education, and personality traits, I am the best candidate for this position." You introduce an interview presentation with this exact purpose: "I have a presentation that communicates how my background, skills, and experience match the critical requirements for this position and makes me an excellent candidate. May I share it with you?"

***Critical information.** The critical information in an interview is how well you can perform the job. Performing well consists of doing the job tasks with high quality, fitting into the company culture, and getting along with others. To communicate your ability to do the job, there must be agreement about the job requirements. The first part of the presentation addresses the job requirements: "These are what I consider to be the critical job requirements for this position. I would like to discuss them with you to make sure we are in agreement about them." This aligns your and the hiring manager's expectations. When there is agreement about the requirements, the rest of the presentation focuses on your match to the requirements.

*Benefits. Every person listening to a presentation is thinking, "How does this affect me or benefit me?" If there is no effect or benefit, the person quickly loses interest. Each item mentioned in an interview presentation should link to a benefit for the hiring manager. For example, "You're looking for a person with experience in new consumer product introduction. In my previous position, I introduced three mass consumer hardware products that accounted for $4.5 million in sales. As part of the introduction, I was responsible for consumer research, product development, marketing strategy, and sales. As you introduce new products, I'll be able to provide expert leadership in each of these areas, which means that you will require fewer managers, save personnel costs, and bring products to market more quickly and successfully."

A visual presentation (which makes an excellent leave-behind) with all these elements and good, insightful questions make up the most powerful way to communicate in an interview. Candidates who have used interview presentations report dramatic results, and hiring managers are bowled over by their level of preparation, professionalism, and organization. And even without a written document, developing an interview presentation as part of the interview-preparation process is an excellent way to organize critical information that you can present when there is an opportunity in the interview.

> A Candidate's Feedback about Her Interview Presentation from an Interviewer
>
> Beth,
>
> Thanks. I don't usually respond to interview follow-up emails, but you deserve congratulations for the effort you put into developing very professional materials. If all your sales calls were like that, you'd be doing very well here.
>
> Of course, you're in a competitive environment, and we have seen quite a few people, so I don't want to raise your hopes (and as you correctly surmised, Greg's the decision-maker).
>
> Whatever the outcome, keep up what you're doing, because it places you head and shoulders above most of the candidates we have seen.
>
> Regards,
>
> Ronald, Senior Manager, Business Development

An Interview Presentation Goes Way Beyond a Resume

A resume is a sales brochure that has a specific goal: to get you to an interview. When you have landed an interview, a resume has served its purpose and lost its value. Salespeople use sales brochures to engage a prospect and interest them in a face-to-face sales call. At the sales call, they do not use the brochure; they use a sales presentation.

A resume is a backward-looking document; it is all about what you have done. The focus of an interview presentation is forward-looking—it is on the value you will bring to the job. There will be some information about qualifications in the presentation, and this is historical; however, the overarching message is, "Here is the value I will bring to the job once you hire me."

In addition, a resume is written to be read independently and has a lot of content. An interview presentation is for discussion and has brief bullet points that serve to focus the interview conversation and keep the discussion on track.

"Your interview presentation template was exactly what I needed. The presentation not only enabled me to highlight my skill set, but it allowed me to take it to the next level, where I could match my skill sets with what the employer defined in the job description. I think the information that comes from the actual presentation provided the employer with a benchmark of how I would perform in an environment where you have to present information to others. Additionally, the opportunity for a prospective employer to see me present myself objectively demonstrated my commitment to the hiring process. I'm sure the other candidates did not approach the process the same way. I believe the interview presentation was responsible for creating the initial interest the company had in me. I still had to get through the aptitude exam and the four executive interviews to get the offer. However, I think the interview presentation provided the edge and positioned me ahead of the other candidates. My final comp package is about $150,000 to start. I think the interview presentation had some impact!"

Stephen, Senior Production Manager, technology company

Preparation Is 90 Percent of the Value

Before everything else, getting ready is the secret of <u>success</u>.

—<u>Henry Ford</u>, American industrialist

An interview presentation has a great deal of value when delivered during an interview or used as a leave-behind. However, the greatest value is in developing the presentation. Thinking through each section forces you to prepare to answer the three basic interview questions as well as communicate your brand and determine powerful questions to ask. Having developed the presentation, you'll feel far better prepared and more confident about the interview. As confidence increases, fear decreases and performance improves.

"I used the interview presentation with three separate companies. It went over extremely well with all three. Just the process of preparing the presentation was fantastically helpful. As I developed the presentation, I had to think through the critical job requirements—how I matched those requirements and the outstanding skills and experience I could bring to each organization. I also had to prepare an action plan and some good questions. Once my presentation was done, I was ready and confident for the interviews. Each hiring manager I met with was receptive to the presentation, and each was very impressed with my level of preparation and the professional quality of the presentation. How well did I do? Well, two out of three job offers (one company hired from within) is very good in my book. I have accepted one of the offers, and I am on the job."

Sarah, Business Development Specialist

Presenting Is a Basic Professional Skill

For salespeople, it is obvious that presenting is a basic job skill. However, in our knowledge economy, assembling information into a presentation and giving the presentation to a boss is an important skill in almost every job. Even if the situation is simply going into your boss's office to discuss sales figures, production numbers, or turnover rates, you are making a presentation. Watching how well you prepare and present information reduces the hiring manager's FUD (fear, uncertainty, and doubt) and increases his confidence about hiring you. In addition, the presentation provides an opportunity for the interviewer to ask questions and demonstrates how you think on your feet—also an important job skill.

The Eight Parts of a Powerful Interview Presentation

An interview presentation consists of eight sections each of which contributes to answering the three basic interview questions powerfully and succinctly. The presentation does this by creating a conversation about each of the questions during which you can communicate the information you want the interviewer to know. The sections include:

Presenting Your Personal Brand

Your personal brand communicates what you want the interviewers to think and feel about you. It helps the interviewers form a distinct and positive impression of the skills, experience, and personal traits that will make you successful in the position. By proactively and clearly communicating your brand on the cover and throughout the presentation, you don't leave your brand to the arbitrary decision of the interviewer.

Matching Your Background and Experience with Critical Position Requirements

The number-one question in any interview is whether you can do the job. Answering this question is a two-step process. First, you must clarify what the job requires, which is usually not well defined in the job description, and second, you must clearly match your background, skills, and experience with the requirements. The interview presentation accomplishes this by first presenting a list of the critical job requirements, which stimulates a conversation clarifying the requirements. Then, using the list of requirements, you can match your experience to each requirement, verifying that you have the skills and experience to do the job well.

Highlighting Additional Areas of Expertise You Bring to the Job

You can assume that each candidate interviewed matches the basic job requirements. Additional areas of expertise, or your "value-adds" that you will bring to the job, may make you the standout job-winning candidate. The interview presentation gives you the opportunity to list these areas of expertise and tell the interviewer about the benefits she will derive from these value-adds.

Highlighting Career Accomplishments and Outstanding Experiences

People love to hear stories and we all have success stories to share. During this section of the presentation, you share brief stories about times in your career or life when you used your skills, experience, and knowledge to accomplish something notable or outstanding. The stories bring your accomplishments to life, engages the interviewer's interest, and gives the interviewer insight into the contributions you can make to her organization.

Illustrating Personal Qualities That Drive Your Job Success

Companies do not hire solely based on skills and experience, they also hire on personality and cultural fit. During the typical job interview, interviewers must either guess at personal qualities or ask standard questions about situations, hoping to get inklings of personal qualities. Why not proactively give the interviewer the information he is looking for? This section of the interview presentation clearly states the personal qualities that make you successful in the job. And because they have stories and examples attached, they come to life and have impact. Developing a 30/60-Day Strategic Action Plan

When a salesperson presents a service, she talks about how she will implement the service. "Once you purchase our service, here is how we'll get started providing its value. Step one, step two, step three...." Your service is no different. Once hired, what are your goals for the first 30 days and the first 60 days (or 60 days and 90 days)? Presenting a flexible list of goals communicates that you know the job and the position requirements and that you want to provide value quickly. It is essentially your services implementation plan.

Presenting the Benefits the Company Gets from Hiring You

Most candidates talk about all their outstanding skills, experience, and accomplishments and omit the important part—the benefits. This section of the presentation does two things: It summarizes and reiterates your match with the critical job requirements, and it specifies the benefits you will provide to the company. The interviewer will not have to guess the benefits you will provide or why you should be hired.

Presenting Important Questions

During every interview, the interviewer will turn to you and ask, "Do you have any questions for me?" This is a critical point in the interview, and most candidates respond pitifully with, "Not really," or, "You answered my questions." This is an example of how candidates sabotage their interview success.

The final section of the interview presentation is a list of powerful questions you want to ask. The questions reflect your knowledge of the industry, the company, and the job, highlighting the preparation you went through and your interest in the job. Even if the questions were answered, you can go through them just to make sure you are clear about the answers. In any event, the written questions show your preparation.

A Presentation Will Fix Your Interview

> Delivering an exceptional presentation will not guarantee a win every time. But you should never lose because your presentation was less than exceptional.
>
> —Timothy Koegel, author of *The Exceptional Presenter*

A well-developed and well-presented interview presentation will fix your interviews. It reduces subjectivity, provides visual learning, answers the three basic interview questions, and compensates for a bad interviewer. It also differentiates you from other candidates, ensures that you are prepared, and boosts your confidence. Does this sound like a miracle cure for broken job interviews? It can be! An interview presentation provides the following benefits:

*Provides an unparalleled preparation process which ensures you are well prepared for your interview

*Impresses the interviewer with your level of preparation and interest and motivation for the job

*Gives you a method for guiding the interview and communicating the information you want the interviewer to learn

*It is the only tool which can be used in an interview to dramatically improve your interview performance

*Serves as a terrific leave behind the interviewer can refer to when making the hiring decision

*Demonstrates your ability to present information and answer questions both of which are critical job skills

*States clearly why you should be hired so the interviewer does not have to make any guesses or assumptions

Assisting the Hiring Manager to Fill a Position

Brian was applying to a major telecommunications company for a position as a senior business developer. The position had been open for six months, which was puzzling for such a high-paying, desirable position. One of the first questions Brian asked the hiring manager was why the position had been open for such a long time. Being candid, the hiring manager told Brian that he had interviewed a number of qualified candidates; however, none had made it through the multiple interviews with peers and bosses. Somewhere along the way, each candidate was rejected by someone for some often-puzzling reason. The hiring manager was very frustrated.

During the interview, Brian used an interview presentation to communicate his match with the job requirements and his fit with the company culture. The hiring manager was impressed and told Brian he was recommending that he continue the selection process.

When Brian got home after his interview, he was surprised to receive a two-page email from the hiring manager. After all, it is typically the candidate who sends the email after an interview. The email had detailed suggestions about how to modify the interview presentation for each subsequent interviewer. The message included interviewer-specific challenges, management styles, values, and suggested language to use with each person. Brian followed the suggestions to the letter and landed the job.

Without the interview presentation, the hiring manager would not have had a platform upon which to base his suggestions. Brian would not have had an interview tool to assist him in customizing his interview to each interviewer's orientation and personality. Using the interview presentation, the hiring manager and Brian collaborated to fill a long-vacant position and land a new job.

Chapter 6 - Creating Your Personal Brand

- You've Got One, So You Might as Well Manage it
- Determine Your Personal Brand
- Your Brand Is a promise of value
- Your Brand: The Flip Side
- Quality and Usability
- Brand Killers
- You've Got It, Now Use It
- Use Your Brand Statement Often
- Your Brand Has to Stand Up to Scrutiny
- Brands Are Hard Won and Easily lost
- Are You an Expert? Probably!
- From Mid-level Manager to World's Foremost Expert
- Your Vision and Mission
- Create Brand Fans
- Your Online identity Communicates Your Brand
- Six Effective Strategies for Building and Improving Your Brand Online
- It's Not Who You Know, It's Who Knows You!
- A Strong Brand Will fix Your Interviews

According to Wikipedia, personal branding, self-positioning, and individual branding were first introduced in the 1981 book *Positioning: The Battle for your Mind*, by Al Ries and Jack Trout. The personal branding movement was then generally popularized in an August 1997 *FastCompany* magazine article entitled "The Brand Called You," by Tom Peters. Peters wrote "Today, in the Age of the Individual, you have to be your own brand. Here's what it takes to be the CEO of Me, Inc."

Personal branding has been around for almost 30 years. But how many individuals do you know who are actively managing their brand? Very few, I bet! So, why is the idea of personal branding finally gaining momentum?

The most important factor is the shift in the employment marketplace. Up until the early 1990s, most people were employed by large corporations for long periods of time. Your personal brand was essentially your job performance within the corporation. You were considered either a good, fair, or poor employee, and your brand was tied to your role within the organization. No one viewed a personal brand as something you owned and managed, something that was portable, and something that had value independent of the company. Only recently have people clearly become the "CEO of Me, Inc."

Along with job longevity came corporate career management. The company was responsible for managing your career, providing training, a career path, and a series of promotions. After all, if you were going to be with a company for 20 years, it made sense for the company to make sure you progressed in your career. Due in part to today's shorter job tenure (averaging three years), companies have abandoned career management; now it's *your* career to manage. Frequent job changes mean that you are in the job marketplace more frequently selling your services. A well-defined and well-articulated personal brand will help your sales efforts.

The second—and equally important—factor in the growth of personal branding is the Internet. Quickly, easily, and for free, anyone can project a personal brand to the world in a multitude of formats. Your personal brand is no longer locked away behind the walls of a corporation. With this freedom, many more people are using mass-media channels, including Facebook, Twitter, blogs, and LinkedIn to communicate their brand to the world. For the first time in history, everyone has open access to the most important brand strategy: visibility.

You've Got One, So You Might as Well Manage It

Corporations spend hundreds of millions of dollars developing, managing, and protecting their brands. Brand "touch points" include their logo, customer service, treatment and training of employees, packaging, advertising, stationery, and quality of products and services. Any means by which the public connects to a brand constitutes a touch point that affects perception of a corporate brand.

Brands have become so important that many have a dollar value attached to them, called *brand equity*, and that value is part of the calculated value of the company. According to *Forbes* magazine, Apples' brand is valued at $309 billion, Microsoft's is valued at $103.1 billion, and the world's number-one brand, Amazon's, is valued at $315 billion. Some companies get acquired solely for their brand!

You have a brand as well—unfortunately, probably not one worth $315 billion. Like a corporate brand, your brand is determined by what people think and feel about you. Look around at your co-workers, family, friends, and neighbors and consider their brands—what you think and feel about them. Some of them will have strong brands. You will think of them as dependable, hardworking, honest, good in a crisis, willing to lend a hand, punctual, smart, expert, and so on. Others are known for spreading rumors, doing shoddy work, being unreliable or lazy, having a temper, or being careless. These characteristics make a weak brand.

Certainly, a person is neither all good nor all bad, and his brand dictates when you turn to him. The person with a bad temper might be a good organizer, and perhaps the honest person doesn't do well in pressure situations. Also, people may have different brands in different roles. A person may have a great brand as a hard worker on the job, but a weak brand as a good family member.

What is your brand? How do your co-workers, family, friends, and neighbors think and feel about you? Your brand is out there in the minds of others—what is it, and how are you managing it?

Determine Your Professional Brand

Your brand is what others think and feel about you, so the best way to determine your brand is to ask others for feedback. Many companies do this as part of an employment evaluation—the process is called *360 feedback*. A 360 questionnaire is given to everyone who works with the employee, including bosses, subordinates, peers, and clients, if appropriate. The questionnaire provides insight about the employee's performance as well as her brand. You can find free 360-feedback tools online; just Google "free 360 feedback."

You also can determine your brand by doing a self-assessment. Typically, personal brands are a combination of the following:

*Values

*Interests

*Personality

*Skills

*Strengths

*Behavioral style

*Motivators

*Leadership profile

*Work-life balance

Considering these elements, answer the following questions to identify your brand. Your answers will be particularly valuable as you prepare to communicate your brand in interviews.

*What do I do that adds remarkable and distinctive value to an organization?

*What do I do that I am most proud of?

*What do I want to be known for?

*What are the two or three outstanding benefits that I bring to an organization?

*If someone interviewed people who know me well, what would they say my gifts are?

*If people around me heard that I had accomplished something of value, what would they guess that would be?

*At a time when I felt I was contributing to others in a satisfying way, what was I doing?

*When I felt that I was most in tune with my gifts and talents, what was I doing?

*What do I consider to be my best contributions to others?

*When people gossip about me, what do they say are my talents?

*What is my most noteworthy personal trait?

When you have answered these questions, you will have good insight into your brand.

Your Brand Is a Promise of Value

"Promise only what you can deliver. Then deliver more than you promise."

—Author unknown

Corporate brands are based on the value they provide customers, employees, investors, and society as a whole. Your brand is your personal values and skills, and the value of your brand is based on the benefits it provides others. As you develop and communicate your brand, focus on the benefits your brand provides. The greater the benefits to others, the stronger your brand. A strong brand:

***Has integrity by delivering on its promises.** This is the most important element of a strong brand. People relate to you by your word and how you fulfill your word. If you say you will return a call by 9 a.m., you should return the call by 9 a.m. If you say you will complete a task by the end of business today, you should complete it by end of business today. Each time you make (or break) a promise (explicit or implicit), you are creating a brand image.

***Is dedicated to learning.** Learning is a lifelong exercise. Knowledge establishes expertise, and expertise creates a powerful brand.

***Contributes to others.** If nobody benefits from your expertise, it is of no use. Unless you contribute to others, you will not grow. People do not value a brand if the brand is not contributing to them.

***Works hard.** No success comes without hard work, and an unsuccessful brand has little value. A powerful personal brand is built on working hard.

How you dress and present yourself, including your language and social skills, are additional important elements of a personal brand. Dress and presentation communicate professionalism and credibility, which create a trust in others about the value you provide.

Your Brand: Using the Flip Side

Most personal brands stand for something, such as efficiency, quality, service, or integrity. However, it is difficult to differentiate your brand from that of other individuals claiming the same brand qualities. One clever way to differentiate yourself is to focus on what you are against. Being opposed to something, such as waste, inefficiency, poor communication, or rudeness, can help interviewers find meaning in your brand.

In an interview, it can be powerful to be against something rather than for something. For example, instead of being *for* accuracy, be *against* sloppy, inaccurate work. Instead of being *for* integrity, be *against* lying and unethical behavior. Let the interviewer know what you are against, but also include how you are fixing those negative issues.

Quality and Usability

People are not interested in high-quality products or services that are not easy to use or in easily used products and services that are of low quality. In the employment marketplace, your value depends on your marketability and employability. Your *marketability* is the value of your skills, experience, and knowledge—the "quality" of your services. *Employability* refers to your ability to get along well with others on the job, sometimes referred to as *soft skills*—the "usability" of your services.

We have all experienced the smart, efficient co-worker who is impossible to get along with and the incompetent co-worker who is a pleasure to work with—if only he could do the work. Your brand needs to encompass both marketability and employability. Consider the technical things you do and the way you do them. Also consider what makes you attractive to other people at work. In an interview presentation, these qualities are referred to as *personal success factors*. Without good personal success factors, your employability is low, and your brand is tarnished.

Brand Killers

There are lots of behaviors that hurt brands, many of which are obvious. Lying, cheating, stealing, spreading rumors, shirking work, and having a sloppy appearance are only a few of the obvious ones. There are other brand killers that are less obvious and committed by even accomplished people. These include:

***Not stopping to think.** Instead of pausing to think in a rational manner, this is when you let emotions hasten decisions. Many of us think we are good intuitive decision makers, but in highly emotional situations, emotions may overtake even good intuition.

***Failing to see what you are doing as others see it.** You might be convinced of the correctness of what you are doing, and you might be correct; however, if others are not in agreement, you are hurting your brand. Are you sure other people view your behaviors as you mean them to be seen? For example, a manager might reduce consultants' time to save money and avoid staff layoffs, but the staff that has to work more hours may see the boss as saving money to increase profits and get a bigger bonus.

***Being often wrong but never in doubt.** Human brains are wired to build a sense of certainty, and this certainty is often expressed as fact rather than as opinion. Ask yourself whether this is verifiable fact or just your thinking or opinion. If it is your thinking or opinion, present it as such: "This is my thinking/opinion, and I may be wrong, but…."

***Failing to see others' perspectives.** This is getting caught up in your own point of view at the expense of ignoring others' opinions. I wish I had a dollar for every time I said, "This is a no-brainer," only to learn that others' brains didn't see it the same way. For example, in my mind an interview presentation is a no-brainer—but is it in your brain?

***Jumping to conclusions.** Human brains learn patterns that work well most of the time, and it automates them, which promotes efficiency. This has become more prevalent as the world has become more complex and we are confronted with many more choices and decisions. However, automatic responses also encourage us to jump to conclusions that may be wrong. Once you start jumping to conclusions, you may then commit the brand killer of being often wrong but never in doubt.

*Missing the bigger picture. This is when you're narrowly focused on the immediate moment or on your role and you miss the bigger picture. You may succeed yourself, but at the cost of your team or the company. Saying, "I got my section done on time, and it was accurate" for a proposal that didn't win the business is an example of missing the big picture. Your brand is connected more to winning the business than to getting your section done. What did you do to help other team members succeed?

*Doing the right things for the wrong reasons. I once had a boss who announced in a meeting that he had gotten tickets for everyone to attend a Phillies game. We were all pleased and grateful until he said, "Yeah, I was at a fundraising auction, and I wasn't going to let this arrogant SOB show me up by outbidding me." The tickets were nice, but they were tainted by the wrong motivation for getting them, and it hurt his brand, which was not strong to start with. It was no surprise that most of the staff was busy the evening of the game and unable to attend. Doing the right thing for the wrong reason causes confusion and ambivalence in the minds of others and is often worse than not doing the thing at all.

Many of these brand-hurting behaviors will undermine your interview performance as well. You can easily imagine how not stopping to think, jumping to conclusions, failing to see others' perspectives, and missing the big picture will hurt you in interviews.

You've Got It, Now Use It!

When you have determined your brand, it is valuable to be able to actively communicate it in a brief, hard-hitting statement. Your brand statement is one to two sentences that communicate what you are best at (value), whom you serve (audience), and how you do it uniquely (unique selling proposition). It sums up the promise of the value you will deliver; it is not a job title. A job title is something others apply to you and how employers label you, so you fit into a corporate structure. Your brand is bigger than that.

Your brand statement also is not your personal mission statement, career objectives, or even life purpose. These are broader, longer-term concepts intended to guide you through your life and career and are not aimed at marketing you today.

A personal brand statement is memorable, punchy, and solution oriented. As opposed to simply saying, "I am a realtor," why not say "I help people achieve the American Dream—I sell houses?" My brand statement could be, "I help people find jobs." Instead, it is, "I help people achieve their career vision and next job using innovation." One of my clients, a website developer, had "I bring clarity to chaos; I develop websites that sell" as his brand statement. Another client, an administrative assistant, uses, "I organize my boss's desk efficiently" as her brand statement. She used her brand statement to great advantage in her interviews:

> "Met with an HR person who pre-screened me…. I also related some stories of mine. She seemed truly interested during this procedure. I repeated my slogan, 'I manage my boss's office efficiently,' four times. One question— 'Why do you think you are more qualified than other candidates?'—I answered with 'Because I manage my boss's office efficiently.' She wrote it down."

—Amy (62 years old), administrative assistant

A current reality show about a person who restores various objects, from vending machines to motorcycles, has a brand statement of, "I restore history." A graphic artist introduces himself with, "Hello! My name is John. I love drawing and hate zombies. I make art for fun and profit. I am a graphic designer living in California." A good brand statement invites conversation by being provocative and engaging: "Wow, you bring clarity to chaos—how do you do that?" "You manage your boss's desk more efficiently—how do you do that?" "You hate zombies? Why—have you met one?"

In brand statements, less is more. Being able to describe exactly what you do in one sentence is a statement about your clarity and professional focus. These brand statements come in handy during networking and interviewing in response to the question, "Tell me what you do," or, "Tell me about yourself."

Use Your Brand Statement Often

Your brand statement focuses on exactly who you are, what you do, and how it benefits potential customers (employers). It should leave no doubt in an employer's mind as to how she will benefit from your services. You can use your brand statement often and in multiple ways—for example, every time you send an email, post to a discussion group, or establish an online profile, refer to your brand. Doing so ensures that your brand image is clear and well distributed.

Also, keeping your brand message front and center will help you communicate a consistent message that establishes and supports your brand. If your brand is about marketing, integrity, and thought leadership, you won't be tempted to tweet or email about frivolous or unconfirmed rumors concerning Justin Bieber. Your goal is to make mental connections that merge your name with what you stand for. Having your brand statement apparent every time your name appears is one of the best ways to help people make that connection.

Your Brand Has to Stand Up to Scrutiny

"Let none presume to wear an undeserved dignity."

—William Shakespeare

Imagine a company trying to claim a false brand—Philip Morris Cigarettes claiming health, British Petroleum claiming safety and corporate responsibility, or Facebook claiming privacy. It wouldn't work, and it would actually hurt their image. I have led team-building meetings where people shared with their co-workers what they thought their personal brand was. Many got nods of agreement, but many got puzzled looks and even expressions of derision: "Yeah, sure—in your dreams."

For your brand to be of value, it must be authentic and true. If you want your brand to be that of a caring leader, you must actually care about people and have good leadership skills. If you want your brand to be as a reliable and trustworthy co-worker, you must be dependable and not break confidences. Everyone wants a positive brand, but you can't have a positive brand simply by declaring it—you have to deserve it. False personal branding is exposed quickly, resulting in an even worse brand.

During interviews, be prepared with stories and examples that support your brand. If you declare yourself a good communicator, have examples of using communication to achieve a success, and be sure you communicate well during the interview. If you brand yourself an expert—which you probably are (see the "Are You an Expert? Probably!" section)—have stories and examples that support your expertise.

Here is an example of a well-supported brand: One of my clients sold large, expensive medical devices, including MRI machines to hospitals. When developing an interview presentation, he chose the personal brand word "competitive" as one of the terms to represent his brand. I asked him, "Joe, every salesperson brands himself as competitive. How are you going to prove your competitive brand?" He replied, "Eric, let me tell you how competitive I am. When I sell large medical equipment, I only have a few competitors. So, when I go into a sales situation, I study the hospital to which I am selling, and I study the salespeople against whom I am competing. I know their strengths, weaknesses, track records, and employment history. So not only do I sell to the hospital, but I sell against my competition. In at least two situations, my competition did so poorly that they fired their entire sales staff—that's how competitive I am." I was convinced!

Brands Are Hard Won and Easily Lost

Every company has a brand. However, brands cannot be declared simply in writing, they are earned over time, through large and small day-to-day actions that build trust of the brand in consumers' minds.

In brands and in human relationships, trust is built slowly and lost quickly. There are numerous examples of companies or individuals that committed an error and tarnished a good brand. A glaring example is Tiger Woods. Tiger was a quality brand with high levels of trust and numerous endorsements one day; the next day, he was a tarnished brand with far fewer endorsements. In retrospect, it's clear that his brand was not authentic, which made his transgressions even more painful for the public. Like many other fallen celebrities—such as Lori Loughlin (by buying her daughters' way into college), to name just one—Tiger's brand is making a good comeback, but it will more carefully controlled steps and tournament wins.

How do the brands of major companies and celebrities such as Tiger Woods and Lori Loughlin relate to you? Your brand is no different; it develops over time, tarnishes quickly, and is reparable if necessary. For example, suppose you established a reputation for being the "go-to" person for getting project bids done on time and accurately. But along comes a major bid, and you are off your game for one of many possible reasons. You deliver your bid response late, it is inaccurate, and your company loses the business. Your brand is now tarnished. It will take winning two or three subsequent bids to get your brand back to its old level.

The message here is to know your brand and then protect it. When you're confronted with a large number of tasks, one way to prioritize them is to consider which of the tasks is most central to your brand. Brand-centric tasks should take priority, and you should make every effort to deliver on your brand's promise.

Are You an Expert? Probably!

When I'm helping clients with resumes and preparing them for interviews, I often get into a debate about using the word "expert." Clients are concerned about overstating their skill and experience, coming off as immodest or arrogant, and turning off the hiring manager. But there is a difference between being *the* expert and being *an* expert. I contend that anyone with three or more years of experience in a profession is probably an expert.

Dictionary.com defines an expert as "a person who has special skill or knowledge in some particular field; specialist; authority." This is differentiated from a novice, who is "new to any science or field of study or activity or social cause and is undergoing training to meet normal requirements of being regarded a mature and equal participant."

Marie-Line Germain, assistant professor of human resources and leadership at Western Carolina University, developed a measure of perception of employee expertise called the *Generalized Expertise Measure* (*GEM*). Ask yourself whether you meet the following criteria for being an expert. Borrowing a line from a well-known comedian, you might be an expert if:

*You have knowledge specific to a field of work.

*You have the education necessary to be an expert in the field.

*You have the qualifications (certifications, licensure) required to be an expert in the field.

*You have been trained in the area of expertise.

*You are ambitious about your work.

*You can assess whether a work-related situation is important.

*You are capable of improving yourself.

*You can deduce things easily from work-related situations.

*You are intuitive in the job.

*You have the drive to become what you are capable of becoming in your field.

*You are self-assured.

*You are self-confident about your profession.

Using these criteria, the term "expert" can be applied to any job. A janitor can be an expert at janitorial services, just as a lawyer can be an expert at criminal law. If you qualify as an expert in your field, include that in your self-image and your brand and communicate your expert status to the world and your interviewer.

From Midlevel Manager to the World's Foremost Expert

One of my clients was part of a massive layoff at a large pharmaceutical company. He was a midlevel manager working in the bowels of the company, heading up a project to install a well-known management information system (MIS) in a drug-production facility. Although the MIS was a well-known system, this was its first application to drug manufacturing.

During our initial meeting, I asked, "What other drug company is using this MIS system for manufacturing?" My client replied that he was not aware of any other company, and even if it was being implemented elsewhere, his company was about two years ahead of everyone else. I then asked him, "Does anyone else in the drug industry have as much experience implementing this software as you?" After some consideration, he replied that no one else did. Then I said to him, "So, you are the foremost expert in the world at implementing this system for managing drug production!"

After I repeated "foremost expert" a few times, a light went on, and my client realized that he was the world's foremost expert. He immediately stopped looking for a job and called the senior vice-president of sales for the MIS system. He told the senior vice-president, "When you go to sell your MIS system to the next drug company, tell them you have a top expert who will implement the system." He received a call a couple of weeks later from a drug company and accepted a very lucrative job.

Not everyone can claim the title of the world's foremost expert, but most people can and should claim expert status as part of their brand.

Your Vision and Mission

In addition to a brand, most corporations have vision and mission statements that inspire their employees and complement their brand. There is nothing more important or attractive in a personal brand than passion and dedication. Think of the people around you who are committed to excellence and make the effort to be excellent. They are typically charismatic people with valuable brands. One way to ignite your passion and establish your brand is to develop a personal vision and mission.

A personal vision is a big, bold goal that articulates your dreams and hopes for your career, reminding you of what you are trying to accomplish. It is a large, often unobtainable goal that inspires you, gives you energy, and directs your career choices. A doctor may have a vision of achieving a 100 percent error-free medicine or a pain-free world. An airline scheduler might have a vision of every plane being on time every day or a 100 percent safety record. My vision is for "everyone in the world to have a job doing the work they love and earning the money they deserve". These are big, inspirational goals that give direction to work, fuel passion, and build personal brands. What is your vision for your career?

A mission statement is how you are going to achieve your vision. The doctor's mission statement might be, "I am achieving an error-free medicine by developing medication tracking systems and protocols that enforce safety procedures and quality assurance routines." My mission statement is, "I am developing innovative hiring procedures and helping employees discover and articulate their value in the employment marketplace." How are you achieving your vision?

During interviews, it is powerful to tell the interviewer, "This is what I am about [vision], and here is how I achieve it [mission]." One of my young clients (25 years old), who has a passion for sports marketing, has established a goal of being recognized as the Top 40 Under 40 in sports marketing. He communicates this goal during interviews. Having a clear and powerful goal helps the hiring manager see how you fit the organization, it projects a valuable brand, it makes you more charismatic, and it answers the question, "Are you motivated for this job?".

In addition, referring to your vision and mission is the most powerful response you can give to the question "Why do you want this job?" Imagine saying "I want this job because my vision is everyone having financial security and being a Financial Educator is a mission that will support my vision".

Create Brand Fans

The new goal in customer relations is moving from customer satisfaction to earning customer advocates or fans. Instead of being simply a supporter, a customer fan actively supports the brand by sharing her experience, praising the company, and providing unsolicited feedback about service and quality. In some situations, fans will go as far as to protect the brand. Perhaps the best example of brand fans is sports fans. Wouldn't it be terrific to have your own cheering section?

The following strategies will build a network of brand fans.

Address Negativity

Do not focus only on friends and supporters. Identify any sources of negativity and fix the root causes of the negativity. To establish brand fans, you must honestly focus on your most common complaints and fix them. As you fix one source of negativity after the next, your fan base will expand, and in times of need you will have strong supporters.

Build a Solid and Positive Experience

Make sure others are satisfied every time they interact with you. Satisfaction and loyalty are critical to the success of your brand. But don't stop there—offer extraordinary experiences. Go that extra mile when others least expect it, and in return you will receive their long-term fan support. For example, is a co-worker struggling with a project deadline? How about staying late or coming in on a weekend to help out? Is a subordinate overwhelmed? How about picking up a lower-level task you don't typically take on?

Build Others' Brands

Supporting the development of others' brands will build your fan base. You can accomplish this by actively supporting their brands through positive word-of-mouth, by supporting their brand-building activities, and by helping them improve their network. For example, a co-worker may be taking on a project in a new area to broaden his brand. Providing support and guidance as he works on the project supports his brand. As another example, use your network to connect people you know would benefit from knowing one another. As they connect and get benefits, your fan base will get stronger. And, don't forget to constantly say nice things about people who deserve it.

Encourage Your Fans to Be Active

Satisfaction and loyalty are important, but they're old news. Forward-thinking companies identify and work with their fans to build the brand, the customer base, and the bottom line. Look at the explosion of online social sites, such as Facebook, where fans actively "like" and work to build brands. Work with your fans to build your brand. Silent fans are okay, but active fans are terrific. Let your fans know what you are doing and invite their participation. Have them participate in your projects; write supportive blogs, emails, and tweets; and help you network. The more active your fans, the stronger your brand.

Reward Your Fans

Many of us are aware that we need to say thank you; however, taking an additional step to express your gratitude creates fans. For example, one of my junior-level clients was referred to a position, which he landed, by a senior executive in the company. He wrote a handwritten thank-you letter. Every time he meets the executive's wife at a party, she mentions the handwritten note. She is a fan—the executive must've been very impressed to share the note with his wife!

As another example, I landed a position after a period of unemployment, and I sent a gift basket of gourmet ketchups to the five most supportive people. The ketchup tasted great, was a bit unusual, and was a step beyond a normal thank you. Think of ways you can "reward" your fans and make a thank you stand out. Also, don't wait until a fan does something huge, and don't make rewarding fans a rare or unusual event.

Your Online Identity Communicates Your Brand

As mentioned previously, everyone has easy and free access to communicating his brand online. Prior to the Internet, companies had printed brochures and employees carried business cards. Today, websites *are* company brochures, and business cards are being replaced rapidly by the electronic transfer of contact information. Using online resources to increase your brand's visibility is critical to building and managing your brand.

My son, Zach, recently worked for a company doing promotion for BMW. He was responsible for setting up events for potential BMW buyers. Prior to the first event, he received a phonebook-size binder with room setup requirements, including everything from car placement to the type of silverware and the acceptable color of flowers and tablecloths. Not one detail was overlooked. BMW considers each requirement part of maintaining and communicating their brand.

Interestingly, most people—2.6 billion and growing on Facebook and 620 million on LinkedIn—are branding themselves online without being aware of it or considering the details. Everything you put online or connect to online reflects your brand. Your choice of music, the pictures you upload or "like" on Facebook, the articles you link to, the groups you join, the products you review—they all communicate your brand. I'm not suggesting that you need to be as fanatical as BMW (although it has worked for them); however, I *do* suggest you pay attention to how your choices communicate your brand. This is particularly important for younger candidates who use the online world to communicate all the details of their lives.

Despite some legal questions, it is standard operating procedure for companies and recruiters to Google candidates and look them up on LinkedIn. Surveys by job-placement firms show that recruiters like candidates whose online identity reflects a professional image, well-rounded skills, and a personality that fits the company's culture.

There are numerous ways to become more visible on the Internet, some as simple as developing a free page on a networking site, such as Facebook or LinkedIn. Or you can do something more complex, such as building your own website optimized for drawing traffic or writing your own blog.

Building your brand online is like building your brand in the real world. It requires a series of small, consistent steps taken over time, adding up to a strong brand presence. Unless you hit the "go viral" lottery and your brand is an overnight success, plan on developing your brand over a number of months or even years. As the saying goes, "The best time to plant a tree was 20 years ago; the next best time is today." Today is the day to get started on your online branding. Once you decide on your level of interest, effort, and budget, you can establish an online strategy that builds your brand online.

Six Effective Strategies for Building and Improving Your Brand Online

There are simple and effective strategies for establishing and maintaining your brand online. Many of them are easily implemented and either inexpensive or free. The following sections discuss these strategies.

Own Your Name

The first strategy is to own your name. Go to a domain registrar, such as GoDaddy.com or 1and**1**.com, and for less than $10 you can register a domain in your name—www.yuorname.com. However, note that your name may already be registered by someone else, particularly if you have a common name. If this is the case, try registering a domain with your middle name or middle initial. When I went to register erickramer.com, it was taken, so I registered ericpkramer.com.

After you have a "yourname" domain, you can build a website, have a custom email address (yourname@ yourname.com), establish an online career portfolio, or write a blog. All of these will be easily searchable, using your name.

Refine and Expand Your Online Network

Having an extensive list of professional contacts is a well-established job search and career-management strategy. Moving your contact list online, establishing a visible (searchable) professional profile, and expanding your network are important branding strategies. The larger and more established networking sites makes this quick and inexpensive; in fact, most are free. Today, the best site for professionals is LinkedIn (owned by Microsoft). Facebook is also moving toward providing a more professional presence.

When you have registered on these sites, develop a robust professional profile. Your online profile is every bit as important as your paper resume today and will probably replace your resume in the near future.

Upgrade Your Resume to the Online World

Just listing your text resume online at major job sites is important, but it's no longer sufficient for a good online branding strategy. Internet technology enables you to include a visual and engaging portfolio about your career. This portfolio includes and supplements your printed resume. A comprehensive portfolio can include your work history, including links to the companies for which you worked, significant career achievements, links to articles, presentations, case studies, recommendations, references, awards, and so on. Also, by using graphics, video, and audio, your portfolio will be a more engaging representation of your skills, experience, and work history.

Write Your Way to the Top

In the online world, you must establish a virtual self and a "home base" from which to connect to others. A blog or a website is the most powerful way to develop a recognizable brand, and either one provides a home base from which you can initiate your connections. Profiles on social-networking sites, such as LinkedIn and Facebook, can also achieve this goal; however, you need to be active on these sites to stand out. Statistics show that only 10% of LinkedIn's 620 million users post content on LinkedIn. If you post content you will stand out.

Once you establish a website or a blog or a LinkedIn profile, remember that you must constantly feed it. (Google likes fresh, new information.) Blogs, websites and LinkedIn profiles with stale, outdated information hurt an online brand.

A quick, easy way to get noticed through writing is to post replies or comments on blogs or the answers section of LinkedIn. Answering questions on LinkedIn or making comments on industry blogs takes only a few minutes and can get you noticed by many people. As suggested earlier, each time you post something online, include your brand.

You do not always have to produce new and proprietary content to communicate online. For example, most tweets on Twitter are simply connections to existing content. Define your content niche and then write original information and link to existing information. The writers to whom you link will appreciate the traffic you send them, as long as you make it clear that it is a link and not your own content.

Keep Your Online Identity Clean

An ExecuNet survey found that 35 percent of recruiters have ruled out job candidates based on what they found on a Google search. Be constantly vigilant about things you do online or things you do in the real world that may end up online (hello, YouTube). Recently, an executive was visiting his son at college. He was walking by a frat house and impulsively drank a beer from a beer bong (a long tube, as long as 20 to 30 feet, with a funnel at one end and the drinker at the other end). One week later, his beer-bong picture was online for the world to see.

Once a picture gets loose on the Internet, it is difficult, if not impossible, to remove. With a camera on every phone today, you must be cautious constantly.

Similarly, think of the possible repercussions of articles you write, blogs to which you contribute, and newsgroups in which you participate. Anything you write online becomes permanent, and when someone searches your name, it will be found. I have a friend with a PhD who was paid to write an article about artisanal beers for a beer connoisseur magazine. Now when you Google her name, her beer article comes up first and gives the impression of a beer-loving partier instead of a serious professional. Also, particularly on LinkedIn, avoid anything controversial such as religion or politics, which may turn a potential employer or recruiter off. For example, if you choose to list your volunteer activities be sure the volunteer groups you list are non-controversial like The Red Cross or Habitat for Humanity.

Track Your Online Brand

A simple, quick, and free way to track your online brand is to set up a Google alert to notify you each time your name is found on the Internet. Simply list your name in an alert, and Google will send you an email message when it finds your name online. How often are you found today? Over time, are you being found more often? When you Google yourself, how high up in the listing are you found, and what information shows up?

Developing and managing your online brand is critical to career management and should be part of your ongoing career management strategy. Prior to any interview, research yourself online to discover what a hiring manager will be reading about you. Be ready with stories and examples about the positive aspects of your online brand—and be ready with explanations for any negative information that might tarnish your brand.

It's Not Who You Know, It's Who Knows You!

Long ago, people moved ahead in their careers simply by knowing things—having expertise. Then, in a networked world, it became about not *what* you knew, but about *who* you knew. Today, with access to online communication and branding, it's not who you know, it's who knows *you*. The question is, if I were looking for someone with your skills and experience, do I already know about you? If not, how easily could I find you? The greater your online presence and the better networked you are, the greater the likelihood that you will be contacted for jobs. Also, having a strong brand that precedes you to an interview significantly increases your credibility and persuasiveness.

A Strong Brand Fixes Your Interviews

Having a well-developed brand provides clarity and direction in how you think about your skills, experience, and value in the marketplace. This clarity enables you to present to the hiring manager your fit with the critical job requirements and why you are the best choice for the job. Without this clarity, your answers become vague, your confidence goes down, and the hiring manager's FUD level goes up. A strong brand provides the following benefits:

*It communicates a powerful message to the interviewer about how she should think and feel about you.

*It differentiates you from other candidates who may have the same skill set.

*It communicates how you fit the culture of the company.

*It provides credibility.

*It communicates your interest and passion for your profession.

*It declares your expertise.

*It increases your confidence level.

Chapter 7 - Critical Job Requirements

- A Good Job Description
- You're a Salesperson, So Go Get the Requirements
- Job Requirements Often Are Broken
- Ask Good Questions
- Many Job Descriptions Are Really Wish Lists
- Be Aware of Fluffy Requirements
- Acknowledge What's Missing
- Knowing the Critical Job Requirements Will fix Your Interviews

The decision to purchase any item or service depends upon a set of requirements that must be met before the item or service is acquired. Think about your purchasing decisions—each one has a set of requirements that determines the item you select. Some requirements are set in stone; if the item does not meet the requirement, there will not be a purchase. Other requirements are nice to have; if the item does not have them, you *might* still purchase the item. In other words, some requirements are critical while others are preferred or optional.

A job description is essentially a set of purchasing requirements, both critical and optional. Unfortunately, most job descriptions are poorly written and don't provide the information a candidate needs to gain a deep understanding of the job, nor do they have enough detailed information to help a hiring team communicate the specific role that a new hire will fill. Providing a poorly developed job description to a candidate is like saying to a computer salesperson, "We want to buy a computer that does the work we need it to do. Got one?"

A Good Job Description

Once you know the elements of a good job description, you will know a good one when you read one. You will also recognize a bad job description when you read one. A good job description is based on a job analysis, which includes examining the tasks and sequences of tasks necessary to perform the job and states the nature of work, tasks to be done, skills expected, responsibilities and duties to be fulfilled, educational eligibility, qualifications needed, and other specifications related to the job. A good job description has the elements discussed in the following sections.

General Job Description

*The job title

*The nature of the job

*Job type: full-time or part-time

*Location of the office

*Work flexibility including work from home options

*Salary and benefits

*Physical demands

Education and Specifications

This covers qualifications and prior experience in the particular field that the applicant must have to be successful in the job, which may include:

*Education level

*Diploma and vocational training

*Experience in prior jobs

*Number of years of experience

*Knowledge/expertise in specific processes or technologies

Duties and Responsibilities

This covers major areas of responsibility and roles the candidate will play, including what the person in the position actually does, the primary goals and objectives of the position, and its overall contribution to the organization.

*Managerial requirements

*Supervisory level

*Any corporate or individual objectives

*Working conditions

*Goals to be met, specified using metrics where possible

*Detailed work activities that are part of the job

Skills and Knowledge

These are attributes the employer is looking for in a candidate to be successful in this job, including knowledge, skill, and abilities required to perform the job tasks. These may include:

*Communication skills

*Networking skills

*Analytical ability

*Teamwork skills

*The ability to deal with stress

*Flexibility

*Persistence

*Technology skills

*Critical Thinking

Look for these elements in a well-written and comprehensive job description. If the job description lacks these elements or is not sufficiently detailed, it becomes your task to find the job description details you need to sell yourself into the job.

You're a Salesperson, So Go Get the Requirements

The beginning stage of any sale is a needs assessment. After all, you can't sell what you have if you don't know what the consumer needs! In the case of a job interview, the more specific a job requirement is, the easier it is to link your skills, education, experience, and brand to the requirement and then communicate the link to the hiring manager. As the candidate, it is your responsibility to get as much information about the job requirements as possible and make selling yourself easier. This section will discuss some strategies to help you do this.

First, read the job listing carefully and look for any requirements that are defined or measurable and specified as "required." For example, is there a requirement for:

*A specific degree or certification?

*A certain number of years of experience in the job or industry?

*A highly specific skill or knowledge?

*A specific level of performance in a job or task?

These requirements are typically important to the position and are an easy way for hiring managers to determine whether a candidate is appropriate for a position. If you don't have the requirements, you probably shouldn't apply for the job. If you don't have the requirements and you have been invited for an interview, it might be a mistake or, more likely, the hiring manager sees something in you that she thinks can be of value—something that you may not even be aware of.

Research the position on the company's website. You might be able to get additional detail about job requirements based on what the company does and what the position does within the company. Call the company and request sales literature, annual reports, technical information, and product brochures. This material might provide you with additional insights about the company and the position.

You can also look for similar positions at other companies and use their job descriptions. Or, call hiring managers for similar positions at other companies and ask about their requirements for the job. Some of my clients have been successful finding additional information by emailing people they connect with on LinkedIn. Do this by finding someone on LinkedIn that either currently works at the company or worked at the company in the past. Ask to connect with them. Once connected you can message them and ask for insights about the company, the job, and hiring manager.

Prior to the interview, call or email the hiring manager and tell him you are preparing for the interview and would like to know the critical job requirements. I can hear you saying, "But no one else does this. Won't the hiring manager be annoyed?" No. This is an "avoid the herd and fix your interview" strategy. Few candidates do this, and why should a hiring manager be annoyed? He should be impressed! The better prepared you are for the interview, the easier the hiring manager's decision will be.

It's an outdated and foolish notion that interviews have to be a think-on-your-feet question-and-answer process with little (if any) preparation. Using the sales analogy, how often is a salesperson invited to a sales call without a thorough briefing by the purchaser about purchase requirements and criteria so that he can prepare his sales presentation?

Job Requirements Often Are Broken

Like many other parts of the job interview, job requirements often are broken. Asking detailed questions about the job before and during your interview clarifies the requirements for both you and the hiring manager.

Here is an interesting phenomenon: When using an interview presentation that listed critical job requirements, many of my clients found that different interviewers did not agree about the critical requirements. Uh oh, a red flag is rising. A client would present the interview presentation to the first interviewer and say, "Based on my understanding of the position at this point, here is a list of what I believe to be the critical job requirements. I'd like to discuss them with you to be sure we are both in agreement that these are the critical requirements." Following a discussion, there would be agreement about the requirements. My client then would go to the next interview and say, "Based on my understanding of the position at this point *and my prior interview(s)*, here is a list of what I believe to be the critical job requirements. I'd like to discuss them with you to be sure we are both in agreement that these are the critical requirements." The second interviewer would look at the list and say, "These are not what I think the critical requirements are."

Despite the disagreement, this can be a good situation for a candidate. Several of my clients became "consultants," helping the company define the position requirements and then selling themselves into the position.

Even with well-defined written job requirements, it is important to understand the requirements from each interviewer's personal perspective. A senior manager will have a different perspective from a direct supervisor or a peer. Like any good salesperson, you should ask questions to understand each interviewer's individual perspective and then present the benefits that you will provide to that individual. Personalizing your benefits to each decision-maker and influencer makes you more persuasive and a better candidate. This is like selling a car to a family. The mother who transports the kids daily may have a different perspective than the father who is more focused on reliability. The salesperson has to address both perspectives.

One of main reasons why employees fail is that they take a position without being fully aware of what the job entails. Then they either fail at the job or leave because they're doing work that they don't enjoy. I've had this experience. I was hired for an account management position at a software development company. The job, as I understood it, was to take an existing software system and manage existing accounts, as well as to sell the software to new accounts. Soon after starting the job, I found out that the system was not developed and implemented, and I became the project manager for a $6 million software development project—for which I was not qualified.

Had I engaged in a conversation about critical job requirements, I would have learned that project management skills were a major part of the job, I would've realized that the project was not as far along as I thought, and I would not have taken the job.

Knowing the critical job requirements and agreeing with the hiring manager about them prevents a bad hiring situation and fixes your interview.

Ask Good Questions

For most positions, there is an initial phone-screening interview with a representative from human resources. Use this phone screening to ask important job-requirement questions. When you ask questions about the requirements, rather than simply answering questions, you appear motivated and professional. Typically, you'll impress the screener, who plays an important role in the hiring decision. The next three sections provide lists of suggested questions. However, be aware depending on the level and skill of the screener, they may not know the answer to these questions, so don't be surprised.

Position Qualifications Questions

*What are three or four "must-have" qualifications a person should have to be selected for this position?

*In addition to the "must haves" for this position, what are some other qualifications that are important to have?

*What criteria will you use to make your hiring decision?

*What personal qualities will it take to get this job done?

*What technical skill are required to be successful in this position?

*What are the most important personal characteristics for a person in this position?

Position Task Questions

*What are the major responsibilities of this position?

*What is the highest priority for a person in this position?

*What important issues need to be addressed immediately?

*Where do you see this position going in the next few years?

*What is a typical day for a person in this position?

*What made the previous person on this job successful (or unsuccessful)?

*What difficulties did the previous person in this position have?

*What kind of planning and organizing does the job entail?

*What do you consider the greatest challenge(s) of this position?

*Could you tell me about the way the job has been performed in the past? And what improvements you'd like to see happen?

*What are the biggest obstacles to performing this job well?

*What would represent success for a person in this position in six months?

In 12 months?

*What are the major challenges a person in this position will face over the next six months?

*Do you foresee any major changes in this position over the next six months?

The next 12 months?

*What are the challenges I would face in this position over the next three months?

*What surprising and positive thing could a new person do in first 90 days?

*What is the first assignment you intend to give the person you hire?

*What are three accomplishments I will need to have checked off at three, six, and twelve months from starting this role? How do these support the department, division, and corporate strategic objectives? What resources are already allocated to accomplish these goals?

*What are the two or three things I would need to do to make sure the major goal of the job was accomplished?

*What could I do in the position that would surprise and amaze you?

Organizational Questions

*To whom does this position report?

*Tell me about some of the people that a person in this position will interact with on a regular basis

*Is this a new position? If it is new, why are you adding it at this time?

*What types of people tend to excel in this company?

The answers to these questions will give you excellent insight into the critical requirements for the job. When you have the insights, you are ready to prepare for your interview, including identifying the problem(s) to be solved, anticipating questions, developing questions to ask, and preparing an interview presentation.

Many Job Descriptions Are Really Wish Lists

I would love to have a car that flies like a plane, sails like a boat, is the size of a recreational vehicle for camping, and gets 100 miles per gallon on used frying oil. I have been looking but haven't been able to locate one yet.

Many job descriptions are like my fantasy car. Hiring managers include everything they want in job descriptions, hoping they will get most of it. If you are experienced in the profession, you quickly realize that no one person could possibly have all the qualifications the hiring manager listed. In this situation, it becomes even more important to find out the critical job requirements and focus your interview on addressing those requirements. It is also important not to be concerned or discouraged if you lack some of the job requirements; your competition is lacking some requirements as well and may not fit the culture.

Be Aware of Fluffy Requirements

Fluffy requirements make job descriptions longer but don't add any selection insights. For example, "good communication skills" is a fluffy requirement. What are good communications skills, how do we measure them in an interview, and would we really hire someone who cannot communicate well? Likewise, "good problem-solving skills" is a fluffy requirement. Unless we are hiring for a position that has no problems to be solved, shouldn't *everyone* have good problem-solving skills?

Fluffy requirements are different from critical job requirements, such as "3+ years of experience working as a system tester in the IT industry" or "Strong fundamental understanding of engineering thermodynamics, including vapor compression refrigeration cycle, air-side psychometrics, and energy relationships." Critical job requirements are the hiring criteria at the center of your interview presentation. Separating fluff requirements from the critical requirements so you can focus on the important requirements is part of your interview preparation.

Acknowledge What's Missing

Even with realistic job requirements, no candidate is a perfect fit. If you're missing skills or experience in an important job requirement, don't avoid the missing requirement—meet it head on. You are at the interview, so you obviously fit enough of the job description to be considered for the job.

As part of your preparation, plan to address the gap as a conversation topic during your interview. Address the missing qualification and then point to a compensating qualification as closely linked as possible to the missing one. For example, you might say, "I don't have experience working in a college setting [requirement]; however, I have worked with students in summer programs, and I'm active in leadership development groups, which have many college-age members." Proactively addressing an obvious deficit demonstrates strength, honesty, and trustworthiness as well as diffuses the interviewer's concern (FUD).

Knowing the Critical Job Requirements Fixes Your Interview

Having the right people in the right jobs results in higher <u>employee retention,</u> increased productivity, and better performance, all of which are critical to the bottom-line success of any company. Getting the right people in the right jobs begins with a good job description, which attracts the right people and gives them the information they need to interview well. Unfortunately, most job descriptions do not provide the information the hiring manager or a candidate needs to assess job fit. As a candidate in a sales mode, it's your responsibility to discern the critical job requirements and using those requirements to prepare and manage your interview. Knowing the critical job requirements provides the following benefits:

*It enables you to focus your interview preparation on critical issues.

*It helps you anticipate questions that the interviewer may ask.

*It helps you prepare examples and stories about having fulfilled similar job requirements for other employers.

*It positions you as a knowledgeable and conscientious professional.

*It raises your confidence level.

*It enables you to sell yourself—particularly your benefits—in the interview.

*It helps you determine whether the job is of interest to you.

Chapter 8 - Link Your Background to the Critical Job Requirements

- Differentiation is Your Biggest Challenge
- Interviewers Like Similarities
- Linking Your background to the Critical Job Requirements Will Fix Your Interviews

When purchasing a service, buyers want to know who has used the service, where it has been used, and how successful it was. They use this information to decide whether the service will be of value to them—this is why user reviews have become so popular on Internet retailer sites like Amazon. Most purchasers are looking for prior uses of a product or service that have a great deal of similarity to their own circumstances. The greater the similarity, the lower the purchaser's FUD (fear, uncertainty, and doubt) level, and the higher his buying confidence.

Hiring managers seek the same information about your services. Who else has used your services, where else have they been used, and how successful were you? Because this information is historical, a lot of it is in your resume. However, as mentioned previously, your resume is of little value during your interview. A resume is a static, backward-looking document that doesn't address the benefits you will bring to the company with which you are interviewing. In addition, when you wrote your resume, you didn't know the details of the critical job requirements as you do now.

Differentiation Is Your Biggest Challenge

Throughout your interview, you have the goal of differentiating yourself and persuading the hiring manager that you are the candidate of choice. This is most challenging as you link your background, skills, and experience to the critical job requirements, because everyone interviewed has the required background and can link up. Your strategy here is to be the most memorable, the most persuasive, the most likable and to leave no doubt in the hiring manager's mind that you fit the requirements like a glove. Using your brand, selling techniques, and an interview presentation will enable you to impress the hiring manager with your match to the critical requirements and win the interview.

Interviewers Like Similarities

As interviewers listen to you speak about your previous experience, they are wondering constantly, "Is that the same as we do here?" They attempt to reduce FUD by confirming that you have done the same things in much the same way at a similar company. This gives them comfort that you will be able to do the job for which you are applying at their company.

Early in my career, I sold forensic testing—that is, drug testing. The company I worked for did tens of thousands of drug tests every year for major corporations in heavily regulated industries, including airlines, trucking, telecommunications, and manufacturing. A bank called me to talk about drug-testing their employees. During my sales presentation, I was asked whether we had any experience with drug-testing bank employees, which we did not. I had to use a great deal of persuasion to convince the bankers that we could manage to get their employees to pee in a cup, even though we hadn't previously tested bank employees.

If you're applying for a job in an industry in which you have already worked, you won't face this hurdle. Candidates applying to do the same job in a different industry have to overcome this bias, though. Career changers have an even bigger hurdle to get over. Regardless, it is important to eliminate as much as you can any perceived differences between your experience and the job. The following sections will provide strategies to help you reduce perceived differences.

Use the Same Language

Every industry and profession has its own terminology and jargon. It is important to use the appropriate terminology and jargon so the hiring manager feels comfortable that you know the industry. It is also important to know the language so you can understand industry- or profession-specific questions. If you're changing careers or industries, study the language prior to your interview. One way of doing this is to read industry-related articles.

Different companies use different terms for the same jobs and activities. One company may have a purchasing manager, while another has a supply chain manager. One company may have an accounts receivable clerk, while another has a revenue specialist. Hiring managers are looking for people who have done similar jobs at other companies. Using the same job titles will make it easier for a hiring manager to relate you to her position.

Use the interviewer's exact words. If the interviewer says, "We're disappointed about our previous quarter's performance," don't use the word "concerned" if you refer to the previous quarter—use "disappointed." If the interviewer refers to "team meetings" as "huddles," use the word "huddles" when talking about meetings. Active listening at the beginning of your interview will give you a lot of information about company-specific language. Also, don't hesitate to ask the definition of a word or term you don't know—it may be a company-specific word or term that you couldn't have known and need to understand.

You Have Exclusive Information, So Use It!

Studies show that exclusive information is viewed as more valuable and more persuasive. If you've worked in a similar position at another company, chances are you have information about processes and procedures that are unique to your prior company. Without disclosing proprietary information, you can suggest that you have exclusive information that would be of value to the hiring manager. You might mention this by saying, "At my previous company, I was responsible for many of the tasks you require in this position. We were pretty advanced in our business procedures, and I'm sure some of the advanced processes I used there would be of great value to your organization. For example, we figured out how to shorten time to market by two weeks, which saved us approximately $10,000 per product." If the interviewer asks for more detailed information, smile and say, "When you hire me, I'll be happy to answer your question."

During your job search, you may learn exclusive information from other job seekers, networking meetings, and time spent studying your industry. All of this is valuable information you can use in your interview. If you share exclusive information and don't label it as such, you are losing an opportunity to differentiate yourself and increase you persuasiveness. When you share exclusive information, preface it with, "This is something I learned from a meeting with…and few people know this."

Tell Stories and Give Examples

The typical candidate simply talks about having performed the required tasks at previous employers. For example, the interviewer asks, "Have you done month-end closing?" and the candidate replies, "Yes, that was part of my job at Previous Co. I did them every month, and I'm quite good at doing them." It's boring, not memorable, and not persuasive.

Take a lesson from Hollywood. Give your stories interesting characters and dialogue, plus some drama to which the interviewer can relate:

> "Month-end closing was an important part of my job that I really enjoyed. At Previous Co., each month we had about $300,000 in revenue, and reconciling that amount was challenging. My boss, John Smith, was very exacting about having the books 100 percent accurate, and I'm proud to say I met that goal every month. John actually commented to the CEO in front of me that I was the most accurate bookkeeper he had ever worked with. I'm very proud of that comment. I look forward to bringing the same level of accuracy to the position here."

The second answer is far more compelling and engaging. It also has the benefit of allowing you to brag about yourself without obviously boasting. Write a series of these success stories before your interview so you are ready to tell them when an opportunity arises. See Chapter 10, "Tell Stories That Engage and Persuade," for more information about telling stories during an interview.

Numbers Tell a Story

Numbers are persuasive, so whenever possible, include numbers in your answers. Instead of saying, "I supervised a staff of people in a number of locations," say, "I supervised a staff of 12 people in three locations with a budget of $450,000."

It can take some creativity to derive numbers, but you will find that it is far easier to attach numbers to your performance than you might think. For example, perhaps as an administrative assistant, you modified an expense form, which reduced the amount of time required to fill out the form from 30 minutes to 10 minutes. Twenty managers were required to submit the form every week. Do some simple math: You saved 400 minutes per week, or a total of nearly seven hours (rounded up). Seven hours multiplied by 50 weeks equal 350 hours a year. Now plug in the hourly rate of each manager—say, $40 per hour, and you saved the company $14,000 per year, or 15 percent of your salary, by modifying one form.

Something like this would be a good story to relate in response to a question about taking initiative or improving operations. If the interviewer says, "Tell me about a time when you took initiative to improve your work," you could reply, "We were using an expense form that was difficult to fill out. The managers hated it and often submitted it late, and it took a lot of time to administer. I reformatted the form in Excel, which shortened the time required to fill out the form from 30 minutes to 10 minutes. As a result, the 20 managers who filled out the form were far happier. They began to get the forms in on time, and the change saved the company $14,000 per year. My supervisor made a special point of recognizing the improvement during a team meeting and said it was an excellent example of taking initiative."

Linking Your Background to the Critical Job Requirements Will Fix Your Interview

The number-one question interviews are supposed to answer is, "Can the candidate do the job and do it well?" This question is answered in large part by determining whether the candidate has done similar work in a previous job. Thus, it is very important for you to actively link your background and experience to the job's critical job requirements. Linking your background to the critical job requirements will have the following benefits:

*It will reduce the hiring manager's FUD and make it more comfortable for her to hire you.

*It will allow you to proactively answer questions the interviewer may have planned to ask.

*It will differentiate you from other candidates.

*It will highlight similarities between your background and experiences and the job tasks.

*It will enable the interviewer to visualize you performing the job.

*It will help you prepare for your interview.

*It will allow you to communicate that not only have you done similar tasks, but you also have done them very well, and you have examples to prove it.

Chapter 9 - Your Value-Adds and Significant Selling Proposition

- Value-Adds
- Effectively Package a Value-Add
- Value-Ads Require Proof
- For Maximum Impact, Attach a Story and a Benefit to Your Value-Add
- Use a Significant Selling Proposition
- Have an SSP, No Story Needed
- Discover Your Value-Adds and SSPs
- A Value-Add is More Valuable if It's Hard to Acquire
- Value-Adds and SSPs Will Fix Your Interviews

In a competitive and crowded marketplace, every product and service must differentiate itself. It is not enough to be simply as good as all the rest, because there are too many "all the rests" in the market. In addition, with easy access to cheap (or even free) Internet advertising, there is a great deal of advertising that makes differentiating services and determining buying decisions difficult—just think of all the pop-up ads you see online. In the employment marketplace, this is exemplified by the tens of thousands of job sites and hundreds of resumes submitted over the Internet in response to advertised jobs. To rise above the flood of advertising, successful companies establish powerful branding and distinct value-adds and/or significant selling propositions (SSPs). You can adopt the same strategy to rise above the flood of your competition in the employment marketplace.

Value-Adds

A *value-add* refers to an extra feature of a service that goes beyond the standard expectations and provides a more compelling reason to purchase. A value-add makes the service more desirable and positively influences the buying decision. However, a value-add has no value if it is not in addition to good service. Having "always on-time delivery" does not make a difference if the pizza tastes terrible.

The worst position for a service is to be a commodity. A service is a commodity when it is equivalent no matter who provides it. A provider of a commodity service is easily exchanged for another provider of the same service who offers a lower price. For example, many dry cleaners provide a commodity service. Customers will change to another dry cleaner if they can find one that costs less. In the employment marketplace, many employees—even mid- and senior-level employees—are commodities in that they provide a service that can be replaced easily. In bad economies, companies replace more expensive "commodity" employees with cheaper employees. Are you a commodity in the employment marketplace?

Establishing your value-adds, which differentiates you and takes you out of the easily replaced commodity category, is a critical part of career management, branding, and interviewing. However, determining value-adds can be challenging, and many candidates face the challenges discussed in the following sections.

Not Really a Value Add

Many of my candidates have been very successful at their jobs. They are good team leaders, they communicate well, they are good salespeople, they know various software packages, they have notable achievements, and so on. Within their organizations, they do things that provide substantial value because they are the only ones who know how to do it or can do it well. However, outside their companies, the skills or knowledge may be commonplace and not a value-add. Even worse, candidates may highlight the skill or experience in a resume or interview and come off as uninformed about the employment marketplace or as a lightweight. For example, "I am really good at Excel," or, "I am a good team leader"—join the herd!

I tell my successful clients that they are stars in a very crowded universe. And even though they are proud of their accomplishments, they need to distinguish value-adds from standard skills. The challenge for these clients is in packaging and presenting their skills. (See the upcoming "Effectively Package a Value-Add" section.)

Not Aware of a Value Add

Other clients have a strong value-add of which they are completely unaware. These clients typically have worked at one company for a long time, have developed valuable skills, view them as regular parts of their job, and have never received recognition for these skills. For example, "I am a negotiator, and [value-add] I successfully negotiate arms treaties between actively hostile international warlords and drug dealers. I do it all the time—no big deal." Okay, a more realistic example might be, "I supervise a call center, and [value-add] I have also done project management for the implementation of a multimillion-dollar text-analytics software package." A call-center manager with project management experience has a valuable value-add.

Clients with unknown value-adds are often very surprised when they begin to look for a job and get an overwhelming positive response. Research shows that as much as 75 percent of the workforce is interested in finding a new job. I wonder how many would be actively looking and making a move if they knew their true value in the marketplace.

Effectively Package a Value Add

Some clients have value-adds that only become valuable when they are "packaged" and presented correctly. For example, I've had several clients who were entrepreneurs and who decided to go to work for a company. Entrepreneurship is not an obvious value-add for a large company—in fact, for some companies it suggests that you're headstrong, too independent, and not a good team member. However, being an entrepreneur means you have an owner's mentality and are aware of issues that employees in large companies pay no attention to, such as cash flow and accounts receivable. Entrepreneurs also tend to have a more urgent timeframe, recognizing speed as a valuable business advantage. The entrepreneur needs to package the value-add of entrepreneurship in a way that presents an obvious benefit to the company.

I started my career as a clinical psychologist. When looking for jobs in management in the corporate world, I packaged my psychology experience as a value-add in terms of working with people, having extraordinary listening skills, and managing team dynamics. (I ran many group-therapy sessions, which are not much different from team meetings at some companies.) I also package my psychology background as a value-add for career coaching, because much of career coaching involves psychological and emotional issues that career coaches without psychology licenses cannot address ethically.

Most people have a combination of skills and experiences that can be packaged and presented as a value-add. I've spoken with a number of candidates who had career changes early in their career—maybe three to four years out of school—that presented an opportunity to package a value-add. For example, one client was applying for jobs selling clinical lab-testing equipment. He had a degree in biology, and immediately out of school, he worked in a high-volume lab doing clinical testing for three to four years. His value-add to a lab-testing equipment company was having actually used lab-testing equipment. He could speak the technicians' language and understood the day-to-day routines of working in a lab. In competition with other candidates who had only backgrounds in selling clinical equipment, he had a job-winning value-add.

Value-Adds Require Proof

For interviewing purposes, a value-add must be a skill that you can prove you have. For example, provable skills might include a language proficiency, a sales approach in which you have been trained, a computer skill that you can perform, a business process in which you are certified, or management skills where you can cite specific results (preferably with numbers attached). Skills such as team leadership, good communication, strong organization, and time management are valuable but too vague to be persuasive during an interview, unless you have objective proof (such as getting the Team Leader of the Year award for three years running or a team leadership training certification).

For Maximum Impact, Attach a Story and a Benefit to Your Value-Add

For a value-add to have maximum impact during your interview, attach a story or an example and benefits to it. Using the previous example of the lab-equipment salesperson, a brief story about the lab where he worked, combined with the benefit the lab experience would provide to the hiring company, would give greater impact to the value-add. He could say the following: "I worked at a CLIA '88 certified high-volume clinical lab where we did more than 300 tests per day. We had five full-time technicians, and we used a variety of test equipment, including a blood urine hematocrit centrifuge and an aggregometer. Having worked in a large, high-volume lab, I know the workflow, equipment requirements, and challenges facing the technicians. I can speak their language, and this enables me to establish trust and position your equipment as the best solution to their clinical requirements. With these advantages, I can quickly establish a pipeline and ramp up sales."

Use a Significant Selling Proposition

A significant selling proposition (SSP) is a feature of a service that makes the service highly desirable, perhaps even unique. When introduced, these products had an SSP:

*Domino's Pizza: "Made-to-order hot pizza delivered to your door in 30 minutes or less—guaranteed." Dominos does not advertise good tasting pizza like all other pizzerias, they advertise their service level.

*FedEx: "When your package absolutely, positively has to get there overnight."

*GEICO: "15 minutes or less could save you 15% off car insurance." GEICO saves you both money and time.

*DeBeers: "A diamond is forever." The proposition points out a diamond will last forever and therefore symbolized undying love.

*Walmart: "Low prices, every day." Walmart has the lowest prices everyday not just during sales.

A pitcher who can win 22 games a season or a basketball player who can average 35 points a game has an SSP. To be an SSP, a skill has to address a need that is going largely unfulfilled within your industry. You know you have an SSP when it can stand as a headline that sells your services.

I had a client who had an SSP: a background in computer compliance in the pharmaceutical industry. The day after being laid off from a major pharmaceutical company, my disheartened client put his resume on Monster.com. He was amazed and buoyed to get 50 responses within two days and a job shortly thereafter. He had a very valuable SSP of which he was completely unaware while working for a company that employed multiple compliance experts. Other companies were dying for his expertise and would have paid him good money to change jobs had he known they were out there looking. It took a layoff for him to be exposed to the employment marketplace and learn about his SSP.

Have an SSP, No Story Needed

SSPs are so powerful that if you have one, it often communicates its own value. The pharmaceutical computer compliance specialist had one. He could've had a one-line resume—Pharmaceutical Computer Compliance Specialist for Hire—and gotten interviews. Another of my clients had a SSP in shipping: "I can sell international shipping, including doing price quotes." There are not many salespeople who, first, have sold international shipping successfully, and, second, can do their own quoting, which is very complex (particularly with all the anti-terrorism requirements). Simply let hiring managers know you have an SSP and then sit back and wait for the job offer. Unfortunately, many of us are not lucky enough to have an SSP. If you *are* so lucky, use it to your advantage.

Discover Your Value-Adds and SSPs

Value-adds and SSPs are compelling reasons why a service is purchased. Every company works very hard to identify compelling value-adds and SSPs, develop them, and then communicate them to their target customers. Imagine going into an interview armed with defined value-adds or SSPs—your confidence would be through the roof, and you would be looking forward to enlightening the hiring manager about why you're the best choice. So how do you identify your value-adds and SSPs?

Know Your Customers and Their Pain Points

Just as a company's value-adds and SSPs are based on their customers' needs, your value-adds and SSPs exist relative to the employment marketplace. Research your industry and its companies to know exactly what they're looking for, what skills they need, and the challenges (pain points) they face.

As stated earlier, you don't want to make the mistake of positioning a common skill as a value-add. You also don't want to make the mistake of positioning a skill that is of no value to a specific company or job as a value-add. For example, you may be able to draw really well; this would be a value-add in advertising but would be of no value in a call-center position.

You can risk generalizing a bit. For example, if you are fluent in Spanish, you can cite this as a value-add for any position requiring contact with the public. With the rapid growth of the Spanish-speaking population in the U.S., you can position this as an immediate value-add. The same is true for social-media experience and Microsoft Office or Google Suite experience. So many companies need employees with these skills that mentioning them as value-adds is a safe bet.

If you know an industry or a company's strategy well, you can make accurate guesses about value-add skills. For example, colleges and universities are constantly constructing new buildings and renovating old ones. You might be going for a tuition-related finance position; however, if you have experience in financing new construction, that is a good value-add to mention. Another example: Suppose a company with which you are interviewing for a product-management position is undergoing a period of growth through acquisition. If you have experience with mergers and acquisitions, that would be a good value-add to mention.

If you correctly identify what the hiring manager would think of as a value-add and then offer it, you'll find that you'll end up with the job because they're getting value from you that they can't get from your competition, and you're no longer a commodity.

Know Your Competition

Figure out what your competition has to offer. This might seem impossible, given that you probably won't know who else is interviewing for the job. However, it's not as difficult as you may think. Think about the skills your co-workers had at previous jobs and compare them to the skills you have. What skills made you distinct and different? What skills did they have that you lack? Your competitors might be citing those skills as their value-adds, and you need to be prepared to counter them.

A great source for learning about your competition is through online sites, such as LinkedIn, and from recruiters. Search LinkedIn for other people who have (or had) a similar title to the job for which you are applying. What is their background, skills, and experience? How do they position themselves? Do they mention or hint at their value-adds in their profiles?

Recruiters who specialize in your industry will know the skills that hiring managers desire. They are constantly looking to fill positions with people who have required skills and "nice to have" skills. Ask these recruiters what they think would be value-adds in the positions for which they are recruiting. Also, ask them about your competition and how you compare.

Know Yourself

Take a complete inventory of your skills. Do not limit the inventory to skills applicable to the job for which you are interviewing; do a full inventory. This inventory should include skills connected to your job, interests, hobbies, and leisure activities. When you have a full inventory, you can choose which skills serve as value-adds for the job for which you're applying.

Know Your Profession

Every profession has areas of concentration and a large skill base. For example, within human resources, you might be applying to be a compensation manager. However, the human resources field has a number of other specialty areas and required skills, such as diversity management, employee retention, job-task analysis, and international employment. You might have experience in international employment, and even though you're applying to be a compensation manager, having international employment experience could be a differentiating value-add for a multinational company or a company that is expanding internationally.

A Value-Add Is More Valuable If It's Hard to Acquire

As an administrative assistant, being a notary public is a nice value-add—you can witness signatures and validate documents, so the boss doesn't have to run out to the local bank when he needs something notarized. However, take a brief course, take an exam, and voilà—you're notary public. It's not a hard value-add to acquire.

Your most valuable value-adds are the ones that you had to work to develop. Do you speak a foreign language? Learning a language is difficult; a second language is not easily acquired. Do you have a project management certification? That is also difficult to acquire. When choosing which value-adds to mention during your interview, mention the most applicable value-add skills first, because regardless of difficulty, they have most impact. Next, mention the value-adds that are the most difficult to acquire.

In today's rapidly changing employment marketplace, the need for certain skills are rapidly disappearing while the need for others are rapidly emerging. For example, many companies are beginning to use Agile processes in their businesses to improve performance. Are you aware of Agile and the impact it is having on corporations, have you become a Scrum Master? To stay marketable in the employment marketplace, you must stay current with the most in-demand skill sets and jobs. This requires continuing your education and attaining degrees or certifications that verify your continuing professional growth. As you attain additional education or certifications be sure to include them to your LinkedIn profile, so they are available for hiring managers to see.

Value-Adds and SSPs Will Fix Your Interview

Using value-adds and SSPs to differentiate yourself from other candidates benefits both you and the hiring manager. You present yourself as a more desirable candidate, increasing your chances of winning the interview and landing the job. The hiring manager learns about your skills outside of the narrow box of the critical job requirements, making his hiring decision easier and more accurate. Presenting value-adds and SSPs has the following benefits:

*It helps you to position yourself against other candidates.

*It provides the hiring manager with important additional information that may not have been revealed in a standard interview.

*It gives you better insight into your value in the employment marketplace.

*It gives you additional rich content to tell stories. The more stories and examples you share during your interview, the more persuasive you will be.

Chapter 10 - Tell Stories That Engage and Persuade

- Our Stories Define Who We Are
- A Story Has a Beginning, a Middle, an End, and Excitement
- Success-Story Format
- We All Have Success Stories
- Success-Stories Memory Joggers
- When to Tell a Story
- Boring is How Your Saying It, Not What You're Saying
- Answer the Dreaded Weakness Question With a Story
- Telling Stories Will Fix Your Interviews

Stories are the fundamental form of human communication. For most of human existence before the advent of the written word, stories were the sole way of communicating knowledge from one generation to another. We've told stories ever since our ancestors in their tribes gathered around the fire to share stories about the tribe's history and daily events. Our brains are hardwired to respond to stories, and stories are persuasive because they engage our emotions as well as our intellect. Think about it—don't you love a good story?

When skilled salespeople sell a service, they tell stories about the service: where the service has been used, who used it, how it was used, the problem it was purchased to solve, and the positive results it provided. Whenever possible, salespeople make the story dramatic and eventful. They give details about the circumstances, the individuals involved, how the service was used, details about the wonderful results, the problems solved, and the crises averted. They infuse the story with energy and excitement, leaving the customer enthusiastic about the service and wanting to purchase. Sounds like the exact outcome you want in your interview, doesn't it?

Our Stories Define Who We Are

Our stories define who we are. Our sense of identity is forged by the stories we tell ourselves and share with others. The success stories of our careers tell about the defining moments when we were at our best, using our strengths, and contributing in meaningful ways. Our stories build and communicate our brand.

Most of us have multiple examples of career successes. The key is to understand that a career or job success is not defined by its size or financial value, but rather by how we feel about it and its contribution to organizations. One person's success story might be about turning around a corporation, saving millions of dollars, and getting her profile in *Forbes* magazine. Another person's success story might be about helping a troubled student feel more confident in school and having him progress to the next grade. Interestingly, both these success stories probably depend on many of the same personal success factors, including creativity, persistence, courage, hope, persuasion, and leadership.

When my clients write success stories, they come alive. They remember the times they felt productive and were fulfilling their purpose in their careers. They become energized and get in touch with the skills and strengths they enjoy using in their jobs. Some realize that they are doing what they love, while others are reminded of things they need to return to. Regardless, the stories are important statements of the contributions they have made in the past and indications of contributions they can make in the future—if they have done it once, they can do it again.

When telling your success stories, you have energy, enthusiasm, and confidence, and you feel a sense of pride. You are persuasive, engaging, and interesting—all the qualities you want to bring to your interviews! Telling success stories in your interviews will help you differentiate yourself, will impress the interviewer, and will make you memorable.

A Story Has a Beginning, a Middle, an End, and Excitement

"People have forgotten how to tell a story. Stories don't have a middle or an end anymore. They usually have a beginning that never stops beginning."

—Steven Spielberg

All success stories are examples of us at our best; however, some stories are more persuasive than others. What makes a story persuasive? What makes this a valuable interview technique? The answer is the emotional connection a story creates with its audience. A generation of neurological research shows that many rational behaviors are strongly influenced by emotions. If you want interviewers to hire you, then you need to create emotionally compelling stories.

A compelling story has several parts, discussed in the following sections.

A Plot

The plot is the action element of the story: what happens, what happens next, what is the outcome—and, most importantly, why. Plot is the fundamental structure of the story that provides critical clues to the story's meaning. You can think of the plot as a map guiding the listener through the story.

A Theme

The theme completes the statement: "This is a story about _____." Themes provide additional context for the plot. A theme for a career success story might be improving operations, building a team, managing a merger, implementing systems, being creative, showing initiative, and so on. Typically, the theme of your story will come from the question in response to which you're telling the story. For example, if you're prompted with, "Please tell me about a time when you had to solve a problem using creativity," the theme of your story will be about using creativity for success.

Dramatic Tension

Dramatic tension comes from conflicts that had to be resolved. These tensions are the source of emotional energy for the audience. If there is no dramatic tension, there is little emotional involvement; nobody cares. For success stories, dramatic tension comes from the problem that had to be solved and the barriers you overcame to solve that problem.

I keep a big, red "That's Easy" button on my desk that I press when something is easy. These days, I don't press it very often. Things in business have gotten more complicated and more challenging. Even the simplest of tasks has barriers I have to overcome to accomplish them. Your success stories have barriers that you cleared on your way to success. Overcoming barriers provides dramatic tension as well as an indication of the skills you employ to get things done. Typically, barriers are caused by lack of time, money, and people. Look to those areas for possible barriers.

Success-Story Format

Putting your success stories into a brief, concise, and standard format makes them easy to develop and easy to communicate during your interviews. Each success story should take no more than two minutes to tell and should follow the same format. After you have told a couple of stories using the same format, the interviewer is conditioned to hear your stories and will feel comfortable with the structure. This is exactly like telling a joke that has a setup and *boom*—the punch line.

Interview experts have their favorite success-story formats. These include:

*CAR: Context, action, result

*SAR: Situation, action, result

*PAR: Problem, action, result

*STAR: Situation, task, action, result

*SBAR: Situation, barriers, action, result

As you might have guessed, my preference is SBAR because it includes barriers, which introduce dramatic tension. The following sections provide a breakdown of the story elements.

Here is a brief and helpful way to think of successes or accomplishments in your career. The formula is – Accomplished (X) as measured by (Y) by doing (X). An example: "I reduced accounting costs by 20% as measured by reduced personnel time by implementing a new tax software package." Once you have a career success in this formula format, you can easily expand it into a success story.

Situation

The *situation* is like a newspaper headline, and it frames the problem. It gives background, the importance of the problem, and a reason why the problem needed solving. For example:

> "I was hired by AVX Development Company to establish a construction project management department capable of successfully managing a large portfolio of construction projects. At the time of my hire, projects totaled about $400 million, with about seven active in the construction phase. Five of the seven projects were behind schedule and were running into severe cost overruns. If we didn't get these projects under control, the company was at risk of going bankrupt."

Barriers

Barriers refer to the obstacles that were in your way to solving the problem. Every problem that needs to be solved has some barriers in the way, or else there would be no problem! Barriers typically are some combination of time, money, lack of staff, and personalities. Continuing the example:

> "The AVX field supervisors didn't want to admit any overruns to corporate. In addition, they didn't have computers for field personnel to track construction progress, so they didn't know the magnitude of their problems. Also, there was a lack of communication and a lack of trust between office and field staff."

Action

Actions refer to the specific things you did to solve the problem. Your actions taken to solve the problem and overcome the barriers tell the interviewer the specific skills and abilities you can bring to the job. Candidates often make a couple of mistakes when recounting actions: Either they don't provide enough detail, or they give too much credit to the team and not enough to themselves for leading the team.

Not Enough Detail

Many candidates give a broad overview of solving the problem but do not provide details about what they did to solve the problem. It's the details that reveal the skills and knowledge you have to offer. For example, a candidate might say:

"To solve the problem at AVX, I set up a project management office and worked with field staff to implement project management procedures."

That's not enough detail—how did you do it exactly?

"I became familiar with the existing projects and learned of their status, how they were being managed, and by whom. I also reviewed existing procedures and policies and found that there were none established before my arrival. I identified the gray area between contracts for the architect and the general contractor and established a standard product design specification.

"I conducted interviews with senior management to gather their opinions of the staff and current project conditions. I then organized meetings with field staff, visited their projects, and spoke with the clients at each project site. I set new standards for my staff, hired personnel that were more capable, and, after a three-month trial period, dismissed those who could not meet the standards.

"After 10 weeks, I presented a detailed report of my findings, identifying what I considered to be the specific problems, prioritizing the issues, and proposing solutions both short and long term. I also provided computers and software to create and monitor schedules. I implemented weekly meetings for all projects and monthly staff project reviews."

These actions demonstrate interdepartmental communications, research, planning, negotiating skills, project management expertise, personnel management, and persistence. These are all excellent and valuable skills that come shining through in the story. The story also has enough detail for an interviewer to ask follow-up questions and gain more information about what the candidate can do for her company.

Too Much Team

Being a good team member or leader is a critical skill in today's companies. However, the company is not hiring your team; they are hiring you. Team-oriented candidates are hesitant to take responsibility for a team's success, and during interviews they talk about how "the team did this" and "the team did that." An interview is *not* the place to be a good team member and share the glory. If appropriate, you should mention that it was a team effort, but then speak about what you specifically did to achieve the results. Don't take credit for tasks performed by others, but detail and highlight your contributions.

Result

This should be the dramatic finale to your story; it should answer the question, "You did these things—so what?" Your results should clearly communicate the success you achieved through your actions and by overcoming the barriers. Depending on how you are feeling and your personality, you can begin the results section with, "And I'm proud to say…." Or, you can use a more straightforward, "And as a result…."

If possible, use numbers, which provide credibility and give a scope to the story. Numbers don't have to be dollars; they can be time, numbers of people, or numbers of locations. Also, include any recognition you received, whether formal or informal: "Out of 300 employees in my division, I received the Employee of the Month award for the project," or, "My boss told me it was a great piece of work."

To continue our AVX example:

"What we accomplished at AVX in one year was a remarkable feat, considering that our project portfolio grew to $1.5 billion, with 17 active projects and 19 projects in preconstruction. This was a 150 percent increase, with one additional staff member. As a result, our overhead impact on development fees was reduced from 1.5 percent to 0.7 percent. We were able to perform additional preconstruction services, essential in minimizing the mistakes once construction began. Our reporting was more concise, our management of issues was noticeably more professional, and we were negotiating better contracts."

Add Likeability Elements to Success Stories

Hiring managers hire people they like. It is difficult to communicate just how likeable you are in interviews. Of course, you are personable, friendly, and engaging in the interview however, interviewers know you are on your best behavior and tend to be skeptical. To communicate your likeability, you can add elements of likeability to your success stories. When you are relating stories, add in elements such as the following to be more likeable:

*You treat others as you want to be treated

*You listen attentively and respond thoughtfully

*You take time to develop meaningful relationships

*You do not give unsolicited advice

*You believe perfection is a journey not a destination

*You apologize when wrong and learn from mistakes

*You have a clear moral compass which guides your behaviors

*You communicate authentically, directly, and honestly

*You avoid arguments and welcome open discussion

*You are confident combined with humility

*You bring humor and fun to work when appropriate

*You ask questions rather than making statements or assumptions

*You are racially and ethnically sensitive and supportive of diversity

For example, when relating an action you took you can state, "In order to understand the challenges our field staff faced, I asked questions rather than making assumptions and I established meaningful relations with the managers which enabled direct and honest communication."

We All Have Success Stories

My clients—especially early-stage career clients—often struggle to identify successes that they think warrant a story. However, I've never had a client who wasn't able to write at least five to seven good success stories. They key is not to think that a success story must be a huge company-shaking event. It can be a small success if it communicates your skills in a compelling way. Recent graduates often use things they did in high school or college to develop success stories. Stay-at-home moms returning to the workforce use things they did at home or while volunteering to develop stories.

Success-Story Memory Joggers

The following list of events will remind you of successes you've had. Have you:

*Accomplished more with the same/fewer resources? (How? Results?)

*Received recognition/special awards? (What? Why?)

*Increased efficiency? (How? Results?)

*Solved difficult problems? (How? Results?)

*Accomplished something for the first time? (What? Results?)

*Developed, created, designed, or invented something? (What? Why is it important?)

*Prepared original papers, reports, or articles? (What? Why is it important?)

*Managed a work group department? (Who? How many people? Results?)

*Saved the company money? (How? How much?)

*Supervised, managed, or trained employees? (Where? How many people? Results?)

*Increased sales? (How? By how much?)

*Been promoted or upgraded? (When? Why is it important?)

*Increased production? (How? Results?)

*Identified problems others didn't see? (What? Results?)

*Developed or implemented a new system or procedure? (What? Benefit?)

*Reduced downtime? (How? How much? Results?)

*Established a safety record? (What? Results?)

*Managed a budget? (How much? Results?)

*Repaired equipment? (Which? Results?)

*Met company standards under unusual or difficult circumstances? (What? How?)

*Helped your community? (How? Results?)

*Decreased costs (How? By how much?)

*Improved asset allocation (How?)

*Improved time-to-profitability (How? By how much?)

*Decreased employee turnover (How? By how much?)

*Increased market share (How? By how much?)

*Reduced cost of goods sold (How? By how much?)

When to Tell a Story

You can use a story or example to respond to almost any question. For example:

> **Interviewer:** "Do you know how to use Excel?"
>
> **Typical candidate:** "Yes, I do. I've been using it for five years to track contacts."
>
> **Smart candidate:** "Yes, I do. Let me give you an example of a project where I used Excel to complete a project successfully."

A popular form of interviewing today is the *competency-based* or *behavioral* interview. Although this interview approach is being used more today, competency-based interviewing originated in the 1970s. In her book *Competency-Based Interviews* (Career Press, 2006), Robin Kessler states:

> "A competency-based interview uses behavioral questions to help the interviewer assess the candidate based on critical competencies that have been identified [as critical to success] by the employer. Behavioral questions are based on the belief that what a person has done in the past they can do in the present. Thus, by asking about prior work situations, the interviewer can determine if the candidate has the required competencies."

An example of a competency is being results-and performance-driven. To determine whether a candidate has this competency, the interviewer might say, "Describe an instance when you were particularly effective in achieving results. What steps did you take to achieve those results?" Competency-based interviewing and behavioral questions are particularly suited to using success stories as responses.

Boring Is How You're Saying It, Not What You're Saying

> "Be amusing: never tell unkind stories; above all, never tell long ones."
>
> —Benjamin Disraeli, British prime minister

Every day, you are faced with a barrage of efforts to persuade you to buy a product or service. Most of these efforts are forgettable and totally unpersuasive. Occasionally, however, one of these communications breaks through the noise, catches your imagination, and speaks to you personally. What is happening? Many times, it's not the service or the brand that gets through, but how the information was communicated.

In every interview, interviewers listen to candidates answering questions to try to persuade them that they are the best candidate for the job. Most of these efforts are forgettable, mundane, and totally unpersuasive—in short, they're boring. You can avoid boring if you have a good delivery.

Good delivery consists of three factors:

***Sincerity and wholeheartedness.** Any success story you tell must be honest and real. Don't make up a story to respond to a question. A fabricated story will lack sincerity; your heart won't be in it, and the interviewer will know!

*Enthusiasm.** These are stories about you at your best, about achievements you are proud of, so being enthusiastic should be easy. Being enthusiastic doesn't mean you have to be artificially animated or jump up and down on a couch; just let your pride in your success shine through. However, don't get too enthusiastic and get carried away—remember, no story should take longer than two minutes.

*Animation.** A great deal of your story is communicated nonverbally, so show some emotion in your gestures, voice, and facial expressions. Smile, move your hands, change the pitch of your voice, and maintain eye contact. A great success story told with a deadpan expression and in a monotone is boring.

Answer the Dreaded Weakness Question with a Story

Being human, we all have strengths and weaknesses; knowing what they are shows maturity acknowledging them shows integrity and strength. When you're asked in an interview about your weaknesses, it's not the weakness that's most important—it's whether you are aware of your weaknesses and what you are doing about them.

When answering this question, be clear, concise, and brief. Don't overstate things, ramble, repeat yourself, become defensive, or explain too much. A good strategy for answering the greatest-weakness question is to state a weakness and then talk about how you are remediating the problem. Use a story to differentiate your answer and provide compelling support that you are working on the problem. For example:

> "My greatest weakness is that I tend to focus on the big picture and at times I miss details, but I'm working on fixing this weakness. Let me give you an example of how this weakness has affected me in the past and how I'm working on it today...."

A tip: When you're responding to this question, never choose a weakness related to the critical requirements of the job. If you're going for an accounting position, don't talk about weaknesses in detail-oriented work or adding numbers.

By the way, telling a story works for the greatest-strengths question as well!

Telling Stories Will Fix Your Interview

Interviewers will understand your skills, background, and experience better when they are presented in the form of stories. (In fact, sometimes they will have trouble understanding them when they *aren't* presented as stories.) Using stories, you will cut through the overwhelming number of facts and opinions that interviewers are hearing in every interview. You'll tap into emotions and get hiring managers to hire you. Through your stories, you'll communicate your brand, be more memorable, and be more charismatic—all interview-winning factors. Telling stories has the following benefits:

*Stories engage the interviewer's emotions and make you more memorable and persuasive.

*Stories give you a powerful format for answering a wide range of questions effectively.

*Stories keep your answers focused and brief.

*Stories highlight the skills and experience you will bring to the job.

*Using stories will make you more effective in managing behavioral interviews.

*Stories make you more personable and charismatic, which supports your efforts to establish a bond with your interviewers.

Chapter 11 - Personal Success Factors

- Interpersonal
- Intrapersonal
- Information
- Personal Success Factors: Choose Seven
- Provide Proof of Your Personal Success Factors
- Brand Versus Personal Success Factors
- Interviewers Aren't Good at Determining Your Personal Success Factors
- Don't Force a Fit
- Talking About Personal Success Factors Will Fix Your Interviews

"One strikingly consistent finding is that today technical and functional expertise matters less at the top than business acumen and "soft" leadership skills do."

—Boris Groysberg, associate professor of business administration at Harvard Business School

Companies do not hire on skills alone; they want employees who fit their culture, are likable, and get along well with others. Sometimes referred to as *soft skills*, *people skills*, or *interpersonal skills*, Personal Success Factors are personal qualities that make you successful on the job. These factors include proficiencies such as communication skills, conflict resolution and negotiation skills, personal effectiveness, creative problem solving, strategic thinking, team building, and influencing and selling skills, to name a few. There are hundreds of Personal Success Factors—far more than I can cover here. However, I have broken Personal Success Factors into three broad categories to give you context—interpersonal, intrapersonal, and information—and I've included examples of each.

Interpersonal

Interpersonal Success Factors impact your relationship with others. They are qualities that make you successful when working with other people. These qualities include:

Leadership

*Helping others see possibilities

*Assembling resources to get things done

*Assessing and evaluating others' work

*Balancing compassion with performance

*Delegating routine and important tasks

*Empowering others

*Having an excellent boardroom presence

Ability to be a team member

*Having knowledge of group behavior and dynamics

*Helping people to align with each other

*Sharing wins and successes

*Working well with cultural diversity

*Taking personal responsibility for resolving problems

*Having knowledge of group behavior and dynamics

*Collaborating with others

Coaching/mentoring

*Asking good questions

*Bringing out the best in people

*Counseling others

*Being eager to teach others

*Fostering innovative thinking

*Being curious about others

*Showing leadership by giving back

Respect for others

*Acknowledging the ideas of others

*Demonstrating empathy

*Having discretion

*Identifying and managing ethical issues

*Reading social situations

*Being sensitive to others

*Listening

"Being" in relation to others

*Calm

*Collaborative regarding problem solving

*Cooperative

*Extroverted

*Generous

*Humorous

*Positive with an energy that is contagious

Intrapersonal

Intrapersonal Success Factors are internal to you and do not involve interaction with others. These factors relate to your individual work. They include:

Character traits

*Active

*Ambitious

*Driven to continual improvement

*Enterprising

*Desire to practice what you teach

*Experimental

*Driven to get things done

Values

*Appreciation and application of social responsibility

*Compassion and humanity

*Conservative in thought and action

*Ethical

*High level of integrity

*Spiritual

*Tolerant

Skills

*Ability to work with little supervision

*Accurate

*Critical thinker

*Ability to deal with obstacles and crises

*Desire to do things right

*Ability to express written and verbal ideas clearly

*Good time management

Flexibility/learning

*Active learner

*Adaptable

*Anticipates obstacles

*Committed to continuous personal improvement

*Learn from experiences

*Love of learning

*Stays abreast of current and future trends

Moods

*Calm

*Animated

*Cheerful

*Easygoing

*Emotionally stable

*Enthusiastic

*Optimistic

Information

Information factors are Personal Success Factors that relate to how you manage information and technology. They include:

Organization

*Ability to spot useful, relevant patterns

*Ability to acquire and evaluate information accurately

*Ability to develop evaluation strategies

*Ability to use resources and time effectively

*Forecasting and predicting skills

*Ability to resolve problems in early stages

*Ability to identify connections between situations

Thinking skills

*Vivid imagination

*Ability to discern relevant, less relevant, and irrelevant facts

*Arithmetical computation and mathematical reasoning

*Ability to anticipate and see around corners

*Ability to detect changes in organizations or events

*Ability to look beyond the obvious

*Rapid decision-making

Systems

*Ability to break down complex tasks into manageable parts

*Ability to identify underlying patterns

*Ability to monitor and correct performance in systems

*Ability to see consequences and implications within a system

*Ability to understand systems

*Strategy management

*Ability to improve and design systems

Technology

*Ability to explain technical issues to a nontechnical audience

*Ability to apply technology to tasks

*Ability to maintain and troubleshoot technology

*Ability to keep abreast of current technology

*Ability to repair equipment or machinery

*Quality control analysis

*Ability to learn new technology quickly

Top Personal Success Factors

As displayed above, there are a multitude of Personal Success Factors. The Gallup Organization did a study examining 550 job roles and 360 unique skills/competencies. They identified the following Personal Success Factors as most essential for achieving excellence in any role:

*Building relationships

*Developing people

*Leading change

*Inspiring others

*Thinking critically

*Communicating clearly

*Creating accountability

Personal Success Factors: Choose Seven

Without a great deal of concentration, the human brain cannot remember a list with more than seven items. This is why phone numbers are seven digits. (Area codes came along after the fact.) In interviews, you should limit all lists to seven items: seven personal brand terms, seven critical job requirements, seven additional areas of expertise, seven success stories, seven Personal Success Factors, and seven questions.

Personal Success Factors are positive desirable traits. You undoubtedly have many Personal Success Factors listed in the previous sections—and that isn't an exhaustive list. Talking about *all* your Personal Success Factors during an interview would take too much time and would be confusing for the interviewer, so pick seven to focus on and emphasize.

Which Personal Success Factors will you pick? I suggest you use the selection criteria described in the following sections.

Personal Success Factors That Relate Most Closely to the Critical Job Requirements

When you are preparing for a specific interview, consider which of your Personal Success Factors are most relevant for that position. If one of your Personal Success Factors is leadership, but the position doesn't require managing others, choose another one of your Personal Success Factors.

Personal Success Factors to Which You Most Strongly Relate

We all have Personal Success Factors that we are proud of and that we believe contribute the most to our success. These are Personal Success Factors about which you will be most enthusiastic and for which you can easily develop success stories and examples.

Personal Success Factors for Which You Have Success Stories

Choose Personal Success Factors that are highlighted by your success stories. You may want to choose Personal Success Factors that are highlighted by the success stories of which you are most proud.

Provide Proof of Your Personal Success Factors

Personal Success Factors are all positive and somewhat general terms; thus, they need definition to be meaningful. You give them meaning by telling a story or giving an example. One of my clients, a senior hospital administrator, chose as a Personal Success Factor "management by walking around," which has become almost a management cliché. Managing by walking around was popularized by Tom Peters and Robert Waterman in the early 1980s because it was thought that managers were becoming isolated from their subordinates. Today's savvy managers know that staying in touch with subordinates is a good management practice and will claim that they "manage by walking around."

When my client told me he wanted to use "management by walking around" as one of his Personal Success Factors, I challenged him to prove it. He told me that in his previous job as a hospital CEO, he would spend numerous shifts, including evenings and weekends, sitting at nursing stations throughout his hospital. As he sat at the nursing stations, he would speak with nurses, doctors, and support staff and hear firsthand what was going on at the hospital, as well as get a feel for staff morale. This was truly management by walking around.

Another client, a website developer, chose "creating clarity from chaos" as one of his Personal Success Factors. He was able to tell a story about combining multiple company websites into one coherent, easily navigable website.

Regardless of the Personal Success Factors you choose, make sure you can tell a story or give examples about them, and be prepared to answer questions about them. Questions might include:

*Please tell me your definition of this Personal Success Factor.

*How does this personal success factor contribute to your success?

*What does it actually look like when you're displaying this personal success factor?

*Please give me a specific instance when you displayed this personal success factor.

*How do you think your Personal Success Factors will mesh with the culture here?

*Of the Personal Success Factors you chose, which is the most dominant?

*Has this personal success factor ever gotten you in trouble with a boss or a co-worker?

Brand versus Personal Success Factors

You might be asking, "What is the difference between a personal success factor and a personal brand?" Think about how companies brand themselves. One of Volvo's Personal Success Factors is safety, and it is part of their brand message. Another one of Volvo's Personal Success Factors is a widespread dealership network, but that is not part of their brand message.

A personal success factor might be part of your personal brand, or it might not. For example, one of your Personal Success Factors might be "assembling resources to get things done." If you want people to think of you as a person who knows how to identify and mobilize resources, this will be part of your personal brand that you communicate to others. You might also have "good time management" as a personal success factor, but you might not want that as part of your personal brand message.

Interviewers Aren't Good at Determining Your Personal Success Factors

Other than what goes on interpersonally during the interview, the interviewer has no way of knowing your Personal Success Factors. Interviewers try to guess what they are by listening to you and maybe by asking behavioral questions. Primarily, they depend on a gut feeling about what you're like on a job. Gut feelings, which are primarily based on unconscious biases, may work for you or against you—do you want to gamble?

During the interview, you can tell the interviewer about your Personal Success Factors. Having prepared a list of Personal Success Factors and stories or examples about each, you can respond to questions by relating your Personal Success Factors. For example, if the interviewer says, "Tell me what makes you a good team member?" you could reply, "One of the things that helps me perform well in a team is my mood, which is typically calm especially in stressful times. Let me give you an example of how my being calm benefitted a team I was on.…" As you will read in Chapter 15, "Develop an Interview-Winning Presentation," you can include a list of Personal Success Factors in your presentation.

Don't Force a Fit

One of the three critical interview questions is about your fit with the company culture. Your fit with the culture depends on how your Personal Success Factors will contribute to (or hinder) your success at that company. For example, one of your Personal Success Factors could be "a vivid imagination." Your vivid imagination would work well at an advertising company but probably not so well at a bank. Similarly, your personal success factor of "easygoing" might fit well as a tour guide but not as a security guard.

As you go through the interview, it might become apparent that the culture doesn't suit you, and you might be tempted to cite Personal Success Factors that fit the job but don't fit you. If you do that, you may end up getting the job, but you likely won't be happy there, and you probably won't stay long.

Talking About Personal Success Factors Will Fix Your Interview

Hiring managers are very concerned about a candidate's fit with the organization's culture, as well as the candidate's general likability. In typical interviews, the hiring manager guesses about the candidate's personal and interpersonal skills based on a series of questions and answers. Talking about your Personal Success Factors has the following benefits:

*It clearly communicates the soft skills that will contribute to your success on the job.

*It helps the hiring manager assess your fit with the culture of the organization.

*It doesn't leave your likability and cultural fit up to the hiring manager's gut feeling, which is highly subjective and often incorrect.

*Identifying and developing examples of your Personal Success Factors helps you determine the benefits you can bring to the organization.

*Your Personal Success Factors are more emotional and less intellectual elements of your job performance. These elements engage the hiring manager's emotions and become persuasive.

Chapter 12 - Your Strategic Action Plan

- Most Frequently Asked Questions
- It's a Conversation
- Be S.M.A.R.T. With Your Goals
- Simple Beats Bold
- Strategic Action Plan Goal Examples
- A Strategic Action Plan Will Fix Your Interviews

As part of a sales presentation, a salesperson tells the customer how the product or service will be implemented: "Once you sign the contract, the first thing we'll do is x, then we will do y and this should be completed in z days." This helps the customer understand and visualize how the service will begin to provide value. A good implementation plan includes several steps or goals and a timeline.

You're selling your services—do you present an implementation plan? Almost all candidates ignore how they will begin their employment, assuming that implementation is up to the employer. But by presenting an implementation plan, you communicate to the interviewer a motivation for the position, knowledge of the position requirements, and a message that you will add value to the organization quickly—all strong "hire me" messages.

A strategic action plan consists up to seven goals that you want to accomplish in the first 30 and 60 days in the position. I suggest this timeframe because it is long enough to develop specific goals but not so long that you will be suggesting goals that require a far better understanding of the position. Some candidates prefer to develop 90-day goals, and some of my clients have been asked in interviews about their goals for the first 100 days. The more senior the position, the more sense it makes to develop longer-range goals.

Most Frequently Asked Questions

When my clients hear my suggestion to develop a 30- and a 60-day strategic action plan, their first questions are, "How do I know appropriate goals?" and, "If I suggest the wrong goals, won't I blow the interview?"

How Do You Know Company-Appropriate Goals?

In the first 30 days of a job, goals are limited. Thirty-day goals relate to establishing yourself at the company, including learning policies and procedures, meeting other staff, establishing goals with the supervisor, getting to know the market, and learning about other departments.

Within the first 60 days, goals are broader but also limited in scope. Goals depend on the level of the position, with lower levels having more concrete, task-related goals and higher-level positions having more assessment and strategy-development goals. For example, an entry-level person might be learning how to use various computer systems, whereas a higher-level person might be reviewing a department's strategic direction and performance.

Goals also depend on the profession. For example, in the first 30 days a salesperson might have the goal of learning sales strategy and tools, whereas a project manager might have the goal of developing a complete understanding of current projects. In 60 days, the salesperson might want to analyze competitor strengths and weaknesses, whereas the project manager might want to prepare a software development project plan.

Base the goals you choose on your knowledge of the profession, your job level, and the position. Establishing 30- and 60-day goals is not difficult if you use your knowledge of the industry and the job, keep the goals limited, and present them as suggested goals rather than as final goals.

What If You Have the Wrong Goals?

So far, none of my clients has had a wrong set of goals—not surprising, given that developing a set of accurate goals is not difficult. Some are more accurate than others, but all goals have been realistic and appropriate and have impressed the interviewer. Consider this: You know your profession, you know the job to which you are applying, and the goals are not highly specific and detailed. In addition, the goals are presented as your thinking based on what you know now and are open to change as you learn more about the job.

Candidates introduce their strategic action plan by saying, "I'm really interested in this position [reinforcing their motivation and interest in the job], and I want to add value to your company quickly. I have developed a set of goals that I think I can accomplish in the first 30 and 60 days, and I want to share them with you. Obviously, these goals are subject to change when I know more about the job, but they are my goals at this point." So far, every interviewer has been very interested in hearing a candidate's strategic action plan. Again, not surprising—why *wouldn't* they be interested in how a person is going to provide value to their company?

It's a Conversation

The best interviews are conversations. Your challenge is to actively create a conversation in your interview and not fall into the broken question-and-answer cross-examination format.

Presenting a strategic action plan creates a conversation. First, hiring managers are intrigued when a candidate mentions a strategic action plan and are eager to learn more. Second, discussing job goals, how you chose them, and how you will accomplish them provides a great deal of rich information for the hiring manager. This rich information typically generates questions that you are well prepared to answer, given that they are about your goals, knowledge, and thinking.

I've heard of several interviews where candidates have presented a strategic action plan, and the interviewer has responded by saying, "Those are good goals; however, we have a few fires going on in the department that need to be put out. How would you deal with…?" This is a great question elicited by the strategic action plan. As a candidate, you can then talk about your approaches to putting out these fires. My clients would not have learned about the fire had they not had a strategic action plan to which the interviewer could respond.

Be S.M.A.R.T. with Your Goals

Coined by George T. Doran in the November 1981 issue of *Management Review*, S.M.A.R.T. is an acronym for goals that are Specific, Measurable, Attainable, Realistic, and Timely. A S.M.A.R.T. goal is a well-defined goal. You probably won't have all the information you need to develop comprehensive S.M.A.R.T goals for your interview, but you should try to come as close as possible. Also, questions interviewers ask are typically related to S.M.A.R.T issues, so you will be prepared to answer the questions.

Specific

You're more likely to accomplish a specific goal than a general one. To set a specific goal, answer the six "W" questions:

*__Who.__ Who is involved?

*__What.__ What do I want to accomplish?

*__Where.__ Where is the location?

*__When.__ What is the timeframe?

*Which. Which requirements and constraints do I need to consider?

*Why. What are the specific reasons, purposes, or benefits of accomplishing the goal?

For example, a general goal would be getting to know the customers. A specific goal would say, "Within the first 60 days, schedule a customer meeting at our headquarters location with the top 10 revenue-producing customers."

Measurable

Establish criteria for measuring progress toward attaining each goal you set. When you measure your progress, you stay on track, reach your target dates, and experience the achievement that motivates you to continue the effort required to reach your goal.

To determine whether your goal is measurable, ask questions such as how much? How many? How will I know when it is accomplished? For example, meeting with the top 10 revenue-producing customers in 60 days is a measurable goal. Becoming 100 percent proficient on company-specific information systems in 30 days is also a measurable goal.

Attainable

Attainable goals are achievable, acceptable, and action oriented. As a strategy for your strategic action plan, focus on smaller attainable goals rather than larger, more audacious goals. For example, restructuring the department's workflow is probably too large, but identifying and fixing one workflow bottleneck is not.

Also, be sure to make your goals active rather than passive. For example, reach out to customers as opposed to waiting for sales numbers to be reported.

Realistic

A realistic goal is one you are willing and able to work toward. The goal is probably realistic if you truly believe you can accomplish it. Also, you know your goal is realistic if you have accomplished something similar in the past; ask yourself what conditions would have to exist to accomplish this goal. For example, if you have been able to implement a new training program or you participated in a training program that had a positive impact in a prior position, implementing that program in a new position may be a realistic goal.

Timely

A goal should be grounded within a timeframe to give it urgency and "trackability." When you have a timeframe, it focuses the goal and makes progress measurable. As suggested earlier in this chapter, the recommended timeframes for strategic action goals are 30 days and 60 days. These timeframes will make your goals timely. For example, "In the first 30 days, I will meet with all the department heads that this position supports and identify their most critical needs."

Simple Beats Bold

Some of my clients want to use the strategic action plan to impress the hiring manager with bold goals that will leave the hiring manager dying to hire them. For example, "Within the first 60 days, I will implement a plan to increase shareholder value by 27 percent while increasing revenue by 40 percent and reducing product error rates by 60 percent." Small, attainable goals are more realistic in a short timeframe, and they portray you as a more conservative, well-grounded employee.

No company wants someone—even a CEO—shaking up the company in the first 60 days. A good 60-day goal for any level of position is "listen 80 percent and speak 20 percent." (Some candidates, particularly entry-level ones, actually put this goal in their interview presentation. Hiring managers like junior employees to be aware that they need to learn a lot.) Also, one of the primary objectives of the strategic action plan is to create a goals conversation. Goals do not have to be big, bold, and risky to stimulate a conversation—small realistic goals work just fine.

Strategic Action Plan Goal Examples

I have included some examples of goals broken down by professions. Just as they would be listed in an interview presentation, the goals are just "headlines," and you would add the S.M.A.R.T. detail during the interview conversation.

General management position goals:

*Listen, observe, and ask questions

*Review people's workloads, priorities, and demands

*Schedule meetings with key decision-makers

*Ask people what they need

*Review departmental budget

*Build internal credibility

Marketing position goals:

*Identify critical industry trends

*Initiate advertising agency review

*Read competitors' annual reports

*Review performance indicators

*Review prices, values, and customer perceptions in the market

*Initiate brand review

*Position marketing as a value-added service

Technical position goals:

*Become fully computer-literate in company programs

*Develop a complete understanding of current projects

*Learn capabilities of the department and company

*Make early decisions on small, quick fixes

*Review team competencies

*Define applications and have customer-strategy sessions

HR position goals:

*Analyze level of HR operational success

*Define HR as a strategic partner

*Evaluate turnover rates

*Forecast workforce needs

*Review policy and procedure manuals

*Review recruiting process

*Review position descriptions

People-related position goals:

*Learn co-workers' styles

*Meet and build relationships with members of the team and key personnel

*Visit existing clients and develop rapport

*Establish support systems

*Establish success metrics

*Begin to build internal network

A Strategic Action Plan Will Fix Your Interview

When is the last time you presented a strategic action plan in an interview or, if you were interviewing, had a plan presented to you? Probably never! Developing a strategic action plan and presenting it during your interview is an enormously powerful strategy. It communicates a high level of motivation and interest, knowledge of the job, and the awareness you must provide value quickly. As you discuss the goals, you will get additional valuable information about the job and your fit with the company. The hiring manager will learn more about your background and skills and how you will apply them to the job. A strategic action plan has the following benefits:

*It presents an implementation plan that helps the hiring manager visualize you on the job and understand how you will perform and fit the company culture.

*As you present your strategic action plan, you may elicit information about pressing insider issues that would not have been discussed otherwise.

*Being proactive with your strategic action plan helps poor interviewers get valuable information they need to make a good hiring decision.

*A strategic action plan generates a goals-based conversation, which enables you to have a greater understanding of the job requirements.

*The interviewer's receptivity to your suggested goals will give you insight into the hiring manager's management style and the company culture.

*Setting realistic goals is a critical job skill. Your strategic action plan will demonstrate your goal-setting capabilities.

*A strategic action plan communicates a willingness to be bold, self-directed, and a contributor to the company's success.

Chapter 13 - Why Hiring You is a Good Idea

- Don't Let Hiring Managers Guess About Hiring You
- Why Hire me?
- What Do Employers Want?
- Features versus Benefits
- Telling the Hiring Manager Why You Should Be Hired Will Fix Your Interviews

Good salespeople lead a buyer through a sales process toward a purchase. They begin by understanding the buyer's needs and linking the features of their service to those needs. They then talk about value-adds, tell success stories about purchasers who've used their service, provide an implementation plan, and finally summarize why they are the best choice based on the benefits their service provides. Good salespeople understand that prospects won't understand why they should buy a service simply because they've been told about it. Buyers need to be informed very directly, in simple language, why the salesperson's service is the best purchasing decision.

The critical element in a purchasing decision is the benefits. No buyer purchases a service without clearly seeing the benefits she will get from the service. But most candidates focus on the skills and experience they bring to the job and don't clearly state the benefits the company will derive from hiring them. They never clearly communicate, "This is why hiring me is a good idea."

Don't Let Hiring Managers Guess about Hiring You

The traditional interview consists of a question-and-answer format resulting in the hiring manager putting together the information she has heard and deciding (guessing) about which candidate to hire. But why let the hiring manager come to her own conclusion? Following your interview(s), the hiring manager should have a clear picture of why hiring you is a good idea—because you have told her exactly why!

Part of your interview preparation is developing a list of the benefits the company will get from hiring you. These benefits are even more powerful if they differentiate you from the competition. Going into an interview with this list of benefits will help you be focused and more confident. However, this list is of value only if you share it with the hiring manager.

Why Hire Me?

During your interview—typically toward the end—make a clear statement about why the company should hire you. This statement combines your features with the benefits the company will get from those features. As discussed previously, the benefits are based 100 percent on the company's needs as you have identified them during the interview process. Your "why hire me" statement should be a summary based on the content you have already shared during your interview and should be as objective as possible. A "why hire me" statement can include a combination of skills and experience as well as personal success factors. Some examples include:

> "As we discussed, I have six years of experience selling office equipment in this territory [feature]. This means I have established relationships with customers and I know the competition [feature]. Based on my knowledge and experience, I can establish a productive sales pipeline within three months and meet or exceed my sales goals within six months [benefit]."

> "As I mentioned, I have worked on public relations campaigns for major companies, including Fancy Electronics and Electronics Shack [feature]. For both of these companies, I was responsible for a wide range of public relations activities, including print and industry shows [feature]. Based on this experience, I can help your company sell to larger clients and then make sure the public relations activities are delivered with a high level of quality and impact [benefits]."

"As I have described, I am good at acquiring and evaluating information accurately [feature]. I will be effective in quickly evaluating the marketing department and determining immediate measures to improve their performance [benefit]."

"We have discussed that I express ideas clearly both verbally and in writing [feature]. This will enable me to implement a new healthcare plan that will be of benefit to the employees and will save the company money [benefit]."

When you make these statements, the hiring manager will understand why hiring you is a good idea; she won't have to guess. In addition, being clear about the benefits you will deliver is a further display of your knowledge of the company and the job.

What Do Employers Want?

In addition to desiring an enthusiastic employee with the skills required to do the job, there is a set of basic personal success factors that all employers want. For early career candidates, including these basic personal success factors in a "why hire me" statement can be an effective interview strategy. These personal success factors include:

*Reliability

*Flexibility

*Willingness/ability to follow rules

*Good attitude

*Personal energy

*Strong work ethic

*Willingness to learn (Learnability)

*Desire to do a good job

*Awareness of how business works

*Commitment to continued training and learning

*Willingness to be a good worker and go beyond the traditional eight-hour day

*Good communication skills with the public, fellow employees, supervisors, and customers

If you are a more experienced candidate, basic personal success factors are expected and will not differentiate you. Hiring managers look for higher-level leadership and strategy-development personal success factors, including:

***Leadership.** Management isn't about getting things done yourself; it's about accomplishing things through others.

***Ability to manage a network.** This entails understanding how power and influence work in organizations and building a network of mutually beneficial relationships to navigate a company's complex political environment and get things done.

***Ability to manage a team.** The involves forging a high-performing team.

*Vision.** This is the ability to see around corners, probe consensus thinking and competitive data with a healthy skepticism, and swiftly make changes when the situation warrants.

*Transformation.** This refers to the capacity to grow and learn.

As you present each of these personal success factors, include the benefits these personal success factors will provide the company.

Features versus Benefits

As I mentioned previously, good salespeople sell on benefits and use features to support claims of the benefits their service provides. Most candidates focus entirely on their features and leave hiring managers to guess about the benefits they will gain. Including a "why hire me" statement in your interview will force you to focus on the benefits you'll bring to the company.

Who Is the Main Benefits Beneficiary?

Hiring managers typically speak about the needs of the company, but they are concerned primarily with their own needs and what will bring them success in their position. When you talk about the benefits your skills provide, focus on how you can be of greatest benefit to the hiring manager. What are his primary challenges, what would reduce his stress, and what would make him look good in the eyes of his boss?

The same goes for personal success factors. Which of your personal success factors would be of greatest benefit to the hiring manager? If the hiring manager prides himself on being a strong team leader, your team-leadership skills may not be of interest to him. Alternatively, the hiring manager may not be an analytical thinker, and having a person to whom he can delegate detailed analysis may make his job easier. Listening intently during the first part of the interview, when you're doing a needs analysis, will provide you with insight into the hiring manager's challenges.

If you listen closely to the hiring manager's challenges, you might hear personal needs that will benefit from your skills and personal success factors. For example, a hiring manager might talk about a hectic travel schedule that keeps her away from her family too much. If you can take on some of the travel-related activities, you will free up the hiring manger to spend more time at home. Include this in your "why hire me" statement: "I have a lot of experience working with clients on the West Coast [feature]. I would be able to take over the West Coast territory, freeing you to focus more on the East Coast and enabling you to be in the office more [benefit]." Notice that this benefit statement doesn't address the personal aspects of the hiring manager's life, but it is clear that staying local will enable her to be home more often.

The Greatest Benefits Are Emotional

When a good Volvo salesperson sells a Volvo, he doesn't sell the benefit of safety, although it is the brand and the primary selling benefit of Volvo. He sells the emotional benefit of the peace of mind that safety brings: "Imagine your family driving in a Volvo. If they got in an accident, heaven forbid, you can be more confident that they will be okay because they are in a Volvo."

When you look below the surface of every need a hiring manager has, there is an emotion connected to that need. Typically, the primary emotion is fear of losing his job. Other emotions include pride in his work, drive for success, and a sense of accomplishment. Try to link your benefits to these emotions. For example, "I have successfully managed multimillion-dollar commercial development projects, making sure they were delivered on time and on budget [feature]. I will be able to do the same for any of your projects that may get in difficulty [benefit]." Another example is, "The last division to which I provided engineering support reduced their error rate by 26 percent. This resulted in the manager getting the Most Improved Department award and a nice bonus [feature]. I'm sure I can provide the same level of improvement, if necessary, to your department [benefit]."

Telling the Hiring Manager Why You Should Be Hired Will Fix Your Interview

> "If you have an important point to make, don't try to be subtle or clever. Use a pile driver. Hit the point once. Then come back and hit it again. Then hit it a third time—a tremendous whack.
>
> —Winston Churchill

Buyers should never have to guess why they should purchase a service; the salesperson should tell them why. In your interviews, stating directly and actively why you should be hired will make it obvious to the hiring manager that you are the best choice. At the end of the interview process, when the hiring manager is trying to figure out why a certain candidate is a good one, she won't be doing the same with you, because you've already told her why. By laying out your reasons to be hired, you make her choice easier. Presenting why you should be hired has the following benefits:

*An interview may take an hour or more. By the end of the interview, the interviewer will recall only 50 percent or less of what he has heard, and he will have forgotten some of your advantages. As you tell him why you should be hired, you reinforce the critical information and benefits you want him to remember about you.

*Your "why hire me" statement focuses you on the benefits you will provide. Benefits are the most persuasive factors you can mention to support your candidacy.

*Buyers are used to hearing a summary of the benefits of buying a service. Hiring managers will be receptive to hearing your summary of why they should engage your services.

*Repetition is an effective persuasion technique. Your "why hire me" statement repeats your greatest benefits and makes you more persuasive.

*Your "why hire me" is one form of a sales close. It stops short of asking directly for the job, but it does state, "This is why you should give me the job."

*Stating clearly that "This is why you should hire me" communicates confidence and assertiveness. Both are desirable traits in an employee, and they will reduce your FUD and your increase credibility.

Chapter 14 - Asking Powerful Questions

- Asking Good Questions is a Critical Business Skill
- Ask Open-Ended Questions
- The Definition of a Good Interview Question
- Use the Proper Terminology in Your Questions
- Ask a Question Then Be Silent
- Ask Follow-Up Questions
- Ask Professional-Personal Questions
- Go Prepared with Questions
- Don't Ask Obvious Questions
- Information You Should have After Your Interview
- The Best Interview Question of All time
- Another Must-Ask Question
- Asking Good Questions Will Fix Your Interviews

"Years ago, as a business consultant, I took pride in always having an answer. Now I realize that in our fast-moving, mile-a-minute world, answers have a very short shelf life. Having the right questions is more important and more valuable."

—Gary Lockwood, business coach

Have you ever been in a sales situation where the salesperson asked really good questions? Didn't those questions inspire your confidence and trust in the salesperson and, in turn, in their product or service? I'm always impressed when a salesperson asks questions that display a high level of expertise and make me aware of issues about which I should be thinking. I remember one instance when I was replacing and extending a deck at my house, and I interviewed a number of contractors, primarily those with excellent carpentry skills. They all showed beautiful examples of decks they had built. However, one contractor asked about drainage issues and suggested putting in a drainage pipe. He got the job, and I was lucky—when it rained, water poured out of the drainage pipe instead of into my basement!

The number-two complaint that interviewers have about candidates (the number-one complaint being that candidates don't know enough about the company) is that they don't have questions or that they have vague, general questions. Having good, powerful questions will differentiate you from other candidates and impress the hiring manager.

Asking Good Questions Is a Critical Business Skill

"When you are a leader, your job is to have all the questions. You have to be incredibly comfortable looking like the dumbest person in the room.

—Jack Welch, CEO of General Electric

An excellent interview strategy is to actively display skills and qualities that make you a good employee. Asking good questions is a valuable skill at any experience level. At lower levels, good questions are focused on answers to operational questions: How do I do this? At senior levels, questions are a valuable management tool that can motivate and direct people as well as get important answers. Good management questions:

*Create a learning atmosphere.

*Show team members how much you respect their insights.

*Encourage people to think independently.

*Teach others how important it is to question assumptions about projects, strategies, competitors, and market forces.

*Promote an effective communications culture where the tough issues are free to be examined and ideas can be suggested.

As you ask good questions during your interview, you will impress the interviewer with your knowledge of what questions to ask and how to ask them.

Ask Open-Ended Questions

Open-ended questions encourage full, meaningful answers—contrary to closed-ended questions, which encourage short or single-word answers. Open-ended questions tend to be more objective and less leading than closed-ended questions. They typically begin with words such as "Why," "How," "What," or "Describe" or phrases such as, "Tell me about…." Often, open-ended questions are not technically *questions*, but rather statements that implicitly ask for a response.

In interviews, open-ended questions are typically more valuable questions. The following table lists some common closed-ended questions and their open-ended counterparts.

Closed Ended Questions	Open Ended Questions
Do you offer training?	Please tell me about your training program.
Does your organization value its employees?	What things has your organization done recently to show that it values its employees?
Do you have a plan in place to manage employee turnover?	What steps have you taken to address employee turnover?
Are there specific success metrics for this position?	How is success measured in this position?

The Definition of a Good Interview Question

A good interview question displays an in-depth knowledge of the industry, the company, the position, and relates to performing the job. Good interview questions are not about personal issues, such as compensation, vacation time, or office space. You can ask questions about personal issues when you are offered the position, or you are considered a strong candidate. The exception to this is if there is a question whose answer would make it obvious that you wouldn't consider the position—for example, if the position pays far less than you need to support yourself or requires far more travel than you would consider or maybe a relocation you aren't willing to do. Hopefully, these issues would be clarified before a first interview during the screening call, and you wouldn't waste your time or the interviewer's in a live interview.

Good questions give you additional information about how the company operates, its challenges, or how to be successful on the job. A good question puts the interviewer in a position to think about the answer, and a great question stimulates a discussion about how to solve a problem. I had a client who knew his industry and its challenges. During an interview, he asked a question that he knew the entire industry was grappling with and about which he had some ideas for solving. His question resulted in a 70-minute strategy discussion, after which the hiring manager created a position for my client. That's a great interview question!

Asking S.M.A.R.T. Interview Question

Despite what you may have read in numerous places, interview questions shouldn't have the goal of discovering information that helps you determine if the job is a good fit. Determining your fit is only important if you are offered the job, and once offered you can ask your fit questions. Really, does it matter if the company has tuition reimbursement or three weeks of vacation the first year if you don't have the job? Asking "fit" questions in interviews wastes valuable interview time. The questions you ask should have the goal of showing how smart you are and creating a conversation! S.M.A.R.T interview questions have the following characteristics:

* Specific – The question should be exclusive to the company for which you are interviewing. The question could not be used verbatim for another interview at another company even for a similar job. For example, "Where do you see your company in five years? can be asked of any job at any company.

* Meaningful – The question is related to the performance of the job. It refers to the critical job requirements and pertains to education, experience, and skills you bringing to the job.

* Analytic –The question collects and analyzes information that is relevant to the job. Once the question is answered and information collected, you can use the information to deepen the conversation.

* Relevant – The question is related to things you have discussed in the interview. Does not open other areas of content which may take the interview off track.

* Transactional – The question creates a conversation (transaction) with the interviewer rather than just a yes/no or brief answer.

The following table presents some typical interview questions, along with S.M.A.R.T. ones.

Typical Question	S.M.A.R.T. Question
What do you see ahead for your company in the next five years?	Given the dramatic changes in social media, including the rapid shift to video delivery of content, what do you see as your dominant social media strategies for the next two years?
How do you see this position relating to the Board of Directors?	With a new chairman of the Board of Directors, do you anticipate the board changing direction, and how do you see this position interacting with the Board?
Do you provide training for your employees?	Your website mentions the company's dedication to the ongoing development of its employees including tuition reimbursement. Please tell me what training and development is expected in the next 6-12 months for a person in this position.
How will the recent acquisitions impact this position?	Having acquired ABC Company with their product line of Y and expanding your services into the area of Z, what will the expectations be for this position internationally?

What do you consider to be your firm's most important assets?	One of your strongest competitors, ABC Company, has recently introduced the *Z* product. What strengths does your company have to compete with this market innovation?
What customer contact will a person in this position have?	I read in an industry trade journal that Acme Company is expanding to the West Coast to take advantage of the technology expertise available there. As an account manager on the Acme account, what will be the day-to-day contact with Acme West Coast?
Does the person in this position have work from home opportunities?	With Covid 19 you have reconfigured your workforce to a work from home model. What are you doing to support your staff to be productive working from home?

Use the Proper Terminology in Your Questions

Know the nature of the organization and the appropriate industry terminology. Not all employing organizations are companies, for example. Governmental agencies and not-for-profit organizations are not accurately referred to as *companies*. Some for-profit organizations may call themselves *firms*, *businesses*, or *agencies*. Supermarkets, manufacturers, and marketing companies may talk about CPG. In these industries, it is important to know that CPG is an acronym for *consumer products goods*.

Most industries have their own terms, acronyms, and language. In addition, many companies have their own way of referring to various activities; one company's *team meeting* is another company's *huddle*. The more your questions reflect industry- and company-specific language, the more prepared and knowledgeable you will appear. Prior to your interview, make a list of terms and acronyms that you want to use in your interview. Also, if an interviewer uses a term or acronym with which you are unfamiliar, ask for a definition. Once you know the definition, try to use the term or acronym later in your interview.

Ask a Question and Then Be Silent

The best technique for asking questions is to ask and then listen. Listening requires silence and concentration. By being silent, you encourage the interviewer to give answers that are more detailed. Listen fully and then ask follow-up questions if appropriate.

Ask Follow-Up Questions

Asking a series of questions is not as effective as asking a question that stimulates a conversation. You can initiate a conversation by responding to an answer or by asking another question based on the answer. This requires listening and then responding to what you've heard. Follow-up questions—particularly open-ended questions—will give you more in-depth information and a better understanding of the organization and the hiring manager's needs.

It often surprises me how accepting people are of vague or misleading answers. For example:

Candidate: How much overtime is required in this position?

Hiring manager: We try to limit overtime as much as possible and only authorize it when absolutely necessary.

Okay, so how many hours is that exactly? Another example:

Candidate: When should I follow up with you?

Hiring manager: We still have a number of candidates to interview.

Okay, so what date is that exactly? Another example,

Candidate: Do you anticipate any layoffs in the next 12 months?

Hiring manager: We try to keep a stable workforce.

Okay, so if I take the job, am I in danger of being laid off?

Listen carefully to answers and be sure you get the exact information you're asking about. Don't hesitate to ask clarifying questions that get you the information you need.

Ask Professional-Personal Questions

Everyone's favorite topic is himself. It's a good idea and perfectly acceptable to ask the interviewer questions about his career or experience at the company. Good questions to ask include, "What has been your path to this position?" or "What do you enjoy most about working here?" These types of questions display an interest in and a curiosity about the interviewer as a person and help to establish rapport. It's important to ask these questions out of a genuine curiosity and not as an interview strategy, though. If the questions aren't genuine, they will come across as hollow and may hurt your chances.

Unless you get into a personal conversation initiated by the interviewer, don't ask questions about the interviewer's personal life outside of the job even if it seems non-intrusive such as "Do you play golf? This may cross a boundary and may undermine your chances at winning the interview.

Go Prepared with Questions

Before your interview, prepare a list of at least seven S.M.A.R.T. questions to ask. Write these down and take them with you. Ask these questions when the interviewer says, "Do you have any questions for me?"

It is perfectly acceptable to look to your list of questions because this shows preparation. If all your questions have been answered already, don't say, "I had a list of questions, but you've answered them all." Instead, say, "I prepared a list of questions to ask. I think you've answered them; however, I'd just like to make sure I'm clear about your answers." Then state one or two questions and the answers as you understand them, and then ask for confirmation from the interviewer. For example, "I have a question about how you measure success in this position. I believe you said it's based on a six-month evaluation that measures progress toward objective goals. Am I correct about this?"

Don't Ask Obvious Questions

Make sure any question you ask cannot be answered by reading the company's website or by doing research about the company. For example, information about how many locations the company has, its products or services, or its primary competitors is easily learned online. Asking questions that are easily answered by doing research reveals that you haven't done enough preparation.

Information You Should Have after Your Interview

If you've conducted your interview correctly and you've asked good questions, you'll know certain information following your interview. This information is important for your follow-through letter, and for subsequent interviews. You should create your information list prior to your interview and make sure you have a corresponding list of questions to get the answers you need. Very important — the following list of questions should be asked at the beginning of the interview not at the end. The answers to these questions will give you good information which you can address during the interview. The following list is not exhaustive; it is simply representative of information you'll want to know:

*The top five to seven critical job requirements

*How success is measured on the job

*The top job priorities in the next three, six, and twelve months

*What makes you a good candidate for the position – Why were you invited for the interview (see First Interview Question below)

*The company culture

*The company's financial strength and stability

*The type of employee who tends to be successful at the company and in this position

*The company's top two or three challenges

*The jobs top two or three challenges

*What keeps the hiring manager up at night and problems that are nagging him

*How the hiring manager got to her position

*Whether this position is new or you will be replacing a person who has left

Keep in mind that you don't have to have all your information after your first interview. Decide what information is appropriate for first, second, or third interviews. For example, after your first interview, you'll want to know about the selection process and how to follow up, but you should wait until a later interview or even the job offer before finding out the details about compensation.

Your Very Important First Interview Question

The first question a good salesperson asks a customer is why they have chosen to consider the service they are offering. "What is it about the sales training program we offer interests you?" The answer to this question reveals what the customer likes and where the salesperson should focus. In an interview you are a salesperson and it is important to know why the hiring manager is interested in your services. The best opening question asked at the very beginning of an interview is "I am excited about being here today learning more about this job and having you get to know me, but before we get started I am curious, what led you to invite me for this interview today?"

The answer to this question provides two important results. The first is you get to learn exactly what the interviewer likes about your experience, skills, and knowledge. She may be interested in something which you didn't think was of much importance, but it is of major significance to her. This will be something you emphasize during your interview. The second, is this question creates a positive bias in your favor. People have a consistency bias. When a person says something, they like to be consistent and will look for information to support their statement. Thus, when the interviewer states what they like about you, you have set up a positive consistency bias and they will look for information to support their positive statements. This is a powerful way to cleverly undermine unconscious negative biases.

The Best Interview Question of All Time

I tell my clients that if they don't ask this question in their interview, they should kick themselves in the behind all the way to their car!

In any sales situation, the salesperson wants an opportunity to hear and respond to all objections. A car salesperson might ask, "Is there any reason why you wouldn't buy this car today?" A realtor might ask, "Do you see anything about this house that would prevent you from making an offer?" Once the salesperson hears the objection, he can gauge the importance of the objection and respond.

Some objections will be deal-breakers:

> **Client:** We need a house with three bedrooms, and this one only has two.

Deal over. But other objections can be overcome:

> **Customer:** I really wanted the car in blue, and this is red.

> **Salesperson:** If I can get a red car for you by the end of today, would you buy the car?

Deal closed.

At the end of your interviews, you need to find out how you did. One way is to hear about any objections to hiring you. Hard-sell proponents suggest asking questions such as, "Is there any reason why you wouldn't offer me the job?" or "Will I be asked back for the next round of interviews?" Both questions are "sales close" questions, and the interviewer can avoid them by simply saying, "We have more candidates to interview before we can make that decision." Even if they like you, avoiding the answer is a prudent response, in case subsequent candidates are better suited to the job.

The challenge is to ask a question that elicits an open, honest, non-defensive answer from the interviewer that raises any objections and gives you an indication of how well you did in the interview. The #1 suggested question:

> "Based on my background, experience, and skills, what do you think would be the greatest challenges for me in this position?"

There are a few variations of this best question:

"Now that we've had a chance to talk, how does my background measure up to the requirements of the job? Are there any gaps?"

"Are there issues that cause you concern about my candidacy?"

The next several sections will detail the types of responses you may get to this question.

Vague or General Answers

A poor interviewer response to this question is one that applies to all candidates regardless of their individual experience, skills, or personal success factors. For example, "Your greatest challenge will be getting to know our internal communications system. It is a proprietary system, and it takes a while to learn."

Every new employee has the same challenge, and this answer doesn't reveal any objections the interviewer may have about you personally. Use further questions to improve the interviewer's answers. For example, you can ask, "Is there anything about my background and skills that makes you think this would be a more difficult task for me than for other candidates?" This is a gentle way of suggesting that the answer is not specific enough. Follow up by asking, "Can you think of any challenges related specifically to my background and skills?"

No Challenges or Minor Challenges

If the interviewer genuinely states that there are no challenges or only minor, manageable challenges, it is an indication that you did well in the interview, and you may be under consideration for the position.

A Challenge in an Important Job Area

When a challenge is mentioned, ask how important it is: "How critical is that to the job?" Some challenges are minor "nice-to-haves" and will not disqualify you. Other challenges are very important or even critical. If you cannot address critical challenges, you are not a viable candidate for the job. For example, if the challenge is that you don't speak a required foreign language or you don't have the required level of skill in a complex technology, you won't get the job. But at least you will know this immediately and won't waste time waiting for your phone to ring after the interview.

A Challenge in an Area That Was Not Mentioned in the Interview

The interviewer might mention challenges in areas that weren't mentioned in the interview, but where you have skills and experiences. You now have an opportunity to share the information and correct the interviewer's concerns. For example, if the interviewer says, "Your greatest challenge is that you haven't had direct customer service experience." You can reply, "Actually, I have; we just haven't discussed it. Let me tell you about working directly with customers at...."

A Challenge You Can Provide a Strategy to Overcome

The interviewer might mention a challenge for which you can provide a strategy to overcome. Perhaps there was an opportunity for you to overcome a similar challenge on a previous job. Use that experience to tell the interviewer how you will overcome the challenge on this job. For example, "You are correct that I'm not very experienced with Microsoft Access. However, when I started my previous job, I wasn't proficient at PowerPoint. Immediately after being hired, I took a two-day course, purchased training books, and practiced. Within four weeks, I was producing good PowerPoint presentations, and within eight weeks, I was considered a highly skilled PowerPoint producer. Once hired, I would learn Access the same way."

If you haven't overcome a similar challenge, lay out a plan for overcoming the challenge and ask the interviewer if she thinks your plan is viable.

A Challenge That Is a Misconception

One of my clients was interviewing for a chief financial officer position. He had a strong background in implementing accounting systems and spoke about this experience during the interview. At the end of the interview, he asked the "best interview question of all time." The CEO responded by saying, "Your greatest challenge is that you're going to want to implement a new accounting system, and we cannot afford that at this time." My client responded, clarifying the CEO's misconception: "I wouldn't just implement a new system. I would evaluate the system you have and see whether it can be upgraded, and if it is costing the company money in lost revenue or time, I would put a plan in place to replace it." His answer satisfied the CEO, and he got the job.

Had he not asked the best interview question of all time directly after the interview, the CEO would've said to the rest of the interview team, "This guy just wants to spend our money on expensive new systems; we can't hire him." Interviews lead to many misconceptions that go unaddressed—unless you ask the best interview question of all time.

Addressing the challenges that the hiring manager sees is one of the primary ways you will reduce his FUD (fear, uncertainty, and doubt). As I said earlier in this book, reducing the hiring manager's FUD is your primary goal in your interview.

Challenges Are Often Good News

In sales situations, salespeople know that prospects who aren't going to buy don't waste time raising objections. An objection is an invitation to sell. It's the same in interviews. If a hiring manager doesn't consider you a viable candidate, she won't waste her time talking about challenges, because she's not interested in anything you have to offer. Thus, a challenge can be a sign that the hiring manager is interested and wants to clear up a potential roadblock reducing FUD.

Lean into Challenges

When you hear a challenge it's like hearing a criticism, and it might cause you to become fearful and withdraw. When you do this, you often sit back and assume a defensive posture. Once you ask the best interview question of all time, be prepared to hear a challenge. Remember that it is a positive thing and physically lean forward. When you lean forward, your body language communicates that you aren't concerned about the challenge and you're eager to discuss it. This lack of defensiveness will come across as confidence, and your answer will have more credibility.

It Is Best to Know

The best response a salesperson can get is, "We are interested, and we want to purchase." The second is, "We are not interested, and we definitely won't purchase." When a customer who is not interested gets a salesperson off the phone by saying, "Send me a proposal," or, "Call me again in six weeks," the salesperson wastes time following up. Good salespeople want to know whether or not the customer is interested.

When you get an answer to the one best interview question, it mitigates one of the most uncomfortable parts of the job-search process—waiting for the hiring manager to call after an interview. If the hiring manager made it clear that there are significant challenges to you performing the job, you can stop wondering whether you'll get the second interview or the job, and you can move on. It will be disappointing, but you won't be left wondering how and when to follow up and waiting for a call that won't come. If no challenges were stated or you overcame challenges, you can maintain hope and be assertive in your follow-through.

Another Must-Ask Question

Many candidates leave interviews without a clue about when or how to follow up. They are left agonizing over when and how they should contact the hiring manager. There is a quick and simple way to avoid this agony—simply ask, "How and when should I follow up with you?"

When you ask this question, don't accept a vague answer; get a firm commitment. A typical answer is, "We're interviewing through the rest of the week. We'll contact you next week." This answer is too vague and often results in no contact. In response, you can say, "That's great. If I don't hear from you by Wednesday, do you suggest I call you?" This gives you a timeframe and a method of contact. If you haven't heard from the hiring manager by the following Wednesday, you can place a call and say, "As you suggested, I'm calling to follow up on our interview from last week." This obligates the hiring manager to respond.

Asking Good Questions Fixes Your Interview

> "There isn't a pat answer anymore to this world, so the best we can do for students is to have them ask the right questions."
>
> —Nancy Cantor, chancellor of Syracuse University

One of the primary reasons why people fail on jobs is that they take a job with a misunderstanding of what the job entails. They don't realize that the job requires as much travel as it does or that it requires very long hours during certain times of the year. They don't know what skills are actually required or that they will have limited supervision or training. Maybe they are thinking account management, and the job is actually sales or project management. You can fix this missing information and these misconceptions by asking good questions, paying close attention to the answers, and asking follow-up questions. Asking good questions often clarifies the position in the hiring manager's mind as well, which supports your candidacy for the position.

Leaving the interview with unanswered objections will doom your chances for winning the interview and getting the job. Asking the best interview question of all time can save your interview by reducing the hiring manager's FUD and clearing the way for you to be the candidate of choice. Asking good questions has the following benefits:

*It demonstrates a high level of interview preparation and motivation.

*It demonstrates a critical job-success skill—asking good questions.

*It helps expose concerns about hiring you and allows you to correct misconceptions.

*It creates additional opportunities for quality conversations.

*It allows you to demonstrate your knowledge of the industry, company, and job, thus increasing your credibility.

*It addresses one of interviewers' primary criticisms of candidates—lack of questions which implies lack of preparation, motivation and interest.

Chapter 15 - Develop an Interview-Winning Presentation

- Why a Printed Presentation?
- Is an Interview Presentation Appropriate for a Job in...?
- What to Use to Develop a Presentation
- Introducing Your Interview Presentation
- Interview Presentation Sections
- Interview Presentation Tips
- Another Radical Idea: A Networking Presentation
- Apply All the Principles of an Interview Presentation
- Using an Interview Presentation Will Fix Your Interviews

"Never interrupt someone doing something you said couldn't be done."

—Amelia Earhart

Imagine walking into an interview with a high-quality printed and bound presentation that clearly communicates why you are the best candidate for the job—you cannot fail to impress the hiring manager. The previous chapters have detailed the components of a powerful interview presentation. This chapter will walk you through the process of developing a printed presentation you can actively use to win your interview. (See Appendix A for examples of interview presentations.)

In my experience, 85 percent of all candidates who develop presentations use a printed presentation (a copy can be sent via email prior to the interview or displayed via screen share) in their interview. Fifteen percent choose not to for various reasons—they don't sense an opening to introduce the presentation, they're uncomfortable with the presentation idea, or it's a very structured interview that leaves no time for the presentation. However, 100 percent of all candidates use their presentation as a leave-behind for the interviewer.

All my clients state emphatically that developing a presentation is the best preparation they have ever done for an interview. Developing each presentation section takes you through a thought process that helps define your message and become clear about why you are a good candidate for the job. Your confidence will increase, and your fear will decrease. Thus, even if you don't want to use a printed presentation during your interview, it is important to develop one. Who knows—once you see how good it looks, you might change your mind about using it!

As you have read, an interview has the goal of answering three basic questions:

1.Does this candidate's skill set and knowledge match the critical job requirements such that she can perform the job at a high level of quality?

2.Is this candidate interested in and motivated for this position?

3.Does the candidate's personality and character traits match the culture of the company, and will he work well with me, the hiring manager, and other employees?

The interview presentation is a special form of "sales presentation," and it actively and powerfully answer the basic interview questions using the following content:

*Cover page (Questions 2 and 3)

*Your personal brand (Questions 1 and 3)

*Job requirements (Question 1)

*Your background, experience, and skills match with the job requirements (Question 1)

*Your additional areas of expertise (Question 1)

*Your job-related success stories or accomplishments (Questions 1 and 3)

*Your outstanding personal qualities and characteristics that contribute to your success on the job (Question 3)

*A 30- and 60-day position-specific strategic action plan (Questions 1 and 2)

*A summary of the major selling points of why you are a good choice for this position (Questions 1 and 3)

*Important questions about the company, the job, and the interview (Questions 1 and 2)

Why a Printed Presentation?

"Men trust their ears less than their eyes."

—Herodotus, Greek historian

A printed presentation works terrifically well in many ways, including the following:

*A well-crafted visual presentation communicates that you are well prepared and highly motivated for the interview.

*It clearly differentiates you from other candidates.

*It shows your ability to assemble and communicate pertinent information in a clear and succinct manner.

*It demonstrates important job-related behaviors—presenting information and then responding to questions.

*It can reduce unconscious biases

*It contains the information the hiring manager needs to know to make an informed hiring decision.

*The visual nature of the presentation increases the hiring manger's retention and your persuasiveness.

*A presentation reduces the hiring manager's FUD level and makes it easier for her to hire you.

*It serves as a powerful leave-behind that the interviewer can refer to as she begins to compare candidates.

In addition, according to David Peoples, author of *Presentations Plus* (Wiley, 1992), using visual aids results in:

*The audience being 43 percent more likely to be persuaded.

*The presenter covering the same material in 25 to 40 percent less time.

*The listener's learning improving up to 200 percent.

*Retention improving by 38 percent.

*The presenter being perceived as more professional, persuasive, credible, and interesting and better prepared.

Why should your presentation be printed in this on-line, interactive, electronic world? Using a laptop or projecting a presentation interferes with eye contact and rapport during an interview either in person or via a video interview. As you will learn, each bullet point in your presentation is very brief—no more than 170 characters—and quickly read. The goal is to introduce a topic, speak to it, initiate a conversation, and not have the interviewer distracted by reading the information. Also, even in today's electronic age, having a printed and bound document on which one can make notes communicates credibility and professionalism.

Is an Interview Presentation Appropriate for a Job in...?

When I talk about using a presentation in an interview, I often get the response, "But I'm an accountant/software developer/project manager/financial analyst/…. I don't think a presentation is really appropriate for my profession. I think it is really for a marketing or sales position." All I can say is that candidates in every profession who have used an interview presentation have gotten excellent results. Even technical professionals, such as software developers and engineers, benefit from addressing non-technical qualities they bring to the job and selling themselves in the interview. The issue is not the profession; it is how comfortable you are with using a presentation in an interview. If you choose not to use a presentation, that's fine—just know that it works for your profession, and your competition may be using one.

A related question is, "Isn't an interview presentation good only for senior executives?" Again, I can say that interview presentations have been used very successfully by recent college graduates applying for their first job and senior professionals applying for CEO positions. Recent graduates can be more impressive than senior professionals when they arrive at an interview with a polished, professional document and make a powerful presentation. Hiring managers don't expect such a high level of preparation and professionalism from a recent graduate, and they are duly impressed.

> "I received positive and quick feedback from an interviewer that my materials—the interview presentation—was far superior to and more professional than anything the other candidates were using during their interviews. I believe using the interview presentation as a discussion tool and a leave-behind was instrumental in securing my current position."

> —Richard, academic administrator

Using a Presentation to Land a First Job

Allan, a friend of my son Zach, graduated the same year as Zach from Penn State—into the teeth of the 2007 recession. For 12 months, Allan had been experiencing the recent-graduate career blues, which includes working at low-level temporary positions with minimal compensation, having lots of failed interviews, and living at home with his parents. Allan had been actively job seeking and had eight interviews with no success and, of course, no feedback about why.

With a great deal of networking and persistence, Allan landed an interview with a marketing agency in New York for an assistant account executive position—a dream job. He was about to blow another interview by preparing and interviewing the same way he had interviewed for the previous eight jobs—until he spoke with Zach. He told Zach about his upcoming interview, and Zach, having landed two jobs using an interview presentation, said, "Dude, like, you should totally get your interview on and use an interview presentation if you don't want to screw up again and live with your 'rents forever." Actually, I'm sure Zach, being a Penn State graduate, was more articulate than that, and he *did* convince Allan to use a presentation.

Using a presentation strategy, Allan was well prepared for the interview, impressed the hiring manager, differentiated himself from the other candidates, and landed the job. The only people more excited about the job than Allan were his parents.

What to Use to Develop a Presentation

A presentation is most effective when it's presented in a printed and spiral-bound format. The best interview presentation development tool is the InterviewBest program (www.interviewbest.com), which I developed. The online InterviewBest program will walk you through developing an interview presentation section by section and it results in a high-quality presentation ready for printing. In addition, the InterviewBest program has extensive expert libraries, and the interviewbest.com site has additional presentation examples. Expert libraries (samples of which are in Appendix C) are lists of suggested content you can use in your interview presentation. Expert libraries make developing an interview presentation quick and focused. The InterviewBest program has a free trial, so you can experience the advantages of the guided process and the expert libraries.

Introducing Your Interview Presentation

You can introduce presentations in several places during interviews. Many candidates introduce their presentation at the beginning of the interview. As soon as they sit down they say,

> " I am excited about this opportunity and I have developed a presentation about how my background and experience match the critical requirements of the job and why I think I am an excellent candidate. If we have time, I would like to share that with you".

Another excellent place to introduce a presentation is in response to the question, "Tell me about yourself." Another opportunity is when the interviewer asks a question that you have addressed in your presentation—you can use this as an opportunity to introduce your presentation. For example, "What are your goals for the first 60 days?" or "Tell me about a time when you were particularly effective in your job."

Using a presentation to save the day

One recent college graduate introduced his presentation at the very end of his interview and saved the day. Ben was interviewing with a human resources (HR) representative for an entry-level marketing job at an advertising company. After 20 minutes, the HR representative was ending the interview, which had not gone very well. You know the negative signs—a short interview being closed down with vague expressions such as, "Thanks for coming in. We have a lot of people to interview. We'll let you know." Just before he was ushered out the door, Ben said, "I've put together a presentation about my qualifications for this job. Can I share it with you?" The HR representative agreed, and Ben gave her a copy of his bound presentation and took her through the presentation. Halfway through the presentation, the rep stopped Ben and said, "Our vice president of marketing loves presentations. When you interview with her, you have to show this to her." Ben got through to the second round, though unfortunately he didn't get the job, which was never filled. But without using his interview presentation, he likely wouldn't have even made it to the second interview.

For most hiring managers, having a candidate use an interview presentation will be a new and unfamiliar Active Interview strategy. Thus, it is best to introduce the presentation in a way that enables the hiring manager to accept or reject the use of it, maintaining her "control" over the interview. Again, the following is an example of how you can introduce your presentation:

> "I am very interested in this job, and I've developed a brief presentation about how my background, skills, and experience match the critical requirements of this position, what I can contribute to [use company name here], and why I'm an excellent candidate for this job. May I share it with you?"

The typical interviewer response will be, "Sure, let me see what you have." Note that when you ask permission to "share" the presentation, the interviewer has a chance to say no. They rarely do, but this helps the interviewer maintain her feeling of control over the interview.

Interview Presentation Sections

The following sections contain descriptions of each section of a comprehensive interview presentation. Except for the first two main sections—job requirements and your match with the requirements—all sections are optional. However, results have shown that candidates who prepare and present a complete presentation perform better and win more interviews.

See Appendix D, "Interview Presentation Worksheets," for interview-presentation development forms.

Cover Page

An interview presentation is a high-quality, professional document. The cover page gives you an opportunity to make a strong first impression and communicate your personal brand. The next few sections will describe the components of the cover page.

Tagline

Located at the top of the cover page, the tagline provides a heading and incorporates the name of the company with which you are interviewing. Write a tagline that represents your desired outcome in the position. Possible taglines include:

*Partnering with [company name] to Increase Sales

*Accelerating [company's] Success in the [name of industry] Marketplace

*Partnering with [company name] for Excellence in Product Development

*Providing [company name] with Important Marketing Services

*Supporting [company name] to Provide an Excellent Customer Experience

Cover Graphic

Use a high-quality graphic on the front of your presentation. The picture can represent business in general, your specific industry, or something that relates to you as an employee. For example, a candidate applying for a management position might use a picture of a conference room or several people meeting. A candidate applying for a job in transportation might use a picture of a truck or a train. A person who prides himself on his computer skills might use a technology-related picture, such as a circuit board or a computer.

A number of websites provide free graphics. Just Google "free graphics" and select a professional-looking graphic that communicates the message you want the interviewer to receive.

Company Logo

Including the logo of the company for which you are interviewing customizes the presentation and communicates a high level of motivation for the job. You can usually copy a logo from the company's website. If the logo on the company website is in a banner and cannot be copied, try Googling the company and then selecting "Images" this usually will yield logo images that are easily copied.

Contact Information

Include your phone number, email address and LinkedIn URL so the hiring manager doesn't have to search for your resume for contact information and she can go to your profile on LinkedIn quickly.

Personal-Brand Words

As you now know, a personal brand is what you want others to think or feel about you and a promise of the value you will deliver. On the cover page, include up to four personal-brand terms that represent you. Limit the list to four terms that best represent your brand in relation to this position. More than four will dilute your brand message and confuse the interviewer.

Be prepared to answer questions about your personal-brand terms, including:

*Please tell me the meaning of each of your personal brand terms.

*Please give me an example of a time when you displayed behaviors associated with your personal brand.

*How do you think your personal brand will make you more effective in this position?

*Was there a time when you had to compromise your personal brand?

*What do you do to reinforce and maintain your personal brand?

*Do you think this personal brand is different or distinctive?

*How does your personal brand differentiate you from others?

Critical Job Requirements Section

The most important selection criterion for the hiring decision is how well you can perform the critical job requirements. It is important that you and the hiring manager understand each of the requirements and agree that they are the critical success factors for the job.

The job requirements section gives you an opportunity to engage in a conversation with the hiring manager about the specific requirements of the job and come to a common understanding. Once you have a clear understanding of and mutual agreement about the requirements, you have the information to powerfully align your background and skills to the requirements and be more persuasive. This will significantly improve the hiring manager's ability to determine the fit, reduce FUD, and make an informed hiring decision.

Selecting Job Requirements for Your Presentation

In Chapter 6, you learned questions to ask to help you determine the critical job requirements. When you have a list of critical requirements, categorize them in the following way:

*"**Must-have**" **requirements.** These may include years of experience, specific skills or experience, or certain training, certifications, or licenses—for example, "Required, mortgage agent license plus five years of experience in mortgage lending for a mid- or large-size financial institution."

*Clearly defined requirements that highlight a specific skill set or experience. For example, "The ability to segment markets and develop targeted advertising using online and offline media," or, "Experience working with a multinational corporation managing compensation programs." Further categorize these requirements on the basis of your strongest to weakest match with the requirements.

*Vague requirements. These include having good communication skills or being highly motivated.

Just as you do in all lists in your presentation, limit your list of job requirements to seven items. Choose the seven items using the prioritized list above. First, list the "must haves," and then progress to the clearly defined "best match" requirements. List the requirements in order of your strongest to weakest match. These are the requirements you will talk about in the second section of the presentation: your match with the job requirements.

This list of requirements should be a conversation starter. While you present the list of requirements to the interviewer, ask questions including:

*Do you consider this a comprehensive list of the critical job requirements?

*If you were to put the requirements in order of importance, what would they be?

*Please give me more detail about this requirement.

*Of these requirements, which do you think is the most critical?

During the interview, ask clarifying questions about the critical job requirements. For example, if a requirement reads, "Manage all business systems activities," ask what the specific business systems are and what manage means. Does "manage" refer to hands-on day-to-day computer systems operations or managing a team of people who operate the computer systems? As the hiring manager engages in this conversation and provides details, you will get a better understanding of the requirements, and you'll be able to make a more targeted presentation.

Good References

Some candidates list a job requirement of "excellent references." Then, in the next section of their presentation, they list three or four references. The strategy is to list references that will create a conversation. For example, one candidate, a PhD MD applying for a position in a pharmaceutical company, listed several prestigious scientists. This led to a conversation about how he knew the scientists and the work he had done with them.

Other candidates list references that are well known in the industry and may lead to a networking conversation. For example, an interviewer might say in response to a reference, "I also know Sally. I worked with her at ABC Company. Isn't she terrific? How long did you work with her?" Having references in common increases trust levels and creates more of a bond.

It is important to establish that your presentation is your understanding of the position at this point in the selection process. If you establish the presentation as your current understanding, then if you're mistaken about something, it won't be viewed as a mistake—just as a misunderstanding. You can use the following language to introduce this page:

> "First, I'd like to review my understanding of the key success factors and requirements of the position at this point. The purpose of the review is for us to have a common understanding of the requirements. I

understand there may be some important requirements that I've missed, and I'm interested in learning what those may be. However, here are the requirements as I understood them as I prepared for this interview."

Match with Job Requirements Section

This is an opportunity for you to list your experience, skills, and education that match the critical job requirements and communicate your ability to perform the job. For each job requirement listed on the job requirements page, you can use bullet points to highlight the three most relevant points related to jobs, experience, skills, or knowledge that you believe best demonstrate your fit with the requirement. As you speak to each point, the hiring manager will gain a clear understanding of how you match the critical job requirements and what previous positions or experience support your claims.

As you present your match with the requirements, the interviewer will have the opportunity to get a better picture of your experience and ask questions. Be prepared to answer questions about your experience, including:

*Please give me more detail about how your responsibilities in that position match our job requirements.

*What did you do specifically in that position?

*To whom did you report in that position?

*How large a staff did you supervise?

*What kind of training was required for that position?

*How did you land that position?

*What would you say was your greatest accomplishment in that position?

*What would you say was your greatest challenge in that position?

*Your prior position was in the _____ industry. How will that experience translate to this position?

Include specific metrics in your bullet points if possible. Instead of saying, "I supervised a staff," say, "I supervised a staff of 10 people with an annual budget of $650,000." If numbers are not appropriate or available, be as specific and detailed as possible. Another example, if you managed a restaurant include how many tables, how many staff, and number of customers, "I managed a restaurant with 35 tables and a wait staff of 40 serving over 600 people per week."

Using examples and stories while talking about your experience will make your presentation more powerful. For example, instead of simply saying, "I have construction experience—in my job at ABC Company, I led more than 20 construction projects," say, "I have construction experience—in my job at ABC Company, I led more than 20 construction projects. Let me give you an example of the type of projects I worked on…."

You can use the following statement to introduce your section on your match with job requirements:

> "Based on the job requirements we just discussed, I would like to talk about how my background, skills, and experience are an excellent match for these requirements."

Additional Areas of Expertise Section

This page presents additional areas of expertise you can bring to the job that are beyond the basic job requirements. This page lets the interviewer know, "I just communicated how I match the basic job requirements; however, I will also contribute these additional areas of expertise. They are beyond the basic job requirements, and I think they differentiate me from other candidates."

Each profession and each candidate has a wide range of potential additional areas of expertise. To determine additional areas of expertise, first look to other areas of your profession or industry and then look to other relevant skills. For example, you might be applying for a general accounting position, and you may have international tax or forensic accounting as additional areas of expertise. Knowing these accounting areas could be an important differentiator for you.

As another example, suppose you're applying for a project management position, and you have contract negotiating experience. If the position requires a candidate to establish projects with vendors, contract-negotiation skills could be important. And, social-media and website development experience are valuable additional areas of expertise for many positions, as is the ability to use a variety of software programs and write copy. Another rapidly emerging area of expertise is Agile which is a process management approach. If you have Agile experience, it could be a differentiator across a wide range of jobs and industries.

The following list provides examples of areas of expertise from a few professions.

Human resources

*American Disabilities Act

*Benefits administration

*Career pathing

*Change management

*Incentive planning

*Professional recruitment

*Union relations

Engineering

*Capital project management

*Customer management

*Fault analysis

*OSHA requirements

*Project costing

*Regulatory compliance

*Technical briefings

Corporate law

*Criminal law

*Ethics

*Licensing

*Mediation

*Trademark

*SEC affairs

*Risk management

Sales and marketing

*Competitive analysis

*Direct-response marketing

*Distributor management

*High-impact presentations

*Market launch

*Product development

*Solutions selling

General management

*Business reengineering

*Corporate legal affairs

*Global market expansion

*Multi-site operations management

*Startup ventures

*Turnaround management

*Sales management

Some candidates will include high-level certifications or specialized training in the additional areas of expertise section. For example, a salesperson may have been trained in a specific sales technique, such as Sandler or consultative selling. A manufacturing professional might have a Six Sigma Black Belt certification. These certifications and training are not required but can be differentiators.

As you present your additional areas of expertise, the interviewer will have the opportunity to get a better picture of your experience and ask questions. Be prepared to answer questions about your areas of expertise, including:

*How would this additional area of expertise relate to your performance on the job?

*How do you see using this additional area of expertise on the job?

*How do you think this additional area of expertise differentiates you from other candidates?

*How did you develop this additional area of expertise?

*Do you have licensure or certification in this additional area of expertise?

You might have several areas of expertise, so be sure the areas selected for your presentation are pertinent to the specific job. It's wonderful that you know web design, but how does that apply to accounting?

As you talk about the additional areas of expertise, state clearly what the benefit of the expertise will be to the position. For example, "Because I have expertise in public relations, I can expand your marketing efforts with little additional cost," or, "Because I have expertise in web design, I can set up a website to support your departmental communication and improve customer service."

You can use the following statement to introduce your additional areas of expertise:

> "In addition to the skills and experiences we just discussed; these are additional areas of expertise I will bring to [company name]. These are important value-added areas that I believe differentiate me from other candidates and will contribute either immediately or in the future to the success of [company name]."

Outstanding Accomplishments (Successes) Section

> "Story will always be king, no matter how much we love the technology."
>
> —Ethan Marten, film producer

Lou Adler, a recruiting thought leader, advocates a one-question interview. The question is, "Please describe a major project or accomplishment in great depth." He then suggests that the interviewer explore the accomplishment extensively by asking when, where, why, how, and who questions to really understand the scope and impact of the accomplishment. This question-and-answer process is then repeated several times to get a fully rounded picture of the candidate's skills, experience, and personal success factors. His rationale for this approach is that it differentiates candidates who simply interview well from good employees, and it gives a more accurate picture of what the candidate has accomplished.

As you read in Chapter 10, successes told in story form are powerful communicators of skills, abilities, and potential contributions to the hiring organization. In this section of your presentation, list up to seven accomplishments— either job-related or from your personal life—that you think best represent the highest level of skills, knowledge, and experience you can bring to the job. Each accomplishment represents a time when you were at your best. Some of my clients have used awards they received as the basis for accomplishment stories. By exploring each accomplishment, a hiring manager can learn the following information about you:

*Additional skills and experience relative to the job

*Initiative

*Commitment

*Team leadership

*Potential

*Compatibility with company's culture

*Comparability of past job requirements with the current position

*Character

*True personality

*Ability to learn

*Interest and motivation to do the work required

*Additional value to the organization beyond the basic job requirements

As suggested in Chapter 10, use a SBAR story format to relate each accomplishment, and do not take more than two minutes to tell each story. Most candidates find that interviewers are very intrigued with their stories, and the interviewer's questions add a substantial amount of time to them. This is a good sign, and the questioning can take as long as the interviewer wants—just limit your storytelling to two minutes. After you've related your accomplishment, be prepared to answer questions including:

*Were you recognized for this accomplishment and, if so, how?

*How do you think this accomplishment relates to the requirements of this position?

*What company did you work for when you achieved this accomplishment, and what did the company do?

*What was the importance of this accomplishment to your company?

*Why were you were chosen for the project?

*What were the most critical decisions you made?

*What were the most important skills required for this accomplishment?

*Tell me some of the mistakes you made. What did you learn from the mistakes, and what would you do differently?

*How did this accomplishment influence you as a person?

*What were the greatest lessons you learned from this accomplishment?

*What was the most enjoyable aspect of this accomplishment?

*What specifically were other people's responsibilities in this accomplishment?

*Can you identify an action or decision that was most critical to the success of this accomplishment?

As with your entire presentation, the written content should be brief, introducing only your accomplishment and not providing enough detail to distract the interviewer. Think of each listing as a newspaper headline enticing the interviewer to want to learn more. In addition, any numbers or metrics you can put in your headlines will lend credibility and substance. Some examples of good accomplishment headlines include:

*Recruited largest new-member class in the history of Sigma Beta Theta fraternity

*Sold first outsourcing project at Bycom, which accounted for $34M in sales

*Selected to present keynote address about infrastructure technology at annual meeting of International Technology Association

*Implemented systems that met 25% funding-match requirement

*Increased readership of industry journal by 115% in an 18-month period

*Grew website traffic by 64% by posting daily news features and implementing polls and other interactive forums

*Increased profits for Image Group with $35,000 in reprint revenue

*Received award for publication excellence in health and medical writing

You can use the following statement to introduce your accomplishments section:

> "These are examples of times in my career or my life when I was at my best. Each of these accomplishments exemplifies my skills and knowledge in real-life situations. By hearing what I did in these previous situations, you will get good insight into how I will perform at [*company name*]."

Personal Success Factors Section

As you learned in Chapter 11, organizations hire people whose personality and work style fit their culture. You also learned that personal success factors, distinct from skills and knowledge, are personal characteristics that contribute to your success on a job.

Select up to seven personal success factors that you think best represent you in relation to the position. Your choice of personal success factors reveals what you believe to be the most important personal contributions you will make to this job and those that will make you successful in this position. Your choice of personal success factors will give the interviewer information about how you will fit into the organization's culture.

You undoubtedly have a long list of personal success factors. For each position you interview for, choose a set of personal success factors that matches the job requirements. For example, if a position doesn't include supervising others, don't include personal success factors related to leadership. If the job includes working from home, choose personal success factors related to time management and self-supervision.

All personal success factors are highly desirable traits. Select factors that truly represent you and are authentic. You will need to speak about each of the personal success factors and communicate to the interviewer how you display these factors at work. For example, it is not enough for a salesperson to say, "I am competitive"; he must give examples of being competitive in a notable and distinctive way.

Be prepared to answer the following questions about your personal success factors:

*Please tell me your definition of this personal success factor.

*What does it actually look like when you display this personal success factor?

*Please give me a specific instance when you displayed this personal success factor.

*Tell me about how you typically display this personal success factor at work.

*How do you think your personal success factors will mesh with the culture here?

*Of the personal success factors you chose, which is the most dominant?

*Has this personal success factor ever gotten you in trouble with a boss or a co-worker?

You can use the following statement to introduce your personal success factors:

> "These personal success factors are personal traits and skills that make me successful on the job. This list will give you insight into how I like to work, my personal style, and how I will fit the culture of [company name]."

Strategic Action Plan Section

As discussed in Chapter 12, a 30/60-day strategic action plan is your "services" implementation plan, communicating your ideas about how you will approach the position and provide value quickly. It is designed to illustrate "on-target" proactive thinking. It will give the hiring manager insight into your goal-setting process, your understanding of the job requirements, and your level of expertise in the industry and your career.

It is important to present your strategic action plan as your *proposed* goals at this point of the selection process— subject to change when you know more about the position. Being too definitive or strident about the goals may make you come across as aggressive or close-minded. Communicating openness and flexibility about changing the goals will result in a good conversation, and it won't matter if your goals aren't 100 percent accurate. The important part is that you have thought ahead, you know you need to have a good set of S.M.A.R.T. goals (refer to Chapter 12) to guide your performance, and you are prepared for the interview. The hiring manager's focus should be less on the absolute accuracy of the goals and more on the quality of your thinking and the level of sophistication of your goals.

As you introduce the goals, communicate that you will accomplish them in collaboration with the hiring manager and the team, if appropriate.

As you present your goals, be prepared to answer the following questions:

*How did you decide on this goal?

*What do you think may be barriers to achieving this goal?

*Did you achieve this goal in a prior position? How and at what point in your employment?

*Of the goals listed, which do you think will be the most achievable?

*Of the goals listed, which do you think will be the most challenging?

*Please give me details about specifically how you will achieve this goal.

*How will you measure success for this goal?

You can use the following statement to introduce your strategic action plan:

> "As I mentioned, I'm very interested in this position, and I have given a great deal of thought to how I can contribute immediately to [company name]. The following is a list of goals that I think I can accomplish in

the first 30 and 60 days. Certainly, these goals are open to discussion and will be refined as I get to know the job and the company. However, based on what I know at this point, I think these goals are realistic, and I would like to discuss them with you."

Introducing a Presentation to Answer a Question

Jane was applying for a senior management position at a healthcare company, and she spent a great deal of time developing an interview presentation. She had practiced giving her presentation in three mock interviews and had blown away all three of her interviewers. However, during her actual interviews, Jane didn't see an opening to use her presentation—until the last interview of the last round with the CEO of the company.

Halfway through her interview, the CEO asked Jane, "So, what is your 100-day plan?" Jane smiled and responded, "I don't have a 100-day plan, but I do have a 60-day and a 90-day plan. Can I share them with you?" She took her interview presentation out of her portfolio, gave the CEO a copy, and initiated a conversation about her 60- and 90-day strategic action plans. The CEO was impressed and asked Jane to take him through the rest of the presentation, which Jane was happy to do. The CEO was as impressed as her mock interviewers were, and Jane got the job offer.

Using the presentation, Jane was able to tangibly demonstrate that she anticipated an important issue for the CEO and that they were on the same wavelength. The presentation communicated Jane's level of preparation and professionalism and her insights about the position. How could the CEO not be impressed?

Hire Me Because… Section

"I want to inform you that the interview presentation was a great success. It was easy to complete, and the library tools gave me different options to choose from(on www.interviewbest.com). I had two interviews on Wednesday, and they were both impressed and awed by how professional, well-prepared, and organized the presentation was. It was easy for them to view, and they were extremely impressed with the match for position requirements, additional areas of expertise, outstanding accomplishments, personal success factors, and—my favorite—why hire me section.

"I even received a call today (Friday) for a job offer from one of the companies I interviewed with on Wednesday, which is a full-service practice management and billing company. I have another interview today with a Spanish organization, as an executive assistant. I even did the presentation in both languages (English and Spanish). This will determine my future within the company. Thank you for letting me have the opportunity to use this great tool. I would recommend an interview presentation to anyone who wants to land a position with a professional organization."

—Rosita, Medical Billing Specialist

This page contains information that you have already presented. It is an opportunity for you to restate the most important experience, skills, or accomplishments that you think make you the best person for this position. It is a "why hire me" statement based on all the important material you have already shared.

This page gives the hiring manager the opportunity to hear once again your strongest selling points. The hiring manager will also have an opportunity to observe you making a summary statement highlighting the key elements of a detailed presentation. This is a critical skill for most workers in today's knowledge economy.

Do not introduce new material here. It is an opportunity to drive home your most important selling points related to the job's critical success factors—which you have already introduced and discussed. Introducing new information here may confuse the interviewer. In addition, repetition is an excellent sales and persuasion tool.

This section also gives you an excellent opportunity to focus sharply on how the skills, experience, knowledge in your "why hire me" statements will benefit the organization. For example, "I have eight years' experience working in the northeast territory. This means that I already have a network of established contacts that I can quickly convert to prospects and then to customers. I should be able to meet sales quotas four to six weeks sooner than any other salesperson."

Be prepared to answer the following questions:

*Why do you think this item differentiates you?

*Of all the items on this page, which one do you think is most important and why?

*How will this benefit the company?

*In what way is this point related to the critical requirements for this position?

You can use the following statement to introduce your why hire me section:

> "This is a list of items that most strongly support my candidacy for this position. We have spoken about these items already; however, I want to highlight them and point out how they will benefit [*company name*]."

Questions Section

> "Judge of a man by his questions rather than by his answers."
>
> —Voltaire, French writer and historian

The questions section gives you an opportunity to ask the interviewer important questions about the company, the position, and the interview. It neatly handles the dreaded, "Do you have any questions for me?" Because the questions are in writing, you won't forget them, and the interviewer will respond to them. Also, asking questions will transition the interview smoothly from the presentation phase back to a more traditional interview format.

Based on the information you learned in Chapter 14 about asking questions, select up to seven questions you want to ask. I strongly recommend that you always ask the following three questions:

*Based on my background and experience, what do you think would be the greatest challenges for me in this position? As you remember from Chapter 14, this is the best interview question of all time. By including it in your presentation list of questions, you won't forget to ask it, and the interviewer will read the question and answer it. This will save you from beating yourself up after the interview for forgetting to ask the question.

*What are the next steps in the selection process? This is an opportunity for the hiring manager to tell you any next steps in the hiring process. Without this information, you will be left guessing about how long the selection process will take and where they are in the process. Not knowing is a very uncomfortable position to be in.

*How and when would you like me to follow up with you? The answer to this question will tell you exactly how and when to follow up. A good answer would be, "We're interviewing through the rest of the week, so give me a call early next week to follow up," or, "We're interviewing through the rest of the week, and we'll contact you early next week to let you know our decision." You'll know exactly how and when to contact the hiring manager or expect to hear from him. When asking this question, attempt to get a very specific answer. If the hiring manager says, "I will contact you early next week," respond by saying, "If I don't hear from you by Tuesday, can I call you on Wednesday?"

You can use the following statement to introduce your closing questions section:

> "I have some questions that I'd like to ask you. We may have touched upon some of these questions already; however, I'd like to make sure I'm clear about the answers."

Saving an Interview and Landing a Job

Joe, a senior salesperson for a digital machine company, was contacted by an executive recruiter about a position at another digital machine company. Joe was interested in the position and asked the recruiter to set up an appointment with Ron, the hiring manager. As is often the case with busy executives, finding a time to meet was difficult, and the meeting was rescheduled multiple times over several weeks. While Joe and Ron were finding a time to meet, Ron's company identified an internal candidate and offered her the position.

Because Joe was a senior executive and Ron did not want to cancel again, Ron decided to meet with Joe even though the job had already been offered to an internal candidate who was still deciding about taking the job. The meeting was on a hot July day in the late afternoon in a hotel in Center City Philadelphia. Due to traffic and parking, both men arrived a little late, sweaty, and harried. Wanting to limit the interview time, upon sitting down Ron told Joe that he had a dinner with a client scheduled and that he had about 45 minutes to meet. Joe had prepared an interview presentation, and he said, "I've prepared a presentation about how my background and skills match the critical requirements of the job and why I'm a good candidate for the position. Because our time is short, maybe we can just go through presentation together."

Ron was relieved to have Joe take the lead and not have to run a potentially "lame duck" interview. Joe took Ron through the presentation page by page. Because he knew the industry, in the questions section Joe included a question about a challenge with which every digital machine company was struggling. Ron said, "We're trying to come up with strategies for this problem—let me tell you some of our thinking." Ron went and got a napkin and began to draw diagrams.

Forty-five minutes later, Joe and Ron were still discussing potential strategies to solve the problem. Did Joe get the job? No, he didn't, because the internal candidate got it. However, Ron went back to his boss, showed him the interview presentation, and convinced him to create a position for Joe, which Joe took. Without the presentation, Joe and Ron would have met for 45 minutes, and Joe would've been forgotten as soon as Ron's dinner started. The presentation gave Joe a way to structure the interview and present information he wanted Ron to know in a brief amount of time, and it gave Ron a printed document to show his boss. The presentation was an interview- and life-changer for Joe.

Interview Presentation Tips

The following are a series of tips you can use as you develop an interview presentation. Some tips are related to the content of the presentation, and other tips are related to the presentation itself.

Leave Out Extraneous Words

Messages that are harder to read are judged as less truthful. Read each of the bullet points in your presentation, and if you can delete a word without changing the meaning of the point, delete it. The fewer words the better. For example, "Instrumental in developing and implementing a customer service department" reads better as, "Developed and implemented a customer service department." As another example, "Initiated and compiled Form 8858 organization chart to show a path to the IRS" reads better as, "Compiled Form 8858 organization chart showing a path to the IRS."

One way to limit your words is to limit the number of characters in each bullet point. The InterviewBest presentation program (www.interviewbest.com) limits each bullet point to 170 characters. The 170-character limit will force you to consider each word and make sure your bullet points are not lengthy sentences or, even worse, a paragraph.

Bind It

A presentation looks most impressive when it is bound. After you have developed your presentation, you can send or take the file to a print center at your local office store. Ask for spiral binding with a clear plastic cover and a solid-colored cardboard back.

Depending on how busy they are, print centers often can turn around a presentation within 20 to 30 minutes. However, it is advisable to leave one day for printing and binding, just to be safe.

When video interviewing, email a copy to the interviewer. You can suggest to the interviewer that they print the presentation so they have something tangible they can write on, "May I suggest you print a copy of this presentation so you have something convenient to write on".

Use Regular Paper

When it's printed and bound, your presentation will be impressive. There is no reason to pay extra for high-grade, fancy paper.

Make a Copy for Each Interviewer

Before you go for your interview, find out how many people you will be interviewing with and make a copy of the presentation for each interviewer. Bring one or two extra copies just in case, and don't forget a copy for yourself. Similarly, email a copy to each interviewer for video interviews.

Simple Is Better

Unless you're going for a job as a graphic artist, a simple presentation with only a few graphics and a minimal number of different fonts works best. Fancy presentations with lots of pictures and different fonts can be distracting.

Mind Your Font Size

Many candidates use presentation software, such as PowerPoint or Google Slides to develop their presentations. Most presentation software is geared toward projecting presentations, and they tend to default to larger fonts (anywhere from 24- to 40-point). Your interview presentation will be printed, so limit your font sizes to 24 points for section titles and 20 points for text.

Fix Any Typos or Misspellings

Your presentation is like your resume; it cannot have any errors. Pay particular attention to items that spell-check will not catch, such as the company name or special industry terminology.

Another Radical Idea: A Networking Presentation

I've had a number of clients take their interview presentation and modify it for networking. Because they've had so much success, I've included a section about a networking presentation, even though it isn't specifically for interviewing. But it's related—if you use a networking presentation correctly, you'll have more interviews!

See the networking presentation in Appendix B for an example of a networking presentation.

It is a commonly accepted fact that most jobs are found through networking. In fact, research shows that as many as 70 percent of all jobs are found through networking. Networking for jobs takes many forms, from online networking, to networking at conferences and lectures, to one-to-one networking meetings. Typically, before a networking contact will make a job referral, there will be a one-to-one networking meeting over breakfast or lunch. This all-important one-to-one meeting suffers from many of the same issues as broken interviews. The exchange is verbal, retention is 50 percent or less, and the lasting thoughts and feeling are subjective, based on gut feelings. Using a networking presentation can fix this.

The ultimate goal of any networking contact is to establish enough trust so the contact feels comfortable introducing you to his valuable network. This often is a challenge during job search, where you may be meeting numerous people with whom you don't have an established trusting relationship. In addition, the person with whom you are networking—particularly if she is well-networked—may be meeting with numerous people seeking her help. Like an interview, your challenge is to establish trust, talk about your skills and experience, and communicate your potential benefits to a company. When you leave your networking meeting, you will have been successful if your contact is willing to refer you to two or three other people.

One of the critical keys to successful networking is making it as easy as possible for your networking contact to help you. The more information she has about you, the easier it is for her to help you. Important information includes both technical information about your skills and abilities and information about your soft skills. As mentioned earlier, most networking meetings are a conversation, usually accompanied by a resume. If your networking contact is an executive, she has seen hundreds of resumes, and yours is just one more—not a real differentiator that makes you memorable.

A networking presentation is a simplified version of an interview presentation with many of the same elements. Like an interview presentation, a network presentation is a printed and bound document to be used during a networking meeting. A networking presentation consists of the following sections.

Your Personal Brand

Your personal brand communicates what you want your networking contact to think and feel about you. It helps the contact form a distinct and positive impression of the skills, experience, and personal traits that will make you successful in a position. By proactively and clearly communicating your brand on the cover and throughout the presentation, you don't leave your brand to the arbitrary decision of the contact.

Positions to Which You Can Bring Value

This section tells your contact titles of positions in which you have interest. This helps her understand and categorize the types of jobs you are seeking and thus the jobs to which she can refer you. Be as specific as possible with the job titles and be prepared to discuss the tasks associated with the jobs. As with the interview presentation, this list and all other lists have the goal of supporting a productive conversation.

Areas of Expertise You Bring to the Job

This is a list of the areas of expertise you bring to the job. Expertise supports your claim of being able to perform a job well and helps your contact become more confident about referring you to a job. Unlike in the interview presentation, these are basic job-related skills and not value-adds. You might want to include significant selling propositions because these are clear and powerful differentiators.

Career Accomplishments and Outstanding Experiences

In this section of the presentation, you share brief stories about times in your career or life when you used your skills, experience, and knowledge to accomplish something notable or outstanding. The stories bring your accomplishments to life, engage the contact's interest, and give the contact insight into the contributions you can make to an organization.

Personal Qualities That Drive Your Job Success

Companies do not hire based solely on skills and experience; they also hire on personality and cultural fit. Similarly, networking contacts want to feel comfortable with a person's personality before they make referrals. During the typical networking meeting, contacts have to guess at personal qualities and will rely on subjective gut feelings. This section proactively gives your contact the information he is looking for. This section of the network presentation clearly states the personal qualities that make you successful in the job. And because they have stories and examples attached, they come to life and have impact.

Your Ideal Job

This section lists the individual responsibilities and tasks of your ideal job. This helps your contact understand what you want to do on a day-to-day basis and helps her get deeper insight into your job targets. This list may also help your contact suggest positions you weren't considering.

Types of Companies You Are Seeking to Work With

Your contact needs to know the types of companies for which you would consider working so he can make appropriate referrals. This includes both the characteristics of the company—size, location, and industry—and specific companies for which you would like to work. When you provide a list of specific companies, it helps the contact make connections if she knows people at the companies.

Why a Company Would Hire You

This is similar to a sales closing summation. It is the benefits a company would derive from hiring you, and it gives contacts reasons why they can give a referral for interviewing you. This list, along with the rest of the presentation, helps your contact "sell" you to a referral. Once again, the focus here is on the benefits you provide to companies.

Closing Questions

The final section of the network presentation is a list of questions you want to ask. The questions will help clarify whether your contact has gained an adequate level of understanding of your goals, your potential benefit to a company, and target companies to which he can refer you. It asks whether the contact has developed a level of trust substantial enough to feel comfortable referring you to his network. It also asks the most important networking question: "How can I help you?"

Apply All the Principles of an Interview Presentation

Every interview presentation principle applies to a network presentation. This includes using stories and examples, using powerful language, creating a conversation, presenting powerfully, and so on. The most distinguishing difference is that you aren't applying to a specific job. However, you are in a sales mode, persuading a contact to refer you to people who may help you. This is no different from a salesperson asking for a referral to someone who might want to purchase her services. Also, like an interview presentation, a network presentation makes a great leave-behind.

Using an Interview Presentation Will Fix Your Interview

> "The presentation was an invaluable tool, as it allowed me to better control and affect the interviews. Capturing the flow of the typical interview and providing pointed, quantitative evidence of my achievements enabled me to be on top of my game and anticipate follow-up questions as the interviewers sought details. The sheer creation of the presentation was a fabulous way to prepare, as it forced me to complete my due diligence and stay focused on winning the interview with short, succinct responses. I feel confident that this tool, if not *the* deciding factor, was instrumental in me receiving an offer."
>
> —Sarah, VP of global product management, consumer products

An interview presentation is the cornerstone of Active Interviewing. It enables you to prepare for your interview and gives you a tool to powerfully guide the interview. There is no other interview tool or strategy you can take into your interview that has the same impressive interview-winning impact. Using an interview presentation will have the following benefits:

*A written presentation transforms your interview from only verbal to verbal and visual. With the addition of a visual component, the interviewer retains more information, and you become more persuasive.

*An interview presentation will focus your interview and ensure that you communicate the information you want the interviewer to know. You won't have to depend on the interviewing skills of the interviewer to elicit the information.

*An interview presentation will ensure that you communicate the persuasive benefits of hiring you, increasing your chances of winning the interview.

*An interview presentation will make sure that all your pre-interview preparation is not forgotten and is communicated during your interview.

*An interview presentation will impress the hiring manager with your level of motivation and interest in the job.

*An interview presentation fosters a high-level, information-rich conversation, which increases trust and rapport with the interviewer.

*The interview presentation gives you the opportunity to talk about your personal success factors, which are typically not communicated well during an interview.

Chapter 16 - Present with Impact

- You Have All the Elements of a Great Presentation
- Give a STAR Interview
- Show Confidence and Enthusiasm
- Use a Conversational Style
- Use Powerful Language
- Communicate Using Body Language
- Presenting to a Group
- Avoid Perfection
- Presenting with Impact Will Fix Your Interviews

"Presentations are the *lingua franca* of business, and those who master communicating with them rise faster than their peers, reach more customers than their competitors, and turn causes into a groundswell."

—Nancy Duarte, presentation expert

Selling is about persuading, and persuading is about actively communicating compelling reasons for a buyer to purchase a service. As you actively sell your services in your interview, your ability to communicate your ideas and the compelling reasons to hire you depends on the content of your presentation and how you deliver it. As I mentioned previously, most candidates focus solely on being able to answer questions. Answering questions is important; however, moving from responding to questions to presenting elevates your game, differentiates you from other candidate, and ensures that the interviewer hears the information you think is important.

You Have All the Elements of a Great Presentation

There is a lot of information in books and on the Internet about presenting. Amazon alone lists more than 26,000 books about presenting. Fortunately, you don't have to read these books. Having now developed your interview presentation, you have all the elements of a great presentation! Let me explain. According to Todd Smith, author of *Little Things Matter* (Success Books), the key elements of effective presentations include knowing your audience, knowing the goal of your presentation, communicating a clear point of view, communicating the benefits to the audience, using stories and examples, and using appropriate quotes and supportive information. As you will read next, your presentation covers all these important areas.

Knowing Your Audience

The more you know about your audience, the more you can connect with them. Who are they? What's their profile? Why should they care about what you have to say? Having prepared for your interview, you'll know the answer to these questions. You will have researched the company, the industry, and the people with whom you'll be interviewing, if possible. Why they care about what you have to say is obvious—they are looking to hire a qualified person, and based on your resume, you appear to be qualified.

Knowing the Goal of Your Presentation

What is the goal of your presentation? Make sure you're clear about what you want the audience to take away from your comments.

Your interview presentation has very clear goals: to answer the three basic interview questions, to match your background and experience with the critical requirements of the job, and to communicate to the hiring manager why you're a good choice for the position.

Communicating a Clear Point of View on the Subject

You need to be clear about your point of view (POV) on the subject—that is, your position on the topic. In your interview, your POV is very clear—you are the best choice for the job. In addition, you have good supporting evidence in stories, examples, and your why-hire-me statement about why you should be selected.

Communicating the Benefits to the Audience

What benefits will your audience gain if they act upon your message? People need to understand the positive results they will experience if they do what you propose.

In this case, you're proposing that the company hire you. In the why-hire-me section of your presentation, you will definitively state the benefits and positive results the company will get from hiring you.

Communicating the Main Body Points

The main body points are the major points of your presentation. Your interview presentation is designed to answer the three basic interview questions; thus, the major points you want to make are in your presentation. Each section of your presentation makes a point that supports your candidacy.

Using Stories and Examples That Communicate the Main Body Points

Your success stories and examples illustrate your main points. These are relevant illustrations or anecdotes you can tell to make your points memorable.

Using Appropriate Quotes and Supportive Information

Reputable sources add credibility; include or list them in your presentation.

Your interview presentation is filled with information that actively, clearly, and powerfully supports hiring you. The information includes stories and examples of your skills and experiences that demonstrate you can do the job.

As you can see, the elements of your presentation are very solid. Your next challenge is to present them well.

Give a STAR Interview

At a marketing conference I attended, one of the presenters pulled down his pants, revealing Snoopy-themed underwear. He commented, "For the rest of your life, you will always remember the guy who pulled down his pants at a conference." That was a STAR (*Something They will Always Remember*) experience, and I do remember it.

Now, I'm not suggesting you pull down your pants during an interview, unless you want to make one of those "strangest interviewing behaviors" lists. However, I *am* suggesting that you be memorable. Having a well-developed interview presentation is a good start to making you memorable. One candidate writes:

> "As the interview concluded, the members of the three-person committee with which I interviewed all agreed on one point: The presentation they had just seen and heard was the most professional they had experienced during an interview. The panel's final question of the interview was, 'How much is it going to cost us to get you?' I accepted the position as a mid-level manager with a generous six-figure salary and all the perks."
>
> —Jim, pharmaceutical operations manager

In addition to having a printed presentation, presenting well will make you memorable. Presenting well includes the strategies and techniques discussed in the following sections.

Show Confidence and Enthusiasm

Presenting with confidence and enthusiasm is critical to having your presentation impact your interview. The first step is to be excited about the opportunity. If you are uncertain about the position, it's difficult to be enthusiastic and communicate motivation for the job. If you find yourself feeling lackluster about the position, focus on the positive aspects of the job; try to see opportunities the job will offer you and picture yourself doing a great job. When you are feeling enthusiastic, make sure you're well prepared to increase your confidence; then, bring this confidence and enthusiasm to your interview through your presentation.

An interview presentation is all about you—your strengths, your successes, and the benefits you bring to an employer. How can you *not* be excited about telling your story? Let the excitement shine through. You can communicate excitement in several ways, discussed in the following sections.

Consider Tone of Voice

Modulate your tone of voice. Modulating your voice means moving the pitch up and down. The alternative is to keep an even pitch throughout the sentence—which, at best, will sound odd and, at worst, will sound dull, boring, or confusing. By modulating your tone, you can emphasize certain points and focus the interviewer's attention.

In addition, pay attention to the other dimensions of your voice, including:

***Tempo.** The speed of your speech.

***Rhythm.** What parts of words you stress.

***Emphasis.** The importance or prominence you give to a word.

***Pauses.** Breaks in speech, which add clarity and emphasis.

Research shows that the changes in the tone of your voice add emphasis and meaning to the content of what you are communicating.

Use Positive Expressions

Use positive expressions as you give examples and tell stories. Positive expressions include:

*"It was challenging and exciting."

*"I really enjoyed…"

*"This is important…"

*"I was proud of…"

*"That was an accomplishment I will always remember."

*"It was difficult, but I persevered."

*"And best of all…"

Positive expressions convey energy, enthusiasm, and motivation, which are key selection criteria for any position.

Use Emotional Words

When you're giving examples and speaking about events, use emotional words. Emotional words resonate with interviewers, and they will be more connected to what you're saying. Positive emotional words include:

Amazed	Amused	Angry	Astonished
Attracted	Calm	Caring	Cautious
Cheerful	Comfortable	Confident	Curious
Delighted	Elated	Encouraged	Enthused
Envious	Excited	Exhilarated	Fond
Funny	Glad	Happy	Hopeful
Impatient	Liked	Loved	Nice
Optimistic	Pleased	Proud	Relieved
Satisfied	Sorry	Stressed	Surprised
Thrilled	Triumphant	Victorious	Wonderful

For example, you might say, "I was very enthusiastic about the challenge and was elated about the results."

Also, be sure to differentiate between saying "I think" and "I feel." Many candidates confuse the two. If you use the word "feel," it must be followed by a word that expresses emotion. If you aren't going to use a feeling word, use the word "think" instead. Saying, "I feel I'm the best candidate" is inaccurate; saying, "I think I'm the best candidate" is accurate. Saying, "I feel honored to be considered for the position" is accurate; saying, "I think I'm honored to be considered for the position" is not.

Use a Conversational Style

Although you've a prepared presentation, the goal is to establish a conversation that will build rapport with the interviewer. To accomplish this as you present, ask for the interviewer's thoughts and opinions. For example, during the job requirements section, you can ask, "Is this a comprehensive list of requirements?" or say, "Please tell me more details about this requirement." During the strategic action plan section, ask, "Are there additional goals that you would suggest?"

You should also leave openings for the interviewer to make comments. During your presentation, you should pause, which provides an opening for the interviewer to jump in. If you are intent on getting through your presentation, the interviewer may not see an easy way to ask questions and engage you in conversation. As the interviewer becomes engaged in a conversation, he will be more attentive, will get to know you better, and will get information he needs to make a hiring decision.

Use Powerful Language

"The difference between the almost right word and the right word is really a large matter—it's the difference between the lightning bug and the lightning."

—Mark Twain

I recently prepared a client for an interview for a full-time accounting position. He was doing an internship for large multinational media company, where he was finalizing international tax forms for dozens of companies. When I asked him to tell me about what he was doing, he said, "I'm helping out with getting forms done for international taxes, which are sort of complicated, and I think I'm going to get them done mostly on time." I was almost asleep before he finished speaking.

Using powerful language during your interview will make a greater impact on the interviewers. Powerful language:

*Is more exact, using words that express the complete idea.** For example, instead of saying "sort of complicated," using the phrase "highly complex with multiple detailed sections" communicates far better the challenge of completing the forms.

*Is more active and uses a strong voice.** Instead of saying, "I'm helping out with getting forms done," say, "I'm responsible for making sure forms are completed correctly and in a timely fashion." Instead of saying, "I think I'm going to get them done mostly on time," say, "With my direction, the forms are being completed quickly, and I'm confident that they all will be done on time."

*Uses words that are shorter and less complex.** Using words such as "ask" instead of "question" and "use" instead of "utilize" makes your words more powerful and sets a more conversational tone for your presentation.

*Uses shorter and less complex sentences.** Whenever an interviewer must spend time figuring out what you said, you've lost her. At best, she will ask a question to clarify the confusion; at worst, she will lose the meaning of what you're saying and will tune out.

Powerful language uses powerful words, and each profession has powerful words associated with it. For example, for someone in the same line of work as my accounting client, the following words communicate power: analyzed, audited, justified, verified, prepared, processed, reported, researched, reviewed. For a healthcare worker, assigned, assessed, assisted, cared, charged, provided, monitored, nursed, and secured are power words.

Avoid Filler Language

Filler language consists of words that contribute no meaning to what you're saying. They weaken your message. When people become stressed, as they often do during an interview, they tend to use more filler language. Do away with any words that do not change the meaning of your message when dropped. Filler words include:

*Um.** As in, "Um, we…um…need to…um…move ahead…um…with this project."

"We need to move ahead with this project"

*Uh.** As in, "Uh, we…uh…need to…uh…move ahead…uh…with this project."

*Clearly.** As in, "We clearly must make a decision about this."

"We must make a decision about this."

*Actually. As in, "We actually went to his office to speak with him."

We went to his office to speak with him.

*To be honest. As in, "To be honest, I don't agree with that approach."

"I don't agree with this approach"

*Quite frankly. As in, "Quite frankly, I'm not happy with the outcome."

"I am not happy with the outcome"

*Like I said before. As in, "Like I said before, we are focusing on the problems."

"We are focusing on the problem"

*Well. As in, "Well, I don't think we should go."

"I don't think we should go"

*I mean. As in, "I mean, they were really good at the game."

"They were really good at the game"

*I guess. As in, "I guess it's time to begin the meeting."

"It's time to begin the meeting"

*Okay. As in, "After you complete this form, return it to me, okay?"

"After you complete this form, return it to me"

*In fact. As in, "If, in fact, you have the authority to make the decision"

"If you have the authority to make the decision"

*If you will. As in, "Getting people to agree on this topic is like pushing a rock up the hill, if you will."

"Getting people to agree on this topic is like pushing a rock up the hill"

*Like. As in, "It's like, when I went to the meeting, like, it was very apparent that people weren't, like, going to be, like, in agreement."

"When I went to the meeting it was very apparent that people weren't going to be in agreement."

*Sorta. As in, "When I work at home, it's sorta like being on my own."

"When I work at home, it's like being on my own."

*Kinda. As in, "I want to show you something that's kinda strange."

"I want to show you something that's strange."

*You know. As in, "I work well with teams, and, you know, it's good to be part of, you know, a strong team."

"I work well with teams, and it's good to be part of a strong team."

As you read each of the above sentences with and without the filler language, you see how much more direct and powerful it becomes.

"You" Is Really "I"

Have you ever noticed that most people use "you" instead of "I" or "me" when referring to themselves? I recently listened to President Obama being interviewed by Bill O'Reilly, and he did this exact thing. In response to the surprising question, "Does it disturb you that so many people hate you?" the president responded, "The people who dislike *you* don't know *you*. The folks who hate *you*, they don't know *you*." He added, "What they hate is whatever funhouse mirror image of *you* that's out there. They don't know *you*. And so, *you* don't take it personally."

Let's try that again with "I" and "me" instead of "you": "The people who dislike *me* don't know *me*. The folks who hate *me*, they don't know *me*.... What they hate is whatever funhouse mirror image of *me* that's out there. They don't know *me*. And so, *I* don't take it personally."

Speaking about yourself by using "you" instead of "me" or "I" distances you from the content of the message, story, or example and weakens its impact. Using "I" and "me" makes language more accurate and powerful. Consider this during your interview and your everyday conversations, and always refer to yourself using "I" and "me."

Replace "But" with "And"

There might be occasions when you disagree with the interviewer. This may happen when the interviewer questions or expresses concern about your qualifications. In these situations, and throughout your interview, avoid using the word "but" as much as possible. For example, "I understand your concern, but...." The word "but" tends to make a listener feel wrong, defensive, and more attached to his ideas. The alternative is to use "and." You could say, "I understand your concern, and...."

Even if you are disagreeing with the interviewer's concern, the word "and" communicates that he is right and that you simply have a different take on the issue. This maintains a good level of communication, helps the interviewer be receptive to your ideas, and gives you the opportunity to disagree without seeming disagreeable.

Communicate Using Body Language

Body language is an important part of communication, and it can constitute 50 percent or more of the message you communicate. You might be surprised by how many different types of body language people use to communicate their message. Body language types include:

*__Aggressive.__ You're showing a physical threat.

*__Attentive.__ You have real interest in the conversation.

*__Open.__ You're open and receptive to others.

*__Bored.__ You aren't interested.

*__Closed.__ You aren't open to listening.

*__Deceptive.__ You're trying to cover up a lie or other deception.

*__Defensive.__ You're protecting yourself from verbal attack.

*__Dominant.__ You're trying to dominate others.

*__Emotional.__ You're identifying your feelings.

*__Evaluating.__ You're judging and deciding about something.

*__Greeting.__ These include meeting rituals, such as handshakes, smiles, and eye contact.

*__Power.__ You're displaying your power.

*__Ready.__ You're wanting to act and waiting for the trigger.

*__Relaxed.__ You're comfortable and not stressed.

*__Romantic.__ You're showing attraction to others.

*__Submissive.__ You're showing you are prepared to give in.

During an interview, it is most important to display attentive and open body language. You can demonstrate attentive body language by:

*Ignoring any distractions. Be sure your cell phone is turned off.

*Being still, with relatively little body movement when listening.

*Leaning forward.

*Tilting your head slightly forward.

*Maintaining steady eye contact. Looking at a person shows that you acknowledge and are interested in him.

*Furrowing your brow to show that you are concentrating.

*Begin patient. Wait until the other person is finished speaking before you say something.

You can demonstrate open body language by:

*Not crossing your arms across your chest.

*Being animated and responding to what is being said.

*Opening your hands to show that nothing is being concealed. Don't sit with your fists tightly clenched.

*Sitting with legs that are not crossed. Usually your legs will be parallel, with your feet pointing to the floor or to one side.

*Directing your head toward the other person or looking around at others in the rom. Eye contact should be relaxed and prolonged but not a stare.

*Wearing loose clothing that does not appear tight and binding.

You don't want to exhibit (or see from the interviewer) bored or closed body language. If the interviewer displays boredom or closed body language, your interview is in trouble, and you need to change your strategy.

The language of boredom includes:

*Appearing distracted by looking anywhere but at the person who is talking.

*Doodling.

*Talking with others or looking around the room.

*Taking an "important" call in the middle of the interview.

*Performing repetitive actions, such as tapping toes, swinging feet, or drumming fingers. The repetition may escalate as the boredom increases.

*Displaying tiredness by yawning or slouching. The person's face may show a distinct lack of interest and appear blank.

Closed body language includes:

*Having arms closed with one or both arms across the central line of the body. Less obvious arm-crossing may include resting an arm on a table or a leg or loosely crossing the arms at the wrists.

*Having legs crossed, such as the ankle cross, knee cross, figure-four (the ankle on the opposite knee), or the tense wraparound with the foot tucked behind the calf.

*Looking down or away. The person's head may be inclined away from the person who is speaking, or it may be tucked down.

Presenting to a Group

"If I went back to college again, I'd concentrate on two areas: learning to write and to speak before an audience. Nothing in life is more important than the ability to communicate effectively."

—Gerald Ford, 38th U.S. president

You may be interviewed by a panel of people. In a panel interview (also called a *group* or *committee* interview), you will be interviewed by several individuals at the same time. My clients have been in panel interviews with up to six interviewers. Panel interviews, first used in academia and the healthcare industry, are becoming more popular in the corporate sector due to efficiency and the ability for all interviewers to observe the same behavior and hear the same responses.

Interview presentations are very successful in panel interviews. One candidate wrote:

"Last but not least was your recommendation that I use an interview presentation. I gave the presentation about nine times during the course of interviewing—six with my eventual employer. The three biggest things it did were:

*Gave me confidence knowing that I was going to be prepared.

*Separated me from the rest of the competition and provided the employer with a leave-behind document that was thorough and professional.

*One last very important benefit of using the interview presentation was that, in my group interview, when I indicated that I had prepared a presentation, you could immediately feel and see the tension leave the room.

"I believe they were all impressed and, as a result, I got a better offer than they intended to make. They just promoted my title to senior sales engineer. It was truly amazing."

—Robert, Biomedical Sales Engineer

In a panel interview, use the presentation strategies discussed in the following sections.

Make Eye Contact with Everyone

As you present, scan from one face to the next, pausing for two to three seconds on each. When you're asked a question, make eye contact and address your answer to the individual who asked the question. Then make eye contact with the other interviewers. As you finish your answer, return your focus to the person who asked the question. Be careful not to break eye contact with a person in the middle of a sentence or a thought.

Learn the Roles

In the initial part of the meeting, ask about each person's role. It is important for you to understand each person's responsibilities and how she interacts with the position. Do not go by title alone; ask for a description of the interaction. As each person speaks, take notes. It is often helpful to make a seating chart with names, titles, and roles that you can refer to during the interview. Also, during the interview, don't make the mistake of ignoring people at lower levels; their opinion has weight in the ultimate selection.

Address Everyone

In a group interview, often one or two individuals are quiet. However, even though they are quiet during the interview, they will have an opinion about hiring you. Try to get everyone involved by addressing questions to each member of the group. You can do this by asking a "supportive" question of the quiet individuals. Without commenting on a person being quiet, you can say, "Larry, I know you work closely with the person in this position, so I value your opinion. What do you think are the critical job requirements?"

People like to hear their names during your interview, so be sure to refer to each of the interviewers by name.

Don't Lock on to the Friendly Faces

In many panel interviews, there will be one or two people who are attentive and smiling. There may also be several people who appear disinterested and unfriendly. It is easier to focus on the friendly people and avoid the "rejection" of the unfriendly people. However, ignoring the unfriendly may cost you their support. They are in the interview, so pay them the same attention you pay to all the other panel members. This means making eye contact and asking them questions.

Avoid Perfection

Audiences rarely relate well to people who come across as too polished, and perfection is not the goal in your interview. We are most influenced by authentic people who share challenges similar to our own. Your greatest position of influence is being alongside your audience, not speaking down to them as if you're a subject-matter expert.

Presenting with Impact Will Fix Your Interview

All sales presentations have a goal of moving people from where they are to where the salesperson wants them to be—from a prospect to a customer. During your interview, you want to actively move a hiring manager from considering you to hiring you. The most effective way to accomplish this is by presenting yourself powerfully. Presenting with impact has the following benefits:

*It will make you memorable, differentiating you from your competition.

*It will make you more effective in panel interviews where you need to persuade multiple people at the same time.

*Your language will be more powerful and exact. Powerful and exact language will make you more credible and persuasive.

*Presenting takes pressure off of interviewers to manage the interview and proactively gets them the information they need to make a good hiring decision.

*Presenting well will create a conversation that fosters rapport and trust with the interviewer.

*A high-quality presentation during your interview demonstrates your presentation ability, which is a critical business skill.

Chapter 17 - Advanced Interview Tips

- Before the Interview
- During the Interview
- After the Interview
- Using Advanced Interview Tips Will Fix Your Interviews

As I mentioned in the introduction, I developed Active Interviewing to challenge you to use higher-level active strategies and tactics that differentiate you and help you win job interviews. There is a huge amount of interview information readily available to you in more than 3,000 books and tens of thousands of Internet sites. Ninety-nine percent of the information is basic interview information that is repeated over and over again. The most written-about interview information includes advice on:

*Dressing professionally.

*Giving a good handshake.

*Being on time.

*Bring extra copies of your resume.

*Don't lie on your resume.

*Mimic the way your interviewer sits and moves.

*Being prepared.

*Having questions to ask.

*Being enthusiastic.

*Answering tough interview questions.

*Staying positive about prior employers.

*Listening.

*Being well rested.

*Emphasizing your positive qualities.

*Not doing unprofessional things, such as answering your phone or playing with items on the interviewer's desk.

*Not rambling or talking too much.

*Not flirting with the interviewer.

*Not chewing gum.

*Being yourself.

*Not getting too personal.

*Not using bad words.

*Getting the names of everyone involved with your interview so you can send them individual thank-you notes. (Ask for a business card.)

This book's goal is to offer interview strategies and techniques that move beyond the basics and elevate your interview game. Yes, it is important to pay attention to interview basics, and I suggest you read about the basics—

you just won't read about them here. Also, certain topics, such as negotiating, are so vast that I can write about them only selectively. I suggest you read more in-depth books and articles about negotiating elsewhere.

The following advanced interview tips come from my experience in working with thousands of job seekers and learning from them what made a difference in their interviews. For clarity, I have broken these advanced tips into three categories:

*Before the interview

*During the interview

*After the interview

Before the Interview

This section has a list of suggestions for things you can do prior to the interview to be better prepared. As mentioned earlier, they are not typical suggestions, and they will provide you with a distinct advantage.

You will see that there are no suggestions about one of candidates' primary concerns—how to dress. When my clients ask me how they should dress, I typically tell them, "Dress a half-step up from the way employees at the company dress." If you are interviewing for a software-developer job where the typical dress is anything decent, wear a nice pair of slacks and a button-down shirt. If you are applying for a job where the dress is business casual, wear a suit.

Manage Your Brain

> "I used to think that the brain was the most wonderful organ in my body. Then I realized who was telling me this."
>
> —Emo Philips, comedian

Interviewing success follows an 80/20 rule. Eighty percent is attitude and 20 percent is content, presentation, fit, and so on. Does 80 percent seem like a high number? To explain how I arrived at that number, let me quickly describe our primitive brain.

Human beings have brains that are better adapted to survival in caves than in modern society. As our fear level and heart rate, blood pressure, and stress increase, our brain functioning decreases. At very high fear levels, our thinking completely collapses, and all we have left is a fight-or-flight response—well suited to escaping large predators, but not so well suited to the 21st century. This explains all the stupid behavior we see on police-based reality shows, where dozens of police cars and a helicopter are pursuing one car with flattened tires. Don't you often wonder what the guy is thinking, as there is no way he's going to escape? The answer is that he *isn't* thinking. His fear response is so high that he is fully in a flight response.

This is an extreme example; however, at far lower levels of fear, our thinking begins to decrease. Have you ever had an experience where you're having a contentious discussion with someone, and as soon as you leave the room or get off the phone, you get a flash of something you should have said? "Darn, I should have said…" While engaged in the conversation, your heart rate, pulse, and stress level were up, and you didn't have access to your full thinking capacity. As soon as the conversation ended, you calmed down, and your thinking expanded.

Interviews are fearful situations, and the more fearful you are, the less access you have to mental acuity, creativity, flexibility, logic, and the ability to answer questions—all important abilities to access during an interview. The more positive your attitude, the calmer you are and the better your thought process.

You can adjust your attitude by being confident about your interview. Confidence comes from being secure in your skills and preparation and being ready to present yourself as the best candidate. It also comes from being ready to engage the interviewer as another human being and not as someone who is judging you and making a life-changing decision for you.

Assume Power Postures

New research about body language by Amy C. J. Cuddy, a social psychologist at Harvard Business School, indicates that holding a "high power" pose for two minutes that opens up your body and takes up space will alter hormone levels, make you feel more powerful, more in charge, and help you perform better in interviews.

The prototypical high-power pose is the Superman stance - feet wide shoulders back hands on hips. Another pose is sitting in a chair in front of a desk, with your feet resting on the desk, leaning back, and your hands clasped behind your head. Both poses take up space, which is an expression of power. In contrast, low-power postures, such as hands clasped on thighs, legs together with arms folded, and legs crossed decreases your power.

Based on Cuddy's research, which links body postures with mental state and hormone levels, candidate should spend their pre-interview time in a power pose consisting of expansive postures, such as the Superman standing pose. Compare this to the typical pre-interview time spent sitting hunched in a chair, staring at a cell phone in a waiting area.

Research the Position

As mentioned earlier, most interviewers' number-one complaint is that candidates don't have enough information about the job and the company. Even entry-level candidates know they must research the job; however, even senior-level candidates don't do a thorough research job.

There are two types of position and employer information. The first is from primary sources produced by the employer, including:

*The organization's website

*Annual and other reports

*Promotional materials

*Prospectuses

*Information presented at an information session or another employer-hosted event

*Newsletters

Primary sources give you an understanding of an employer's priorities, values, and culture and how the employer perceives itself.

The second type of source is secondary, produced by groups outside the organization. Secondary sources may include:

*Articles about the employer in the popular press or in trade and professional journals

*Chapters in—or even entire—books about a field or industry

*Social media content

These sources can provide an external view of an organization's leaders, culture, goals, strategies, products, services, reputation, and effectiveness. These primary and secondary resources can help you use the advanced strategies that follow.

Contact the Hiring Manager

> "Nothing kills an idea faster than common sense."
>
> —Luke Williams, freelance graphic designer

As part of your preparation for your interview, contact the hiring manager. This seems like a ridiculous idea to many candidates; after all, the hiring manager is crazy busy, has no time to spend talking with you about an upcoming interview, and will only be annoyed at you for being pushy. Let me ask you—what is a greater priority for the hiring manager than hiring the best qualified person? Shouldn't she take time to help you and other candidates present your best in the interview?

I suggest the following strategy: Email the hiring manager, requesting 15 to 20 minutes of her time to ask questions about the basic job requirements. During the call, have a list of five to seven questions you want to ask. Make sure the questions will provide information you need to develop your interview presentation and maintain a strict 20-minute time limit. See the list of questions in Chapter 7.

Admittedly, this strategy is rife with obstacles. There may be an administrative assistant or an internal recruiter who is running interference for the hiring manager. The hiring manager might want to avoid any contact with a candidate that could influence the hiring decision. And greatest of all, it's just not how it's usually done. Having had a number of clients follow this strategy, I can report the following:

*Some were successful, having a very productive 20-minute conversation.

*Even when there wasn't a conversation, several hiring managers were impressed by my clients' attempts to be well prepared for their interviews.

*Not one client reported any negative consequences of reaching out to the hiring manager.

Tap into the Company's Network

Shortly after graduation from college, my son Zach had an interview with the New York Rangers for an entry-level marketing position. Like any good job seeker and career manager, Zach had joined numerous groups on LinkedIn related to his desired profession, sports marketing. As he prepared for the interview, he searched for anyone related to the NY Rangers in his network and his groups. He was able to establish email contact with a former Rangers' employee and find out about the marketing department—and he got a request to "give the VP of marketing my regards." During his interview, Zach mentioned his contact's name and communicated the regards; the VP was impressed. Unfortunately, she was not so impressed that Zach got the job—the position went to an intern.

Former employees are excellent sources of information, as well as good networking connections. Using sites such as LinkedIn makes it possible to find employees who have worked at the company or who have worked with the hiring manager in the past. I always tell my clients that the first question they should ask when they see a job is, "Who do I know who can connect me to this position?" Once you have an interview, ask yourself, "Who do I know or how can I get connected to the hiring manager?"

Read the 10-K (Publicly Traded Companies Only)

The number-one suggestion for interviewing is to be prepared. Amazingly, 78 percent of all candidates simply wing it in interviews. This is particularly egregious today, when so much information is easily accessible on the web. Even with candidates who do prepare, few do the in-depth preparation that will distinguish them from other candidates.

Reading a 10-K will give you very in-depth information. 10-Ks are documents that the SEC requires every publicly traded company to file at the end of their fiscal year. They are accessible at EDGAR, at the company's website, or at Yahoo! Financials. 10-Ks are all pretty much a standard format and consist of the following sections.

Business

This section introduces you to the company, its business, and the industry. It outlines the history of the company and any recent developments, and it gives an overview of the industry and its competitors. It's a good way to determine whether the company has a good plan and what macroeconomic factors impact the company's industry positively or negatively. It's an excellent source for powerful questions!

Legal Proceedings

This section talks about any serious litigation the company is facing. It is not unusual for companies to face multiple lawsuits, most of which either will be dismissed or will have an insignificant impact on the company. The SEC requires companies to disclose their estimated liability amounts if they face an adverse ruling or if they feel that outcome is likely, or the amount is significant. What you find in this section may influence your decision to join the company.

Management's Discussion and Analysis

Here, management discusses and compares past and present results and what they expect for the future. For example, costs and revenues might have changed since last period. What drove those changes, and do they expect more? This is one of the key parts of the 10-K and is worth reading if you read nothing else. Accounting policy changes are discussed in this section as well.

Toward the end of this section is a part called "Liquidity and Capital Resources" that discusses how management intends to raise money for future plans. For example, if the company plans to acquire other companies or open new plants, do they have sufficient funding to do so? If not, are they planning to issue more debt? Or sell more shares of stock? How strong is their financial position?

This section also discloses risk factors. For example, does the bulk of the company's revenue come from only a handful of customers? What are key macroeconomic factors that might cause a downturn in their industry or company? Are they in a highly regulated industry?

Financial Statements

Here you will find the company's income statement, balance sheet, and cash flow statement, or information on where they are located in the document. These three financial statements comprise the bulk of information on how the company has performed.

As you can tell from the descriptions of the 10-K sections, the document contains a wealth of company-related information. After you have read the 10-K, you will be able to develop a good set of powerful questions to ask.

Read the News

There are a number of good and easy resources from which you can get current information about the company. These include:

***Company press releases.** Many companies keep a list of press releases on their website. Read through the releases to see the latest company news and read what the company is saying about itself.

***Google Alerts.** Google Alerts (www.google.com/alerts) are email updates of the latest relevant Google results (web, news, and so on) based on your choice of query or topic. When you set up an Alert, you will be emailed any Internet results containing information about that alert. For example, you can set up alerts for a company, their major competitors, company products, company employees, and industry trends.

***LinkedIn.** LinkedIn (www.linkedin.com) has a feature where you can follow a company. Based on the LinkedIn profiles of employees at that company, you can see recent hires and departures, employees who have changed titles, geographic location of employees, and job listings. By using member's profiles, LinkedIn offers information not found elsewhere on the Internet.

***Business databases.** A number of business databases have company information. These include Hoovers, Harris InfoSource, and Dun & Bradstreet. These databases are typically free for limited information and charge a fee for premium information.

Prepare Your Portfolio

The best thing to carry to an interview is a portfolio. Inexpensive and found at any office supply store, a portfolio is a leather (or faux leather) file with a document pocket and a pad for writing. As mentioned earlier, an interview is a nerve-wracking situation that will result in some loss of thinking and memory. Use the pad in your portfolio to write down things you want to remember during the interview. Include information such as success stories and questions to ask, as well as behaviors you want to do or avoid. Think about positive behaviors you want to exhibit and negative behaviors you do when you're nervous; write these down.

Jay Berger, a former top-10 tennis player from the United States, wrote a list of catchphrases before every match and then read them and reread them on every changeover. Long retired, he still remembers them all: "Watch the ball," "Stay down low," "Run down every ball," "Keep the ball in play," and "Have fun."

For example:

Do

*Smile

*Maintain eye contact

*Keep an open posture

*Breathe

*Get a business card

*Be enthusiastic

*Refer to yourself as "I," rather than "you"

Don't

*Cross your arms

*Say "um" or "uh" (or use other language fillers)

*Play with your hair

*Answer your phone

*Tap your feet or hands

*Put your hands near your face (which makes you look insecure)

*Interrupt

During your interview, take notes on your pad. As you look down to take notes, you will be reminded of things you should and shouldn't be doing.

Schedule Your Interview in the Morning

If you have a choice, schedule your interview in the morning. You and the interviewer are fresher, and there's less of a chance that the interviewer is fatigued or will be distracted by work that has piled up throughout the day. Recent research also shows that as a person becomes fatigued, he tends to choose less difficult decisions. In interviewing, the easiest decision is to reject someone. If you cannot schedule your interview in the morning, choose a time just after a lunch break.

I've been asked whether it is better to be the first candidate interviewed or the last. Research on this is inconclusive. Some research says that the first candidate sets the bar and all others compete against her, which is an advantage for the first one. Other research says that the last tends to be remembered. So it's your choice; intuitively, I would go with being the last and blowing them away with your presentation.

Prepare Exit Statements

Interviewers frequently ask, "Why did you leave (or why are you leaving) that employer?" This is a difficult question for many candidates to handle well. If a candidate was let go for cause, answering is an embarrassment. Even in a bad economy, where the reason is a layoff, a candidate may get defensive and tend to ramble with his answer. To effectively answer this question, prepare an exit statement for each employer for whom you worked. The statements should be brief, factual, and not defensive. Some examples include:

*Candidates who've been laid off

> "Due to declining market conditions, Konix underwent a major reorganization. This resulted in the elimination of more than100 positions from the national sales force, including mine."

> "Due to market conditions, Mileage Automotive has reduced the size of their workforce by 350 positions. I was able to retain my job through two rounds of layoffs; however, my position was eliminated in the third round."

*Candidates who are working and looking for another job

> "Although I'm performing very well as a senior business analyst with Capital Tech, I have learned that there are no opportunities there at the level appropriate for me, especially across the disciplines in which I work best. Therefore, I'm exploring senior-level management positions that will leverage my understanding of technology, marketing, communications, and sales."

*Candidates who've been fired

> "The culture at my last company was not a good fit for me. My style is to bridge differences to find common ground. I believe that's the most effective way to move forward when two sides disagree. That style was instrumental in the successful resolution of several serious negotiations at Zenox Company, but at Stricker, I found the situation to be quite different. In fact, when I tried to intervene to resolve a problem that had brought our new product group to a standstill, my manager pulled me out of the group and told me he thought the creative differences would result in a better product. This trend continued for the 18 months I was there, so I wasn't really surprised when I was asked to leave."

A few rules about exit statements:

***Never be negative about the employer.** Even if the layoffs were due to terrible planning or you were let go because of a bad boss, do not be negative. Notice that in the first exit examples, layoffs were due to "market conditions," not bad corporate planning. If you were fired, don't blame your boss; talk about strategic differences or differences in work philosophies.

***Keep it simple.** The briefer the better. Only give pertinent information, and do not go into detail. Long explanations make you sound as if you're being defensive and covering up something. If the interviewer wants more detail, he will ask for it.

***Communicate magnitude.** If you were part of a large layoff, include numbers. Being one of 15 or one of 2,000 (depending on the company's size) makes it clear you weren't singled out.

***Mention multiple rounds of layoffs.** Often, companies lay off workers in multiple rounds. The common perception is that the first round of layoffs consists of marginal workers the company wanted to get rid of anyway.

The subsequent rounds begin to include good employees. If you were in a second or third round of layoffs, mention that in your exit statement.

Think about Hiring Yourself

There is no way you can guess the questions you'll be asked during your interview. One of my clients was asked this question: "If you were in a personality supermarket, what two personality traits would you buy?" She certainly didn't see that question coming!

Because you cannot predict the interviewer's questions, prepare to answer questions you would ask if you were hiring someone for the position. What would you want to know? What are the skills, experience, education, and personal traits a person should possess to be successful in the position? You will not predict 100 percent of the questions, but you will be prepared to answer questions that are the most pertinent to the position.

The more you know about the industry, company, and position, the better you will be able to predict possible questions and respond to offbeat questions.

As an aside, in my client's situation, she was applying for a position that entailed a great deal of exacting, detailed work, which also required persistence. She did not want to purchase these traits because she was supposed to have them already. Instead, she chose two traits that would be nice to have but that were not required to do the job.

Eliminate Energy Drains

You need to be focused and free of distractions to perform well during your interview. If you have a number of things about which you are worried—so-called *energy drains*—you won't be able to focus 100 percent. For example, don't schedule another appointment too close to your interview. The last thing you need is to sit in an interview that is going well and worry about being late to your next appointment or to pick up your child. If you're looking to change jobs, clear your schedule for a job interview with integrity. Schedule the interview after hours or take a vacation day. Don't interview during a "client meeting" or call in sick and expend energy worrying that your boss will find out.

During the Interview

The following strategies are used during the interview. Once again, they are more advanced Active Interview strategies and not your run-of-the-mill strategies.

You're Not Perfect, So Don't Try to Be

> "Nobody is perfect, and no company is perfect. It alienates customers when executives and salespeople try to pretend that they're like Superman and will fix all their problems. Now that I've taken a more humble approach that admits our limitations, customers are drawn in and believe what I tell them, because they know I'm not posing as something or someone that knows it all."
>
> —John Burke, Oracle's group vice president for global sales

Candidates are very concerned about making mistakes during interviews. Most candidates focus on how well they answer questions as a gauge of their interview performance. However, interviewers tend to like people similar to themselves, and the interviewer is not perfect. Interviewers also distrust—and don't want to work with—people who know it all.

Many candidates try to fake their way through an answer rather than just being honest and admitting that they don't know the answer. During your interview, it is acceptable and even wise to admit that you don't know or are unsure of something. If you don't know an answer, you often can say, "I'll find out the answer to that question and email you or call you with the information." Admitting to faults or to not knowing an answer makes you more credible and trustworthy.

Out the Elephant

When there is a known issue—the proverbial "elephant in the room"—and it threatens to reduce your chances of winning the job, tackle it head on to defuse its potential impact. By ignoring a potential weakness, you lose control of it. For example, you might say, "Although I have a great deal of expertise in project management, my project management experience is not in the construction industry. I want to discuss your thoughts about how that would affect my performance on the job." Another example: "I realize you require a PhD in chemical engineering; however, I believe my 18 years of experience has given me equivalent knowledge and experience. In fact, I have worked very successfully alongside several PhDs. For example…"

Just because you don't discuss an issue during the interview doesn't mean the issue won't be discussed in meetings as the hiring decision is being made. In addition, bringing up the issue communicates that it is not a concern for you and demonstrates your confidence that you can overcome it.

Suspend Judgment

You may have more experience performing the job than the interviewer does, and you might be eager to tell how much you know and how much the interviewer will benefit from hiring you. However, hold back your opinions and be open to learning about the job from the interviewer's perspective. The critical issue is not your ideas or opinions, it is the ideas and opinions of the hiring manager and you being able to provide the value she is seeking. By withholding your ideas and opinions, you will learn her perceived needs, and then you can be more targeted as you link your background and experience to the job requirements.

State your opinions as your perceptions and make sure the interviewer understands that they are your assumptions and are open to discussion. For example, you might say, "I believe the primary challenge to the newspaper industry is the rapid development of online content. What do you consider to be the primary challenge?"

Establish Points of Connection

Our primitive brain is wired to live in tribal societies. In tribal societies, members of our tribe are safe and secure, and we can trust them, whereas members of other tribes may pose a threat. In modern society, people are members of numerous "tribes," and when meeting others, we quickly try to determine whether they belong to one of our tribes. Tribes include hometown, schools, hobbies, professions, interests, sports teams, religious affiliation, ethnicity, pet owners, people in common, and so on. When you establish a "tribal connection," you'll tend to trust the other person.

Here is an example. My older brother, Jon, was applying for an executive-level job, and the interview wasn't going well. There were uncomfortable exchanges, and there was a disagreement about trends in the industry. Jon and the interviewer weren't connecting, and that was influencing the tone of the interview. Partway through the interview, Jon noticed a picture of a Bernese Mountain dog on the interviewer's desk. Jon, who also owned a Bernese, asked the interviewer, "Is that your Berner?" (That's an insider's term for Bernese mountain dogs.) A lively discussion about owning a "Berner" ensued, and the interview turned completely around. Jon and the interviewer were now members of the tribe of Bernese Mountain dog owners—and Jon got a job offer.

People hire those they trust and finding connections that establish common tribal memberships engenders trust. With our primitive brains, even the smallest connection can make a difference. Detecting connections is typically considered part of the small talk or bonding that occurs at the beginning of an interview. However, it is important to continue to listen for connections throughout the interview and then highlight them. For example, during the interview, an interviewer might say, "Many of our competitors are in the Southeast, and having come from Georgia, I understand their approach to business." Do you have any connections to Georgia? If so, make them known.

Video Interviewing

Due to cost, efficiency, and technology, video interviewing for the screening phases of the selection process has become almost routine particularly with larger companies hiring lots of people. In addition, with the emergence of Covid 19, video interviewing is replacing in-person interviews.

Screening video interviews are replacing telephone screening interviews and are becoming very sophisticated. Typically, you will be asked to login to a website where you will be asked questions by a person in a video. You will be given an opportunity to record your answers using your computer's camera and microphone. The length of your answers will be limited, usually to two minutes, and you may be able to make multiple tries at answering the questions before submitting your final video. Once you submit your video, the video is analyzed using artificial intelligence (AI). The AI analyzes your facial expressions, eye contact, tone of voice, word choice, speed of delivery, and compares them against traits that are considered important for job success. Using AI in video screenings is somewhat controversial however, the cost savings is so substantial that questions about its use may be ignored. For example, in 2018 Unilever Corporation saved 100,000 hours of human interviewing time and over $1MM. You can expect to have video interview screening in your future.

A face-to-face video interview has all the impact and decision influence of a live face-to-face interview. Thus, everything you have read in this book applies to a video interview. You can also use an interview presentation in a video interview; simply send the interviewer an electronic copy of your presentation.

In a video interview, remember the following tips:

*Practice with the technology. Many video interviews are done using Skype, Zoom, GoToMeeting, Google Meet or any of several other video conferencing technologies. Prior to the interview install the chosen technology (if necessary) and be sure you know how to use it.

*Dress in professional interview attire, just as you would for an in-person interview. Even though only your top half will be visible, being fully dressed for the interview will affect your mood and attitude.

*There will be a picture of the person with whom you are interviewing on the screen. Often the person will be off to one side of your screen or if centered their eyes will be lower than your camera on your screen. Maintain eye contact with the camera and speak directly into the lens not into the screen. When you look away, it becomes particularly noticeable, and you may appear unfocused and shifty. Also, when you're not talking, keep looking directly at the lens, as you are still "on camera."

*If possible, shrink the picture of the interviewer and move the picture directly under your camera. Doing this enables you to see the interviewer while looking at your camera.

*Put the camera at eye level so you can look straight ahead. If the camera is below eye level, you risk having the interviewer looking up your nose.

*Make sure your background, which will be part of the video, is neat and uncluttered. A textured background with solid colors works best. Your clothes should contrast with the background color, so you don't fade into the background.

*I suggest you don't use a virtual background. With virtual background you tend to move in and out of the picture and if you move your arm too quickly it disappears. This detracts from your presentation of yourself.

*Have yourself well-lit from behind the camera, not to your side or rear.

*Just as you would write reminders in your portfolio for a face-to-face interview, place reminder signs behind the camera, such as "Smile," "Eye contact," "Speak slowly," and so on

*Being on camera may make you tense, so remember to smile.

*Before you begin the interview, say some tongue twisters to get your mouth moving smoothly. This will help you articulate clearly and not stumble over words.

*If you are wearing a jacket, use a news broadcaster's trick and sit on the bottom so it will stay tight and not bunch up.

*Be aware that your microphone may be sensitive and will pick up small background noises, such as a tapping a pen, sniffling, or people/pets in the next room. It will, also pick up the hum of air conditioning or a fan, turn these off. It is also suggested you invest in a microphone that plugs into your computer and gives better fidelity to your audio.

*Maintain proper distance from the camera. If you are too close to the camera, that's too intimate for the interviewer. If you are so far away from the camera that the interviewer can see all or most of your body (head to toe), that is perceived as being aloof or keeping people at arm's length. The proper distance shows your head to about mid-chest.

*Close all other programs so there is no pop-ups and there is nothing taking up bandwidth.

*Know how to use all functions of the conferencing software. Particularly know how to use screen share so you can share your interview presentation if necessary.

Here are some suggestions for technical interviews

*Ask as many clarifying questions about the problem as possible

*If you are using two screens to work the problem let your interviewer know

*Be sure to over-communicate your thought process so the interaction is collaborative and the interviewer knows your strategy

Take a Deep Breath

During periods of stress, people tend to breathe shallowly or even hold their breath. Shallow breathing increases heart rate and blood pressure, decreasing brain function. Taking a deep breath will slow your heart rate and improve your thinking. Taking a deep breath is one of the reminders to list in your portfolio.

A Word About Modesty

> "If you done it, it ain't bragging."
>
> —Walt Whitman

Don't be modest! As children, most of us were taught to be modest and refrain from bragging about ourselves. This is generally a good idea; however, not during interviews. Many candidates have difficulty turning off their modesty in interviews, and as a result, they don't present themselves powerfully as the best candidate for the job. This often takes a subtle verbal form. For example, one client stated that she "contributed" to a project that reduced product flaws by 20 percent. Upon exploration, it became apparent that she was "instrumental" to the project. The difference is significant - playing a role versus being a critical player. It was her modesty that demoted her from "instrumental" to "contributing" in her mind—and, without corrective coaching, in the hiring manager's mind.

One way to brag without being too arrogant or obnoxious is to let others brag for you. For example, you can use quotes from others: "The project manager for the product flaws project, Jesse Rogers, mentioned to me that my participation on the project was critical to its success." Using others' words gives you credibility without seeming as if you're tooting your own horn.

Behavior versus Performance

It's not prior behavior that predicts success; it's prior performance. Just because a candidate has done a task, that doesn't mean he has done it well. Most interviewers (including those using behavioral interviews) ask questions and focus on the candidate's past behaviors, but they don't adequately tap into performance—another indication of broken interviews. By communicating your performance, you fix your interview.

To fix you interview, talk about your performance not just your behaviors. For example:

> **Interviewer:** "Give me a specific example of a time when you used good judgment and logic in solving a problem."

> **Candidate:** "I was working with a team to determine whether my company should submit a proposal for a $15 million piece of business. The business would have grown the company, but we weren't sure we had the internal systems and personnel to deliver on the project, and failure with this high-profile customer would've severely damaged our reputation and chances for further business. I developed a decision matrix that contained all the pertinent factors and then used the matrix to make the decision."

Where is the performance aspect? A better response would be:

> "… I developed a decision matrix that contained all the pertinent factors and used the matrix to make the decision, which was to pass on the business. This decision turned out to be correct, saving the company a significant loss and positioning me as a thorough and logical problem solver. As a result, I received a nice year-end bonus and was promoted to director."

Adding the performance element will differentiate you from other candidates who simply report their behaviors. It will impress the interviewer and position you as a stronger candidate.

Try Not to Give Away Your Knowledge

This is one of my interview pet peeves—companies ask candidates to solve problems or provide business plans for which a consultant would charge thousands of dollars. A candidate who wants the job finds it difficult to refuse the request.

After being out of work for a year, one of my clients was interviewing for a high-level marketing position at a prestigious marketing company. After his first round of interviews, he was asked to prepare a three-year marketing plan and come back in two weeks to present the plan to the executive group. Because he wanted the job badly, he wrote the plan, including paying for development of a slide presentation. He ended up not getting the job and giving the company a plan that was worth $25,000 to $30,000. Exacerbating this unreasonable request is that the company had two other candidates, so they received $75,000 to $90,000 in free consulting.

Another client was asked to develop a sales plan. She was not willing to give away her knowledge, so instead she provided a high-level outline of a sales plan. She was rejected because her plan "didn't have enough meat on the bones." This is a tough situation to manage, particularly if a candidate is desperate for a job. Some assertive candidates ask whether the company will pay for the knowledge if they aren't hired. Other candidates who can afford to lose the opportunity simply refuse to participate, and still others say, "I'll be happy to share my knowledge once you hire me."

A trap I warn clients about is the "How would you solve this problem?" scenario. In an interview, a candidate is asked to provide solutions to an existing problem. Wanting to display expertise, the candidate begins to provide possible solutions. The trap is that those solutions may have been tried already and may have failed. When the candidate is finished suggesting already-failed solutions, the hiring manager has lost faith in the candidate's ability to provide new thinking and solutions to the organization.

To avoid this trap, I coach my clients to respond to this question by saying, "I don't know enough about your organization to know what solutions have been tried and failed or which ones would work. However, I have approached solving a similar problem by doing the following things.…" Then the candidate can talk about a process for solving the problem instead of solving the problem itself—trap avoided.

Search for the Hidden Meaning

During interviews, there is the question that's being asked, and then there is *why* the interviewer is asking the question. The key is knowing what the interviewer is trying to find out about you with each question.

For example, think about a question such as, "On a scale from one to ten, how competitive are you?" What is the interviewer hoping to learn? The company probably values competitiveness and has identified it as a top desired quality. It would not be a good idea to say you're only a five. As another example, consider the question, "If you could be any animal, what animal would you want to be and why?" It doesn't matter whether you pick a cat, a dog, or a wombat, as long as you can explain your thought process. Again, the interviewer is hoping to learn about your basic qualities and whether they are the qualities desired by the company. During the needs-analysis part of your interview, listen for qualities valued by the company and the hiring manager and then choose answers that communicate those qualities. For example, if the company values speed and flexibility, don't choose to be a turtle. However, if the company values persistence and caution, be the turtle.

Another example: "Are you a person with a lot of hobbies or interests?" You may think it is a positive thing to be an interesting person with hobbies and lots of interests; however, the interviewer might be thinking, "If this person has too many outside distractions, he will be less likely to put in long hours on the job." The way to answer this question would be to say, "I do have interests and hobbies; however, I don't let them get in the way of getting my work done."

When asked a question, take a moment and ask yourself, "Why is the interviewer asking me this? What is she trying to get at?" You may not be able to read the interviewer's mind, but using what you know about the position, you can answer the questions in a way that supports your candidacy. Also, because you are creating a conversation, you can ask the interviewer why she's asking the question: "That's an interesting question; I'm curious why you're asking. What are you hoping to learn?"

Use Power Phrases

A *power phrase* is a brief statement that communicates a memorable idea. When repeated, the phrase becomes part of a brand and a compelling, memorable message. President Barack Obama's campaign power phrase was "Yes we can." President Bill Clinton's campaign power phrase was "Bridge to the future."

One of my clients, a CFO, was particularly proud that he was able to perform all the functions of an accounting department, from strategy development to nuts-and-bolts, day-to-day data entry operations. He thought of himself as a go-to guy when things needed to be done. He chose this as his power phrase and referred to himself multiple times during his interview as the "go-to guy for financial management." For example, "In my prior position at ABC Company, I was considered the go-to guy for solving financial problems," and, "I'm particularly valuable when a company needs a go-to guy to manage financial issues."

Another client, a web developer, prided himself in being able to bring clarity to chaos. He used "Bringing clarity to chaos" as his power phrase during his interviews. For example, "When designing websites, I bring clarity to the chaos of site navigation," and, "Many companies need to have clarity brought to the chaos of their websites."

Another client, a project manager, prided herself on being a trusted advisor to the C-suite. She used this power phrase throughout her interviews while mentioning the qualities that made her so valuable to the most senior management.

What is your power phrase? When you have a phrase, use it multiple times during your interview to make you more memorable and help communicate the value you will bring to the position.

Take Notes

Few candidates take notes during their interviews. However, taking notes is very helpful and consistent with typical business behavior in a meeting. Many hiring managers are impressed by candidates who take notes, displaying interest and conscientiousness. Taking notes also encourages you to listen.

Just be sure to ask permission to take notes during the interview. Taking notes without asking permission may strike some interviewers as presumptuous. Also, be careful not to spend too much time with your head down taking notes, as you'll lose eye contact.

Take notes about the following information:

*Interviewer's name and title

*Details about job requirements

*Numbers, such as expected sales quotas

*Selection process, including timing

*Things about your background and experience that impressed the interviewer

*Things about your background and experience that concerned the interviewer

*Things about the job that particularly impressed you

*Things about the job that concerned you

Information from your notes will be helpful when refining your interview presentation for subsequent rounds of interviews and when writing your follow-through letter.

Use Repetition, Use Repetition, Use Repetition

Don't hesitate to use the phrases, "As I mentioned," or, "Let me repeat," or, "The important thing to remember is...." Follow these phrases with your benefits. For example, "As I mentioned, based on my level of experience in laboratory technology, I will be able to decrease testing time by 20 percent and increase profits by 8 percent." Another example might be, "I think the important thing to remember is that I have experience being a server in a four-star restaurant, and I will bring this experience to your restaurant, improving customer satisfaction." Interviewers remember approximately 50 percent of what they hear, and it is only through repetition that they will remember the most important reasons to hire you.

Take Your Time Answering

Interviews are not a timed verbal test. Many candidates think they must fire off rapid answers to interviewers' questions. This results in undue pressure, an increase in stress, and lowered brain function. Many interview questions require thoughtful answers, and thoughtful answers require time. It is perfectly reasonable to say, "Let me think about that for a moment." Taking 15 to 20 seconds to formulate an answer is fine. While you are thinking, take a breath to calm down. If this were a business meeting, taking time to answer a question accurately and concisely would be expected.

It is also okay to say, "I don't know" or, in response to a behavioral question, "I haven't been in that situation." Interviewers will respond far better to an honest response than to a fabricated answer that sounds inconsistent and raises concerns. Once again, like business meetings, you aren't expected to have all the answers all the time and in 20 seconds or less.

Provide Points of Comparison

The human brain is comfortable making decisions based on comparisons. Without comparisons, buyers have difficulty understanding the differences between services, their FUD factor remains high, and they don't make a purchase.

During your interview, make comparisons between your skills and someone without them. For example, "Unlike other salespeople who don't know the territory, I can set up a lot of sales calls quickly," and, "Unlike many technical people who often don't communicate well, I'm very good at explaining highly technical issues to non-technical people."

Handle the Compensation Question

The bottom line of the compensation question is that you are worth being paid the value you will deliver to the company—your value in the employment marketplace. Throughout the interview, you'll have the opportunity to present the benefits you will deliver to the company and build your perceived value. At the end of the interview, you'll be in a stronger position to discuss compensation, because the hiring manager will understand the value you can deliver. It is in your best interest to delay the salary discussion until the company understands your value and wants to hire you. Once they decide you are their first choice, they don't want to hire number two, and they will be willing to pay more to get you.

The following sections cover suggested compensation-discussion guidelines.

Know Your Value

The most important compensation strategy is to know your worth. Using salary review sites, such as salary.com and payscale.com, know your value in the marketplace. Smart companies will have reviewed the same websites, and your expectations and theirs should be consistent. If the company has not done a salary review, you can inform them of your value.

You also need to know your value relative to the position. Jobs require a certain level of experience, knowledge, and skill. If you have 10 years of experience and are applying for a job that only requires three to five year of experience, your additional years of experience will be discounted. This is unfortunate, but you need to consider it as you determine how much compensation you will ask for.

Stay in the Interview

During your interview—particularly if things are going well—you might be taken on a tour of the office or out to lunch. During these informal parts of an interview, it's easy to let down your guard and do or say something that may hurt your chances. For example, on a tour of the office, you might say, "Wow, these cubicles are so much better than the cramped one I worked in at ABC Company, and the computers are actually from the 21st century!" You might think you're being complimentary; however, you just violated the "don't be negative" rule.

During lunch, the conversation might be informal and more personal, but you are still being interviewed. Keep focused on presenting yourself as the best candidate for the position and try to keep your conversation in the context of the job. For example, saying, "I love to ski, and I'd rather be skiing than doing anything else" does not speak to your motivation for the job.

Small Agreements Get to "Yes"

Getting a small agreement from an interviewer leads to bigger agreements. Begin to get agreement by asking questions that you know the interviewer will answer affirmatively. For example, "Would you agree that this position requires someone with excellent skills in team leadership?" or "Would you agree that the person you hire for this job needs to have excellent written communication skills?" As the interviewer begins to agree with you, he will be more likely to continue to agree with you. You can move on to questions such as, "Would you agree that I have the type of leadership skills this position requires?" and "Wouldn't you agree that my written communication skills are very good?"

Be a Gracious Guest

Respond to the interviewer's hospitality by accepting whatever is offered. Even if you don't drink coffee or if you aren't thirsty for water, if the interviewer offers it, take a sip or two and then just leave the cup. Let the interviewer or the assistant be the host, and you be the gracious guest. This is particularly important if the interviewer has coffee or water; no one likes to drink alone.

Expect the Unexpected and Go with the Flow

I've heard enough unusual and unexpected interview stories that I could write several books on bizarre interviews alone. For example, a client who was interviewing for a high-level sales position flew to Chicago from Philadelphia for an interview, at the expense of the hiring company. Due to a scheduling snafu, after picking up my client at the airport, the VP of sales conducted the interview in his car while driving to a fast-food restaurant for lunch and then back to the airport. After a round of local interviews, my client got a job offer, which she refused.

Another client, an operations VP in finance, was invited to interview for a position by a senior manager at another company. The "interview" consisted of a 45-minute monologue by the manager about himself and the company. As a well-trained interviewee, my client attempted to refocus the interview on her background and skills. The manager rebuffed her efforts, telling her, "This is not an interview. You are already going on to the second round, so just listen." It would've been nice if he had told her it wasn't an interview at the beginning rather than at the end.

After a brief phone interview, a recent college graduate was asked by a major advertising company to submit a two-minute video about why he should be hired. He was hired with no further interviews!

Interruptions, distractions, flubbed scheduling, lost resumes, internal bickering, job requirement confusion, a long interview process, and bad interviewers are only some of the things that may challenge you. Interviewing requires flexibility and a willingness to adapt to the interview format and style. Expect the unexpected, and don't be thrown off your strategy and message.

Use Meta-Communication

Meta-communication is commenting or making an observation about your communication to clarify a situation, overcome barriers, or resolve a problem. For example, "We seem to be having difficulty agreeing on the answer. How about we agree to disagree and move on?"

Meta-communication can be highly effective in managing an interview and establishing rapport. For example, when asked about compensation, using meta-communication you can say, "Compensation is a challenge to talk about. At this early stage of the interview, it's important that we know compensation won't be a barrier if the job is a good fit. Can we agree that the compensation is adequate, and it's worth our time to go through the interview process?" Another example of meta-communication might be, "We have spent a good deal of time talking about the job, and I think I have a good understanding of the requirements. Can we spend time discussing how my background and experience match the job requirements?" Yet another example: "I asked whether you think I have any challenges that would interfere with my performing this job well. You mentioned a challenge that almost every new employee would face. Are there any challenges you can think of that relate specifically to my background and experience?"

In these examples, the candidate is commenting on what is being talked about in the interview and suggesting what to focus on. Consider conversations you have with co-workers and friends; meta-communication is often an important part of those conversations.

Meta-communication requires taking a step back from the give and take of the interview, making an observation about the content of the interview, and then communicating your observation and making a suggestion. It turns the interview into a conversation and improves your connection with the interviewer.

After the Interview

After your face-to-face interview is over, you still have some work to do. The following strategies will support and enhance your chances of landing the job and getting a higher compensation rate.

Human Brains Expect the Worst

In the face of the unknown, human brains tend to anticipate the worst. Following an interview, there are many unknowns, including how well you did, whether you will be offered the job, and when you will notified of the decision. In the face of this uncertainty, most candidates assume that they have been rejected. I've had clients who went through a delay of six months between their first interview and when they eventually landed the job, with little (if any) communication in between.

Not knowing is simply that—not knowing. Trying to guess what is going on in the mind of the hiring manager or internally at the company is a waste of time and energy. Try to get reliable information during the interview and afterward by following up. If you can't, then redirect your focus and energy toward another opportunity. Expect not knowing to be annoying and frustrating; unfortunately, it is a large part of job search.

Debrief Yourself

Treat each interview as a learning experience and review your performance as soon as you can after the interview. Your debriefing will provide insights about your performance as well as critical information for your next round of interviews. You should debrief before you write your follow-through letter. Ask yourself the following debriefing questions:

*What problem(s) does this job solve?

*What are the top five to seven critical job requirements?

*What are the top two or three challenges in this position?

*Did I have comprehensive knowledge of the industry, company, job, and interviewer?

*Did I maintain good body language, including posture and eye contact?

*Were my prepared questions S.M.A.R.T.?

*What questions took me by surprise or found me unprepared?

*Did I establish a good level of comfort and rapport with the interviewer?

*Was I able to communicate to the interviewer all the information I wanted him to know about me? If not, what information did I miss?

*Was I on time (15 minutes prior to the start of the interview)?

*Was I dressed appropriately?

*How would I rate my confidence level going into the interview?

*What interview performance grade would I give myself?

*What three or four things about me was the interviewer was impressed with?

*What three or four things about me was the interviewer was concerned with?

*Did anything unexpected happen during the interview?

*Did I take good notes?

*Did I use my interview presentation effectively?

Make the Most of Your Follow-Through Letter

As I have written previously, send a follow-through letter after every interview to each interviewer. Some candidates will send a letter within minutes (via text message) or hours of the interview; however, this is too fast to have developed a well-thought-out letter. Take time to think through your letter and send it within 24 hours. If appropriate, offer links to information that is valuable to the hiring manager and include letters of reference or other proof of your quality work. Be sure to reiterate your most pertinent skills, experiences, and personal success factors relative to the problem. Your letter should continue the sales process and do the following:

***Define the problem.** Define the problem this position is being filled to solve. "As we discussed, the person in this position will be expected to...."

***Present a solution/plan.** Write about how you will use your combination of skills, experience, and personal success factors to solve the problem. "With my experience in building a successful project management office at XYZ

Company, I will...." Describe the positive impact you will have on the interviewer's organization when you are selected to solve the problem.

*Be specific and measurable. Explain how you will provide your solution, including details about goals, timetables, and implementation plans (30- and 60-day strategic action plans). Include numbers whenever possible.

*Include your value-add(s). Include your value-adds that make you the best candidate for the job.

*Hit the hot buttons. The letter must address the specific concerns of each individual interviewer. For example, engineers want technology solutions, whereas accountants want ROI. Be sure your letter provides your solution in terms the interviewer wants.

*Focus on the interviewer, not on your services. Interviewers are not interested in how this position will benefit you. Make the letter about how you'll solve the interviewer's problems.

*Include examples. Include examples of how you have solved similar problems at other companies. This may be a reiteration of your success stories and can be included in your letter as bullet points.

*Summarize the basic issues and the reasons why the interviewer should hire you. Have a strong close to your letter that summarizes why you are the best choice for the position.

*Express your enthusiasm for the job. Be sure to communicate how much you want the job and how excited you are about the opportunity to provide value to the company. "I am excited about the opportunity to work for XYZ Company as a project manager, and I'm confident I can establish a project management office that will...."

*Be well edited. Make sure your writing is tight, jargon-free, and clear. Use power words and remove any extraneous word that doesn't add meaning or value to your letter. A brief, well-focused letter that displays your writing skills will be most impressive. A follow-through letter should fit easily on one page.

Stay in Touch

Once the interview is over, it may be a while before the hiring decision is made. The challenge is to stay in touch with the hiring manager without being intrusive. Staying in touch requires a combination of creativity and emails to touch base.

Emails to touch base state a continued interest and ask for information about the status of the hiring decision. You can send these emails every two to three weeks. Don't be surprised if your emails don't get any response. It seems that most of the corporate world operates on the premise that if they have nothing new to tell you, they will simply ignore you.

You can also stay in touch by being creative. Following an interview, one of my clients saw an article in an industry journal about the company's 25th anniversary of being in business. The client emailed a copy of the article with a note of congratulations to the hiring manager. Other clients have sent notices of conferences or networking meetings in which the hiring manager may be interested, with a note saying, "I hope to see you there." Use any valid reason to send an email to keep your name foremost in the hiring manager's mind.

If You Are Rejected, Send One More Letter

Being rejected from a job is a painful experience. Most candidates just want to forget about the job and the company and put the rejection behind them. However, there is a 50/50 chance that the person who was hired will not work out and the position will be open again. If you were number two or three, you might be back in the running for the job.

Once notified that you were rejected, send a letter reiterating your interest in the job and asking to be considered if any opportunities open up. You can write something along the lines of, "I regret that you weren't able to use my services at this time; however...." Not only is this a classy thing to do, but it may result in you being contacted for another position at the company or for the same position in the future.

Always Negotiate Your Compensation

> "You don't get what you deserve, you get what you negotiate."

> —Dr. Chester Karrass, developer of Effective Negotiating ®

Price is always a part of the sales process, and a conversation about price is expected when you're selling services. Sellers and purchaser know the initial price is only a beginning point for negotiation. Most senior-level candidates negotiate their compensation, while most mid-level and lower-level candidates do not negotiate salary. The primary reasons why mid-level and lower-level candidates don't negotiate is that they don't think they have negotiating power, and they are fearful that asking for more money, or more benefits like an extra week of vacation, will result in confrontation, bad feelings, and loss of the job offer.

A friend was doing contracted recruiting for a call-center position. It was her responsibility to quickly hire 25 call-center staff. Her compensation instruction was, "Offer new hires $12.50. If they ask for more, you can go up to $15." Understand that my friend was on a short-term contract to hire 25 staff; her performance was judged on how quickly she hired qualified people, and how much the new staff earned was of no concern to her as long as it was $15 per hour or less. For a new hire to make more money, all they had to do was ask, and they could earn as much as $2.50 per hour more. How many of the 25 asked for more money? Not one! The lesson here is, always negotiate compensation.

Ask Why They Hired You

One of your first questions should be, "I'm very flattered and excited by the job offer; however, I'm curious—what led to the decision to hire me over other candidates?" Most candidates don't want to look a gift horse in the mouth, and they are just grateful to get the job offer. However, knowing why you were selected over all other candidates will give you a better understanding of your value and, in turn, will improve your negotiating leverage. If the reason you were selected has to do with a valuable selling proposition that no other candidate had, the company will be willing to spend more to hire you.

Know the Compensation Philosophy and Policies

To be ready to negotiate, it is helpful to know the company's compensation philosophy and policies. A compensation policy explains the values and objectives guiding compensation, including:

*Which skills the organization rewards

*Whether the company pays at the median of the marketplace, above it, or below it

*Which types of rewards are available (stock, bonuses, and so on)

*The process used to determine salary grades

Compensation policies are the specific details, such as the size of the increase when an employee is promoted, the performance-review cycle, and how specific jobs are priced and compensated.

Compensation philosophies address the company's approach to compensation. For example:

*We hire the best candidates and pay the highest salaries in the industry

*We hire the best candidate, pay a competitive salary and reward high performers with generous bonuses

*We hire employees and pay industry standard salaries

According to a survey by the human resources association WorldatWork, 90 percent of all companies have a compensation philosophy; 61 percent have it in writing, but 42 percent say most or all of their employees don't understand the philosophy. By asking about the compensation philosophy, you will be more informed about compensation than most current employees!

Asking about the compensation philosophy is a good, neutral way to begin your negotiations. You can begin negotiations by saying, "Thank you for the job offer—I'm very excited about the opportunity. Before we begin discussing the details of the offer, could you please tell me your compensation philosophy and policies?" Once you know the philosophies and policies, you have a lot more information to guide your negotiations. For example, if the company "Hires the best candidate and pays the highest salary in the industry" you will probably be offered a good salary to start and may have little room to negotiate.

Be Prepared to Talk Dollars

From the very beginning of this book, I have been referring to your value in the employment marketplace. I hope that, having developed your value proposition, personal brand, sales strategies to sell your skills and experience, and an interview presentation, you have a good idea of your value in the marketplace. The next step is to assign a dollar amount to that value.

The dollar amount is based on supply and demand: how much your skill set is in demand in your geographic location and how many other people offer the service. The higher the demand and the lower the supply, the higher the dollar amount—and vice versa. The best way to determine your dollar amount is to do research online at sites such as salary.com, glassdoor.com, and payscale.com.

A very powerful exchange in salary compensation negotiation goes something like this:

>**Hiring manager:** "The salary is…"
>
>**Candidate:** "I was hoping to make more than that."
>
>**Hiring manager:** "You were? How much more?"
>
>**Candidate:** "Other employees with my level of skill and experience in similar jobs at similar companies in this geographic area earn an average of…"

When Negotiating Salary Set an Anchor

Typically, the suggested strategy is to have the hiring company mention a salary number first. However, once a number is mentioned that number becomes the "anchor" from which the negotiating begins. The best strategy is to set the anchor and dictate where the negotiation starts. To do this successfully you need to be sure you know the salary range and then set a mildly aggressive salary. For example, if you know people with your skill and years of experience in your geographic location typically earn between $75,000 and $82,000, you can set the anchor at $85,000. Once set at $85,000, you can give up some salary, negotiate down to $82,000 and end up at the top of the range. With the typical strategy of letting the company set the anchor, they may say $72,000 and then negotiating all the way up to $82,000 is a challenge. Also, keep in mind there is a lot more to compensation than just salary, and there may be richer total benefits at a company that offers a lower salary.

*__Be proactive.__ When you have your first conversation about the job, which is typically a telephone screening interview, you can begin by saying, "Please tell me about the job requirements and the salary range." Asking about salary range as a matter of fact, proactive question may result in the screening interviewer simply disclosing the range. Once you know the range, you can use that knowledge to set your anchor. You can set your anchor at the top of the range or even a bit higher than the top.

*__Be prepared to deflect.__ The best time to discuss salary is after they have selected you as the number one candidate. Try to put off salary negotiation until then. Anticipate and be prepared to answer the compensation question. The first strategy is to deflect the question and suggest that compensation be discussed later in the selection process. For example, "I'm very interested in this opportunity with your firm, and I'm sure that if we decide that I am a good fit for the position, we can come to an agreement about compensation that will be acceptable to both of us."

*__Ask for the salary range.__ Every company has a salary range established for a position. If you are pressured to give a salary number, ask the interviewer to disclose the range. You can say, "I understand it is important to make sure my salary requirements and your salary range are aligned. Please share with me the salary range, and I'll tell you how my salary fits your range." Don't be hesitant to discuss the process of negotiating salary (see the metacommunications section below).

*__If you can't avoid mentioning a number, give a range.__ There are situations where you won't be able to avoid giving a number. Instead of saying just one number, such as $78,000, give a broad range, such as $78,000 to $85,000. This gives you negotiating room without pricing yourself too high or too low for the position. Make sure the lower number is a good anchor.

*__Consider benefits and perks as part of your compensation.__ Compute your total compensation, which is your base salary plus benefits and perks. For example, if your base salary is $60,000, you can add 15 to 20% for benefits and perks. If you are asked, "What did you make in your previous position?" you can say, "My total compensation was $72,000." Be aware that many cities and states are prohibiting companies from asking about prior salaries. This is intended to eliminate salary bias based on the sex of the applicant.

You're Hired; Now Negotiate

Employees generally have the most negotiating power immediately after receiving a job offer. The company has been through a lengthy selection process, and they have decided that you present the greatest chance of being a valuable employee. You are their first choice; they don't want to settle on number two, and they are willing to negotiate.

When you are on the job and working, you likely will receive standard wage increases based on your performance. Where your salary starts will impact your income for the rest of your tenure at the company. Even a small increase at the beginning means significantly more money during your career. Assuming an average annual pay increase of 5 percent, an employee whose starting annual salary was $55,000 rather than $50,000 earns more than an additional $600,000 over the course of a 40-year career!

Confidence Makes a Difference

Negotiating research by Markus Baer, assistant professor of organizational behavior at Washington University in St. Louis, shows there is a "home field" advantage. He found that location makes a difference in the outcome of negotiations, with the advantage going to the person who is in his home location. He concluded that this has to do with comfort and confidence that a person feels in his own surroundings. However, this home-field advantage is neutralized when the visitor had a high level of confidence going into the negotiations.

Salary negotiations always take place on the employer's home court. Thus, your level of confidence impacts the success of your salary negotiations. As mentioned before, once you are selected as number one for the job, you have negotiating power. Knowing the company does not want to lose you and go to their second or third pick should increase your confidence. Prior to the negotiation, remind yourself that you won out over all the other candidates, you will deliver good value to the company, and you deserve to be paid what you're worth.

Negotiation Can Be Very Simple

When people hear the word "negotiation," they think conference tables, complicated documents, complex strategies, and long timeframes. However, negotiating a salary can be brief and easy. I've had clients make more money by simply saying, "I was hoping to make more than that" and then being silent. This simple statement asks for more money in a non-confrontational, easygoing manner, and if there is some room left in the salary range, it could mean some extra dollars. If you make this statement, be prepared to say how much more, and be bold, knowing they will come back with a lower number.

Reduce Risk as a Negotiating Strategy

In employment negotiating, risk is a critical element. If the employer knew how productive and profitable you would be, they could attach a dollar figure and compensate you accordingly. When they hire you, your compensation is a gamble about your value to them—a risk.

I've had several clients successfully negotiate higher salaries by focusing on risk. One client was offered a starting salary lower than she had hoped for with a raise after 12 months. She was able to negotiate for half the offered raise after six months and a more substantial raise after 12 months. She did this by establishing performance criteria to earn the raises. If my client hit her performance marks, she would be well worth the salary she would be receiving, so the company eliminated their risk. If you are willing to base compensation on performance criteria, you can ask for a higher compensation level. You are putting your salary where your mouth is—shouldn't the employer compensate you for reducing the risk?

When negotiating, focus on risk factors for both the company and yourself. You take risks by joining a company, and you should be compensated according to the risks. This is particularly true if you're leaving a job to join another company. Your risk factors include industry trends that may impact the company, company stability, relocation, average employee tenure, and so on. The higher your risks, the higher the compensation. For example, I had a client who was relocating for a job negotiate the costs of moving back to his old city if the job didn't work out.

Compensation Negotiation Can Be Creative

Because compensation consists of so many parts, there is often room to come up with creative compensation structures. Compensation is more than base salary and may consist of:

*Housing (employer-provided or employer-paid)

*Group insurance (health, dental, life, disability, and so on) and when insurance coverage starts.

*Retirement benefits

*Daycare

*Tuition reimbursement (school, conferences, and training)

*Sick leave

*Vacation (paid and non-paid)

*Holidays

*Profit sharing

*Employee-assistance plans

*Relocation support

*Adoption assistance

*Transportation support

*Car allowance

*Title

*To whom you report

*Start date

*Profit sharing

*Working from home including money to set up a home office

For example, many companies have employees wait 30 to 60 days before receiving health benefits. This can be a negotiation point—will the company start benefits earlier or pick up the cost of the interim healthcare coverage? What if your spouse has healthcare coverage—will the company give you the cash value of the healthcare they offer if you use your spouse's coverage?

You can negotiate vacation time as well. During several job changes, I negotiated a week of vacation before having earned the time because I had a trip planned. At one job where I was working, an entire department had three weeks of vacation while one person had four. She negotiated the extra week before she began the job.

It is often easier to negotiate non-salary compensation, such as vacation time, because most companies don't account for non-salary compensation the same way. For example, negotiating the cost of attending one or two national conferences that are important to your career is easier for a company to rationalize than spending an extra $3,000 to $4,000 on salary, even though the cost is the same. In a recent study, Michelle Marks, associate professor at Mason's School of Management, and Crystal Harold, assistant professor at Temple University's Fox School of Business, found that more than half of the people polled who chose to negotiate received at least one additional non-salary gain, such as vacation time. When negotiating compensation, think creatively and ask to be compensated for valuable non-salary items.

Most People Think Because It's Written It's a Law—But It's Not

A common negotiating tactic is appealing to a higher power. In fact, most negotiating books suggest that companies don't have the highest authority or the ultimate decision-maker in the negotiations, because they can always say, "I have to check with the boss about that." In employment negotiations, the higher authority is often a written document known as the employee handbook, as in, "I would love to offer you three weeks of vacation, but the policy in the employee handbook is two weeks." But since when is the employee handbook law?

I recently had a client receive a job offer for a sales position that "required" her to sign a non-compete—the non-compete requirement was in the employee handbook. She was not willing to sign the non-compete and was able to negotiate it out of her employment agreement. Don't let the hiring manager or the HR representative quoting the employee handbook prevent you from exploring and negotiating options.

On the flip side, candidates can use significant others as a higher authority. For example, "I like the offer; however, I have to speak with my significant other about the relocation package to make sure it covers our needs."

Leave Emotions Out of It

Fear and neediness are the biggest obstacles to negotiating a better deal. The fear of losing a much-needed job offer paralyzes many candidates and keeps them from being assertive in negotiations. Of all the clients I have coached through compensation negotiations, not one has lost a job opportunity, and not one began his job on a negative note. If you negotiate in a professional, self-controlled manner, you often gain more respect than you lose. Consider that negotiating is a critical business skill, and if you do a good job negotiating your compensation, it means you will do a good job negotiating for the company.

Because compensation negotiation is such an emotionally charged situation, it is helpful to have a coach or an objective person as a sounding board and advisor. The best person for this role is probably not your spouse or significant other, because she is caught up in the emotions as well. Look for someone who has knowledge of the profession or industry and is willing to be totally honest with you about your value and your negotiating approach.

Let the Offer Percolate

As mentioned, the best time to negotiate is after receiving a job offer; however, don't negotiate based on a verbal offer. Typically, you will receive a phone call with the good news and some discussion about the job offer. Always express interest and enthusiasm and then ask for the job offer in writing so you can "fully understand the details of the offer." It will take a day or two to get the written job offer, and you can take 24 to 48 hours to consider the offer before responding. It may take some time for the initial excitement of a job offer to wear off so that you can think more objectively, so take this time to consider the offer and establish your negotiation points. There is no rush, and a day or two will not make a difference.

Get It All in Writing

Be sure to document every detail of the agreement. I have coached clients to push back when a hiring manager has said things such as, "Let's not put that in writing. We can just agree that we'll do a performance review in six months, and at that point you will be eligible for a raise. I don't want it in writing, because the other staff didn't get the same deal, and I don't know whether my boss would like it."

Not only should the performance review and the raise be in writing, but the performance criteria for the raise should be in writing as well. In six months, the person who hired you may not be around, or your memories may differ.

Onboarding: The Final Step

Congratulations! You have won the interview, landed the job, negotiated your compensation, and accepted the job offer. The next step is to begin the job and be successful. *Onboarding* refers to the process of getting settled into the job and starting to contribute to the success of the organization. It is the shared responsibility of the employer and employee; however, just as you took responsibility for the interview, you should take responsibility for getting a good start on the job. Remember, only 51 percent of all employees are successful. Here are some suggested strategies:

*Learn the company's values and priorities.

*Learn departmental goals and objectives.

*Learn your boss's preferred work style and how she likes to communicate.

*Quickly address any misunderstandings.

*Socialize and work to establish a sense of belonging.

*Define performance expectations.

*Understand and address any feelings of anxiety.

*Listen, listen, listen.

Using Advanced Interview Tips Will Fix Your Interview

I can play a game of chess because I know the basic moves and rules. However, I am far from being good at chess. Interviewing is like chess—it is easy to do but hard to do well and win. Most candidates know how to interview and typically follow the basic moves and rules. However, few candidates know how to win the game. Candidates who make the basic moves lose out to more advanced candidates who use advanced strategies. This entire book advocates an advanced strategy, Active Interviewing, using a sales approach and developing an interview presentation; this chapter focused on specific advanced moves used by expert candidates. Using advanced interview tips has the following benefits:

*It challenges you to improve your interview performance.

*It differentiates you from your competition.

*It reduces your risk of accepting a job that is not a good fit for you.

*It increases your chances of getting a higher compensation package.

*It provides a powerful way to follow through after your interview.

*It helps you learn from each of your interviews, improving your performance at subsequent interviews.

*It increases your chances of acing the interview and winning the job.

Epilogue

"We have enough people who tell it like it is—now we could use a few who tell it like it can be."
—Robert Orben, magician and comedy writer

The job marketplace has changed. The average tenure at a job is 4.5 years, and it's even less for younger workers. Job changing is rampant—not just within industries, but across them. With shorter tenure comes self-directed career management, numerous job changes, and frequent interviews. In this changed employment marketplace, employees have become a company of one, and personal branding and selling one's services have become critical career management skills.

With the higher rate of employee turnover, companies are struggling to identify, hire, and retain talented employees. Unfortunately, the acquiring and selling of talent has not adjusted to market dynamics. Talented people go un-hired, while mismatched employees are hired. The old interview format of questions and answers to identify "good hires" is broken—you have learned about a new approach that will fix it!

It Is Time for You to Think Differently about Interviews

You have now learned that the interview process is broken, but you can fix your interviews. You know you can fix your interviews by using Active Interviewing and changing your thinking about how to prepare for and manage your interview. You know it requires changing your thinking from that of a passive question-answering candidate to that of an active salesperson powerfully advocating for yourself and clearly communicating why you are the best candidate for the job. You're aware that it is taking responsibility for how the interview runs and actively guiding the direction and content of your interviews.

It Is Time for You to Act Differently in Interviews

This book has given you the insights and strategies to sell yourself in an interview—to take the sales skills and presentation skills you have and apply them to your interviews, guiding the direction and quality of your interview. You have learned to brand yourself and develop an interview presentation that will help you prepare for your interview as well as present powerfully in the interview. The option is now yours to follow the more traditional, and broken, path of the standard interview or to be bold and improve interviews to your advantage.

Companies Need to be Smart About Hiring People— You Can Educate Them

Most companies' selection processes result in the hiring of adequate employees only 51 percent of the time. They hire excellent candidates only 25 percent of the time. The selection process is broken, and companies don't know how to fix it—but you can. When you take an Active Interviewing approach, you improve the hiring process for yourself as well as the hiring company. You get a job you can do well, and the company gets an employee who will contribute to its success.

A Glimpse of the Present and the Future

Jobs have become far more competitive, and companies expect higher levels of performance from fewer employees. Landing a job requires a high-level interview performance that convinces the hiring manager that you can perform the job at a high level and better than the other applicants can. You cannot do this using the traditional interview format, even if the hiring manager doesn't know how to interview differently. Today, Active Interviewing is the critical interview strategy you need to bring into your in-person or virtual interviews to beat your competition and win jobs.

Interview presentations are a powerful interview tool, and they will become like resumes—a standard requirement of the hiring process. Interview presentations are important to both preparing for and guiding the interview. They help candidates interview better, and they help the hiring manager be a better interviewer—a win-win. As candidates use an interview presentation and the selection process improves, hiring managers and hiring companies will begin to see interview presentations as a standard part of the interview process. Candidates won't consider going to an interview without a presentation and hiring companies will require a presentation as part of the interview. Having learned about Active Interviewing, you are ready to bring an interview presentation to your interview today and get an interview edge.

My Best Wishes

Interviewing is one of the most challenging things a person does in his or her career. I have dedicated my career to helping people land jobs they love and earn the money they deserve. I hope Active Interviewing helps you land a job you love and earn the money you deserve.

Appendix A - Interview Presentation Samples

The following are real examples of successful interview presentations that have been altered to protect the anonymity of the job-winning candidates. The candidates would be happy to be identified and boast of their success, but companies tend to not be so open – protecting their brand I suppose. The samples span career levels from entry-level through mid-management to senior level. Keep in mind that these are conversation-starting presentations, so the content may not be fully understandable when simply read. Imagine a candidate walking into an interview and giving (or emailing) an interviewer one of these presentations. Pretty impressive wouldn't you say?

An Example of an Entry-Level Interview Presentation

Accelerating the Indiana Granger's Success in the Marketplace

Zach Williams

Ambitious
Dependable
Problem-solver
Work Hard, Play Hard

(610) 567-4834
zw@gmail.com

Operations, People & Change Associate
Position Requirements

❑ Strong client service orientation combined with creative problem-solving skills.

❑ Ability to work effectively as part of a team as well as function well with independent responsibilities.

❑ Flexible and adaptable to ever-changing schedules and work assignments.

❑ Strong written and oral communication skills.

❑ Ability to research pertinent client, industry, and technical matters.

❑ Ability to prioritize and handle multiple tasks.

❑ Excellent references.

I have a strong match with position requirements

✓ Strong client service orientation combined with creative problem-solving skills.

- Served as liaison between clients and sales manager at Campus Solutions.

- Established promotional programs to reward loyal customers (Wash Me Quick, LLC).

✓ The ability to work effectively as part of a team as well as function well with independent responsibilities.

- Member of most successful sales team at Campus Solutions.

- Individual achievements warranted increased workload at Campus Solutions.

I have a strong match with position requirements

- ✓ Be flexible and adaptable to ever-changing schedules and work assignments.
  - Wash Me Quick, LLC operated during busiest country club hours.
  - Workload at Z University varied based on project assignment.
- ✓ Strong written and oral communication skills.
  - Found success through "cold calling" at Campus Solutions.
  - Devised written business plan to contract with country clubs and obtained insurance coverage (Wash Me Quick, LLC).

I have a strong match with position requirements

- ✓ Ability to research pertinent client, industry, and technical matters.
  - Currently researching industries with best client potential for Z University.
  - Researched markets where CS's services are provided to develop successful marketing plans (WVU coupon program).
- ✓ Be able to prioritize and handle multiple tasks.
  - Balanced steady workload with crisis management responsibilities at JKCP.
  - At CS completed various projects between sales calls (e.g., developing marketing materials, market-entry research).

I have a strong match with position requirements

✓ Excellent references.

- Jamie Jones, VP of Operations, CS Inc.

- Robert Brooks, Senior Executive, Union Financial Corporation.

- Steve Roberts, Director of Human Resources, JKCP.

I bring important additional areas of expertise

✓ Entrepreneurship

✓ Personnel management

✓ Microsoft Office products: PowerPoint, Excel, Access, Word

✓ Spanish (conversational)

✓ Business administration

Examples of outstanding career and personal accomplishments

- ✓ Excellent sales performance resulting in multiple pay increases at CS.

- ✓ Recruited largest new member class in the history of Beta Sigma Beta fraternity.

- ✓ Business startup (Wash Me Quick, LLC: "It Smells Like New" auto detailing).

- ✓ Held leadership position with Champions of Caring.

- ✓ Completion of International Baccalaureate program.

These personal traits help me succeed on the job

- ✓ Positive (can-do) mental attitude

- ✓ Determination for achievement

- ✓ Organization

- ✓ Love of learning

- ✓ Adaptability

- ✓ Ability/willingness to follow direction

My "Strategic Action Plan" for providing value quickly

30 Days

- ✓ Be visible/approach others

- ✓ Complete orientation

- ✓ Read, review, and understand company policies

- ✓ Listen, observe, and ask questions

- ✓ Establish relationships with other company professionals

- ✓ Listen 80%, speak 20%

60 Days

- ✓ Identify short-, mid-, and long-term goals for position

- ✓ Build internal credibility

- ✓ Establish support systems

- ✓ Work with supervisor to establish goals and success metrics

- ✓ Gain market knowledge

Hire me because…

I have all the pieces

- ✓ Experience in sales, marketing and general management

- ✓ Track record of success in job, internship, and leadership positions

- ✓ Conversational in Spanish

- ✓ Presentation, negotiation, and leadership skills

- ✓ Excellent references

Important closing questions

Questions:

- ➤ What are the three top strategies for increasing ticket sales?
- ➤ Given your limited advertising channels, how will you increase advertising revenue?
- ➤ How will you attract top athletes to this smaller market?
- ➤ What do you believe to be the top priorities for a sports team in the Indiana market?
- ➤ Based on my background and experience, what do you think would be the greatest challenges for me in this position?
- ➤ How and when should I follow up with you?

Thank you for your time and consideration.

Zach Williams
Ambitious, Dependable, Problem-solver, Work Hard/Play Hard

An Example of a Mid-level Interview Presentation

Workforce Planning Director - Position Requirements

- ❏ Bachelor's degree in Business Administration

- ❏ Ten or more years of HR experience

- ❏ Knowledge of HR staffing, recruiting, compensation, relocation, and visa programs

- ❏ Demonstrated ability to communicate verbally and in writing with all levels of internal and external customers

- ❏ Ability to manage a function requiring confidentiality, discretion, and independent judgment

- ❏ Proficiency in MS Office suite

My Match With Position Requirements

- ✓ Bachelor's degree in Business Administration
  - B.S. in Business Administration, Drexel University
  - Ph.D. in Business Management, Penn State University
  - AIRS (Advanced Internet Recruiting Strategies) trained
  - DDI Targeted Selection Interview trained
  - Certified behavioral analyst

- ✓ Ten or more years of HR experience
  - 14 years in human resources and 10 years in strategically planning workforces
  - 14 years experience in implementing effective training programs
  - Proven ability to design efficient workflows, improve productivity, and expand utilization of available resources

My Match With Position Requirements

- ✓ Knowledge of HR staffing, recruiting, compensation, relocation, and visa programs
  - Expertise in HR staffing programs and recruiting all employee levels in multiple functions
  - Expertise in compensation pay grading, career ladder development, and variable pay
  - Designed relocation programs, partnering with real estate brokers, and H1B visa coordination

- ✓ Demonstrated ability to communicate verbally and in writing with all levels of internal and external customers
  - Exceptional ability to influence and communicate effectively
  - Master of Arts in written communication

Linda Fields
Leadership, Integrity, Team Building, Strategic Vision

My Match With Position Requirements

- ✓ Ability to manage a function requiring confidentiality, discretion, and independent judgment
  - Extensive expertise in working in confidential situations
  - Excellent troubleshooter and problem solver

- ✓ Proficiency in MS Office suite
  - Expert user of Word, Excel, PowerPoint, Outlook, MS Project

Linda Fields
Leadership, Integrity, Team Building, Strategic Vision

Additional Areas of Expertise

- ✓ HR metric development

- ✓ Selection tools

- ✓ Senior-level recruitment

- ✓ Labor budgeting

- ✓ Internship and orientation programs

- ✓ Strong leadership

Linda Fields
Leadership, Integrity, Team Building, Strategic Vision

Outstanding Career Accomplishments

- ✓ Design of relocation program, including H1B visas

- ✓ Selected outstanding HR representative of the year three years running

- ✓ Implemented Career Ladder program, increasing retention by 20%

- ✓ Selected to represent company at global leaders' conference

Linda Fields
Leadership, Integrity, Team Building, Strategic Vision

These Personal Traits Help Me Succeed on the Job

- ✓ Bringing out the best in people
- ✓ Collaborative problem solving
- ✓ Working well with cultural diversity
- ✓ Commitment to continuous personal improvement
- ✓ Big-picture approach and outlook
- ✓ Sensitivity to what is possible
- ✓ Ability to use resources and time effectively

Strategic Action Plan

30 Days

- ✓ Manage alignment of business needs with current programs; prioritize and develop new programs
- ✓ Develop HR metrics to determine most effective sourcing strategy
- ✓ Implement selection tools to determine ideal profiles across top-priority functions
- ✓ Monitor and manage 2009 headcount and staffing budget; begin development of 2010 budget
- ✓ Implement a redeployment process for contractors

60 Days

- ✓ Utilize HRIS or develop Access database to track internal skill sets
- ✓ Align primary functions with internship program
- ✓ Develop and roll out a new-hire orientation program
- ✓ Evaluate relocation program and update with current business needs
- ✓ Develop and utilize recruiting staff according to skill sets and program priorities

Why Hire Linda Fields?

I Have All the Pieces

> 14+ years HR experience

> 10+ years workforce planning

> Effective influencing skills

> Exemplary business acumen

> Skill in candidate selection

> Proven track record for lowering turnover

> Results-oriented mindset

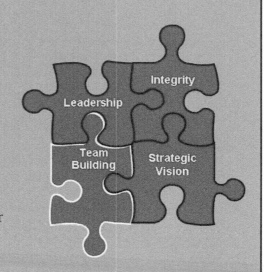

Closing Questions

Questions:

✓ Arcio has had a diversity program for three years. Do you believe you have met your diversity goals?

✓ What training management systems do you use?

✓ Given the recent deregulation, where do you see the market moving?

✓ How is Arcio managing the shortage of H1B visas?

✓ Based on my background and experience, what do you think would be the greatest challenges for me in this position?

✓ How and when should I follow up with you?

Thank you for your time and consideration.

An Example of a Senior-Level Interview Presentation

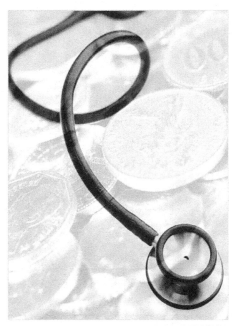

Accelerating **Eastern Medical Center's**
Success in the Marketplace

Stephen James

Leadership
Communication
Strategic Vision
Service Development

Eastern Medical Center

610-787-1590
sjames@optonline.net

Chief Executive Officer Critical Position Requirements

❑ Creating, articulating, and executing the organization's strategic vision

❑ Improving and maintaining strong medical staff relationships

❑ Developing strong community relationships

❑ Governing body relationships

❑ Ensuring financial viability by increasing services, managing revenue, and controlling costs

❑ Taking primary responsibility for higher levels of excellence in patient care, customer service, and employee relations

❑ Excellent references

Stephen James
Leadership, Communication, Strategic Vision, Service Development

Eastern Medical Center

I have a strong match with the position requirements

☑ Creating, articulating, and executing the organization's strategic vision
- Annual management plan and progress report
- Strategic plan for Western Medical Center
- Medical staff development plan (WMC)
- Facility master plan

☑ Improving and maintaining strong medical staff relationships
- Improved physician relationships through visibility, accessibility, and open dialogue
- Development of inpatient medicine program
- Establishment of outpatient care clinic
- Recruitment

Stephen James
Leadership, Communication, Strategic Vision, Service Development

Eastern Medical Center

I have a strong match with the position requirements

☑ Developing strong community relationships

- Community Development Foundation
- Relationship with county, state, and federal leadership (Rural Development Bond)
- Disaster preparedness (Katrina Response)
- Creating and promoting image of the hospital in the community

☑ Governing body relationships

- Improving use of time
- Board meeting efficiency (action summary)
- Education

Stephen James
Leadership, Communication, Strategic Vision, Service Development

Eastern Medical Center

I have a strong match with the position requirements

☑ Ensuring financial viability by increasing services, managing revenue, and controlling costs

- Increased therapy revenue by 225%
- Increased non-surgical outpatient volume by 64% and surgical volume by 37%
- Restructured case-management program
- Eliminated unprofitable services

☑ Taking primary responsibility for higher levels of excellence in patient care, customer service, and employee relations

- Quality council
- Core measure results and patient safety programs
- Chaplaincy program
- Employee meetings and recognition programs

Stephen James
Leadership, Communication, Strategic Vision, Service Development

Eastern Medical Center

I have a strong match with the position requirements

☑ Excellent references

- Jonas Jones, Chairman, Western Hospital Board of Trustees
- Bob Goberts, CEO, Mountain Health System
- Jacqueline Smith, CEO, Riverview Medical Center
- Dale Brady, MD, Western Medical Center, Active Staff Physician & Board Member
- William Brick, SVP Human Resources, Riverview Medical Center

I bring important additional experience to the position

✓ Cost control

✓ Identification and development of new programs and services

✓ Real estate acquisition and joint venture

✓ Construction project design and management

✓ Strategic capital budget development

✓ New technology implementation

Examples of my outstanding career accomplishments

- ✓ Achieved financial viability to initiate $11.2 million expansion/renovation project

- ✓ Added 13 active staff physicians to Western Medical Center

- ✓ Increased funded depreciation by 526%

- ✓ Established successful ambulatory clinic

- ✓ Accomplished facilities improvement programs (aesthetics, lab, OR)

- ✓ Streamlined operations, achieving $1.5 million in annual savings

These personal traits help me succeed on the job

- ✓ Integrity

- ✓ Manage by walking the halls

- ✓ Passion for meeting community healthcare needs

- ✓ Strategic/big-picture thinker

- ✓ Build win-win solutions

- ✓ Excellent boardroom presence

- ✓ Ability to communicate/relate to all levels

My "strategic action plan" for providing value quickly

In the first 30 days

- ✓ Build rapport with medical staff

- ✓ Meet key community leaders

- ✓ Gain knowledge of market demographics, competitors & reimbursement environment

- ✓ Review financials, budget & productivity system

- ✓ Study strategic, medical staff development, and facility master plans

In the first 90 days

- ✓ Gain deeper understanding of services offered and community needs

- ✓ Assess marketing strategies

- ✓ Evaluate leadership team

- ✓ Familiarize myself with quality and customer service programs

- ✓ Maintain visibility and accessibility in facility and community

Eastern Medical Center

Hire me because...

I Have All the Requirements

- ✓ 20 years progressive healthcare leadership experience

- ✓ Proven ability to develop strong relationships with board, medical staff, and community leaders

- ✓ Proven success implementing revenue-generating services

- ✓ Experience creating and executing effective strategic plans

- ✓ A focus on quality and customer service

- ✓ Ability to promote hospital services in the community

Eastern Medical Center

Important closing questions

- ✓ How is EMC going to meet the new healthcare requirements?

- ✓ Based on the large number of new medical staff, what is the impact on HEDIS numbers?

- ✓ Given your aging infrastructure and the demand for the latest medical technology, how are you going to fund improvements?

- ✓ What is the relationship between EMC board, Mountain View, and BHC?

- ✓ Based on my background and experience, what do you think would be the greatest challenges for me in this position?

- ✓ How and when should I follow up with you?

Thank you for your time and consideration.

Eastern Medical Center

Appendix B - Networking Presentation Sample

The following is an example of networking presentation. Like the interview presentations, a real networking presentation has been used with the identifying information changed. Networking presentations have had a very positive impact on my client's ability to turn networking meetings into productive job-search, business-connection, and relationship-building meetings.

An Example of a Networking Presentation

Positions to Which I Can Bring Value

- ✓ VP Strategic Sourcing

- ✓ VP Provider Governance

- ✓ VP Enterprise Project Management Office

- ✓ VP Strategic Project Management

- ✓ VP Transformation

Emma Kane
Leader, Change Agent, Results Driver, Strategic Visionary

Areas of Expertise

- ❖ Strategic Sourcing / Outsourcing / Provider Governance

- ❖ Project Management / Enterprise Project Office

- ❖ Enterprise Transformation

- ❖ Strategic Planning

- ❖ Business Process Reengineering

- ❖ Operations Optimization

- ❖ Mentoring and Team Building

Emma Kane
Leader, Change Agent, Results Driver, Strategic Visionary

Examples of Career Accomplishments

- ❖ Reduced mortgage annual run rate costs by $60M.

- ❖ Expanded enterprise project office to $62M strategic initiatives, $43M products and services, $68M strategic sourcing and provider governance maximizing ROI.

- ❖ Contributed to 16% client revenue growth, acquiring more complex clients using metrics-based vendor governance program.

- ❖ Managed 38% more complex projects with 35% less staff yielding $457K annual savings.

- ❖ Reduced 5,600 client-specific processes to 75 core processes, resulting in a 23% quality improvement.

- ❖ Maintained 14 ISO quality certifications, obtained 5 additional ISO certifications, and penetrated country-specific markets with no additional staff.

Emma Kane
Leader, Change Agent, Results Driver, Strategic Visionary

These Personal Traits Help Me Succeed on the Job

- ❖ Integrity / trust

- ❖ Adaptability at speed of change

- ❖ Quick study

- ❖ Build and manage relationships up, down, and across

- ❖ Strategic / big-picture thinker

- ❖ Building win-win solutions

- ❖ Excellent boardroom presence

- ❖ Innovative problem solving

Emma Kane
Leader, Change Agent, Results Driver, Strategic Visionary

Ideal Job

❖ Work with technical, operational groups, and external partners to align strategy and implementation plans.

❖ Lead and build professional teams.

❖ Create a strategic vision for achieving corporate goals and inspiring teams to collaborate on execution for excellence.

❖ Convert overhead cost centers into strategic marketing advantage/profit centers.

❖ Earn trust as internal consultant to executive team to provide objective assessment of complex issues and to propose options and consequences.

Emma Kane
Leader, Change Agent, Results Driver, Strategic Visionary

Types of Companies I Am Seeking

❖ Midsize to large company
❖ Geographic – Southern NY, New Jersey, Philadelphia & suburbs
❖ Industries:
- Information technology
- Financial services
- Benefit administration
- Insurance
- Healthcare

❖ Companies with whom I would like to work

❖ ED Bank	AMI
❖ Virtual Health	Lincoln Mortgage
❖ Thrifty Bank	Instant Insurance

Emma Kane
Leader, Change Agent, Results Driver, Strategic Visionary

Why a Company Would Hire Me

I provide the following value:

❖ 20 years experience in project management, strategic sourcing, line management, and operations.

❖ Exceptional results in varying domestic/international business environments.

❖ Results-oriented people manager who delivers extraordinary outcomes.

❖ Broad perspective in running an enterprise project office.

❖ Anticipate and adapt at speed of change.

❖ Build trust as internal consultant to executive leadership.

❖ Manage people in a matrix organization and achieve significant project results.

Emma Kane
Leader, Change Agent, Results Driver, Strategic Visionary

Closing Questions

❖ Do you think you have a good feel for my skill sets and potential value to an organization?

❖ Do you know of any companies I may want to target?

❖ Are there other people you would suggest I speak with?

❖ Is there anything else you would want to know about me to feel comfortable referring me to a potential employer?

❖ How can I help you?

Thank you for the opportunity to meet with you.

Emma Kane
Leader, Change Agent, Results Driver, Strategic Visionary

Appendix C - Content Libraries

- Personal Brand Terms
- Personal Success Factors
- Strategic Action Plan

The following are lists of term and strategies you can use in your presentations. The terms include brand terms and personal success factors. The strategies are 30- and 60-day strategic action items. These are only a small representative sample of possible terms and strategies. Their goal is to simply get you thinking in the right direction. You'll find additional and more extensive libraries in the InterviewBest program – www.interviewbest.com.

Personal Brand Terms

Personality

Active	Dynamic
Adaptable	Energetic
Ambitious	Driven
Communicative	Enterprising
Courageous	Intuitive
Curiosity	Flexible
Dependable	Considerate
Diplomatic	Tenacious

Skills

Quality Assurance	Technical
Programmer	Strategist
Customer Service	Mergers and Acquisitions
Dealmaker	Sales
Facilitator	Turn Around Expert
Connector	Strategic
Planner	Transformational
Tactician	Negotiator

Experience

Credible	Road Warrior
Connected	Results

Distinguished	Trend-setting
Diversity	Well-respected
Entrepreneurial	Successful
Experienced	Top Performer
Innovation	Industry Expertise
Global/International	Thought Leader
Promoter	Subject Matter Expert

Personal Qualities

Accurate	Insightful
Achiever	Inspiring
Analytical	Integrity
Astute	Inventive
Authentic	Leader
Bottom-line driven	Learner
Charismatic	Mature
Client-centered	Motivator
Consistent	Open-minded
Contributor	Organized
Creative thinker	Original
Creator	Persistent
Cross-functional	Pioneering
Doer	Problem-solver
Focused	Productive
Forever curious	Resilient
Forward thinking	Resourceful
Future-oriented	Savvy
Good under pressure	Sophisticated
Hands-on	Visionary
Honesty	Vitality

Personal Success Factors

Interpersonal

Leadership

Help others see possibilities	Creating win-win situation
Helping people feel at ease	Developing rapport
Delegating with respect	Good communication skills
Diplomatic	Selling ideas or products
Motivate others	Judging, selecting and developing leaders
Exercising leadership	Polished
Providing support for others	Representing others
Asserting myself	Socially bold
An excellent boardroom presence	Listening
Servant Leadership	Credible

Team Member

Collaborating	Helpfulness
<u>Compassion</u>	Sharing credit
Cooperation	Helping people to align
Dependability	Conveying feelings
Working well with cultural diversity	Listening
<u>Cooperation</u>	Courteous
Being a good team member	Negotiating

Coaching Mentoring

Eagerness to teach others	Counseling
Curiosity	Asking important questions
Active listening	Promote learning

Respect for Others

Discretion	Reading social situations
Non-disclosing	Sensitivity to others
Perceiving other's feelings	Empathy

"Being" in Relationship to Others

Calm	Generosity
Communicative	Desire to "give back"
Connected	Loyalty
Easygoing	Positive energy that is contagious
Extroverted	Community orientation
Formal	Interest in others
Friendliness	Outgoing
Generosity	Supportive

Personal

Skills

Analytical	Methodical
Critical Thinker	Accurate
Entrepreneurial	Have good reading comprehension
Exacting in my work	Organized
Politically aware but not a political operator	Cultured
Able to work with little supervision	Intensely accurate
Take big picture outlook and approach	Service Oriented
Comfortable in unstructured environments	Good time management
Always prepared	Set highly focused personal priorities

Flexibility/Learning

Active Learner	Open to change
Adaptable	Risk taking
Committed to continuous personal improvement	Venturesome
Adventurous	Comfortable with ambiguity

Character Traits

Ambitious	Optimistic
Have a constant drive for improvement	Orderly
Driven	Passionate
Dynamic	Perseverance
Forceful	Persistent
Sense of urgency	Poised
Willing to work hard	Positive attitude
Active	Willingness to go the extra mile
Enterprising	Sensitive to what's possible

Experimental	Productive
Energetic	Resilient
Expressive	Resourceful
High self-esteem	Self-aware
Humorous	Self sufficient
Initiative	Self-confident
Intuitive	Spontaneous
Lively	Straightforward
Mature	Youthful

Moods

Calm	Emotionally stable
Easy going	Enthusiastic
Cheerful	Animated

Values

Ethical	Loyalty
Have high integrity	Tolerant
Honest	Spiritual
Genuine	Dependable
Conservative	Devoted
Conscientiousness	Rule-conscious
I take responsibility	Liberal

Information

Organizing

A broad lens	Gathering information
Acquiring and evaluating information accurately	Identifying problems
Analyzing	Identifying resources

Creating ideas

Defining needs

Developing evaluation strategies

Extracting important information

Forecasting and predicting skills

Imagining alternatives

Interpreting and communicating information clearly

Oral comprehension

Oral expression

Sequencing

Thinking Skills

Problem solving

Ability to think on my feet

Imaginative

Can handle multiple tasks simultaneously

Spend time reflecting on things

Innovative

Excellent ideas

Attention to details

Full of ideas

Creative thinking

Having a good imagination

Creativity

Arithmetical computation and mathematical reasoning

Paying attention to details.

Knowing how to learn

Interested in abstract ideas

A vivid imagination

Quick to understand things

Astute

Solving problems

Accuracy

Imagination

Inventive

Open-minded

Original

Precise

Visionary

Convincing

Forward thinking

Future-oriented

Initiating new ideas

Handling details

Coordinating tasks

Deductive Reasoning

Information Ordering

Mathematical Reasoning

Big picture Outlook and approach

Using logic and reasoning Promoting change

Making decisions

Reasoning

Seeing things in my mind's eye

Solving problems

The ability to reframe

See how the future unfolds from the present

Decision making with others

Managing conflict

Systems
Understanding systems

Improving and designing systems

Monitoring and correcting performance in systems

Organizing complex projects

Technology
Maintaining and troubleshooting technology

Applying technology to tasks

Selecting technology

Applying Agile methods

Strategic Action Plan

Business Related Goals

General Business Goals

Prepare personal positioning statement

Review schedule of upcoming important events

Identify short, mid, and long-term goals for position

Strategize a plan for success leveraging all my resources

Learn my role in contributing to the bottom line

Understand company benefits plan

Identify most important productivity challenge

Develop a productive routine

Listen 80% speak 20%

Learn what the company does

Develop a personal productivity routine

Hold orientation sessions

Set priorities

Identify productivity pressure points

Sales Position Goals

Review pipeline and recent proposals	Assemble database
Develop sales strategy and tools	ID future target accounts
Study success stories and buyer incentives	Review existing contracts
Define who the prospects	Gain understanding of existing CRM issues
Determine potential market size is.	Familiarize myself with existing client base
Strengthen nationwide field sales	Instill a sales culture
Learn the product starting at the manufacturing plant	Meet with key customers
Define sales rep expectations	Evaluate the value proposition

HR Position Goals

Learn existing policies and procedures	Establish "talent brand" to attract the best people
Review staffing	Evaluate turnover rates
Review administrative processes	Evaluate workforce size and requirements
Review policies and procedures manuals	Identify pivotal workers
Review recruitment and retention procedures	Review incentive plans
Identify acceptable behaviors	Review attrition rates
Establish talent management processes	Evaluate human-capital-management technologies
Review position descriptions	Evaluate work-force planning tools

General Management Position Goals

Review budgets	Review administrative processes
Learn current goals for further improvement of department/company success	Develop corporate communications program
Learn about potential obstacles, issues and considerations	Develop Daily "Flash Report"
Establish success metrics	Learn the product starting at the manufacturing plant
Negotiate business partnerships	Establish short term growth plans

Schedule meetings with key decision makers

Initiate market analysis

Establish financial objectives

Build internal credibility

Understand costs

Communicate expectations to management staff

Read recent annual report in entirety

Review in-house talent

Marketing Position Goals

Initiate corporate identity program

Initiate advertising agency review

Read competitor's annual report

Establish a market research program

Review marketing plan

Position marketing as a value added service

Initiate brand review

Identify critical industry trends

Additional Roles

People Related Goals

Meet internal players at {Company}

Circulate letter of introduction

Brainstorm with other successful {Company} sales execs

Meet department heads

Visit existing clients and develop rapport

Establish positive working relationship

Meet and build relationships with members of the team, other departments, customers and key Company personnel.

Learn co-workers styles

Technical Related Goals

Gain Product Knowledge

Introduce improved risk and control methodologies

Learn capabilities of the department & Company

Establish operational controls

Define applications and have customer strategy sessions

Learn the product starting at the manufacturing plant

Learn existing technology systems

Become fully computer literate in company programs

Training Related Goals

Complete necessary training and become familiar with policies and procedures.

Become fully computer literate in company programs

Target areas for improvement and expanded use of training.

Enroll in certificate program

Learn where the product fits with other company products/competition

Complete licensure in…

Learn the product starting at the manufacturing plant

Complete discrimination training

Appendix D - Interview Presentation Worksheet

Use the following worksheet to develop a well-structured interview presentation. Each page represents a section of the presentation as described in Chapter 15. Once you have completed the worksheet, you can use a presentation program listed in Chapter 15 to produce your presentation.

Note: Each item in your presentation represents a speaking point and is not meant to convey an entire thought. Limiting each item to no more than 170 characters will ensure the proper length as well as guarantee you will not lose the interviewer as they read your presentation rather than listen to you.

Note: Use the items in Appendix C "Content Libraries" to fill in content in the worksheet.

You can access this worksheet in an interactive format online at www.interviewbest.com

Cover Page

Your Contact Information

Name: _____

Phone: _____

Email: _____

Company Name

_____

Tagline

This goes at the top of the front page. Tagline examples include:

*Partnering with [Company Name] for Success

*Accelerating [Company Name's] Success in the Marketplace

*Providing [Company Name] with Important Services

_____

Personal Brand Terms

> "Who you are speaks so loudly, I can't hear a word you're saying."
>
> —Ralph Waldo Emerson

The goal of the personal brand words is to communicate your personal brand to a prospective employer. Personal brand words identify the qualities or characteristics that make you distinctive and represent the values, ideas, skills, and personality you want the interviewer(s) to associate with you. Your personal brand words are powerful ideas that support your candidacy for the position.

Answer the following questions to help identify your personal brand:

*Following your interview, if the interviewer(s) were to be asked what they think of you, what would you want them to say?

*What do you do that adds remarkable and distinctive value to an organization?

*What do you do that you are most proud of?

*What do you want to be known for?

*If someone interviewed people who know you, what would they say your gifts are?

*If people around you heard that you had accomplished something of value, what would they guess that would be?

*Think of a time when you felt you were contributing to others in a satisfying way—what were you doing?

*When you felt that you were most in tune with your gifts and talents, what were you doing?

*What do you consider to be your best contributions to others?

*When people gossip about you, what do they say are your talents?

*If you were to create an advertisement for yourself, what would your features and benefits be?

 See the Personal Brand Terms section later in this appendix

1) Personal Brand Terms1) _____

2) _____

3) _____

4) _____

Interview Presentation: Position Requirements/Match with Requirements

Position requirements are the critical elements of the job that you must match to be considered for the position. The first part of the interview presentation lists the requirements, and the second part specifies how your background, skills, experiences, knowledge, and education match the requirements.

The more defined and accurate the critical job requirements, the more targeted and accurate your interview presentation will be. It is important to ask specific and detailed questions about the critical job requirements. These questions can be asked during a phone screening interview, by contacting the hiring manager, or during a first interview.

Position Qualifications Questions

*What are three or four must-have qualifications for a person to be selected for this position?

*In addition to the must-haves for this position, what would be some nice-to-have qualifications?

*What criteria will you use to make your hiring decision?

*What personal qualities will it take to get this job done?

*What skill sets are required to be successful in this position?

*What are the most important personal characteristics for a person in this position?

Position Task Questions

*What are the major responsibilities of this position?

*What is the highest priority for the person in this position?

*What are the important issues that need to be addressed immediately?

*What areas need the immediate attention of the person you hire?

*What does a typical day look like for a person in this position?

*What made the last person in this position successful?

*What were the major challenges for the last person in this position?

*What kind of planning and organizing does the job entail?

*What do you consider the greatest overall challenge(s) of this position?

*Could you tell me about the way the job was performed in the past? And what improvements you'd like to see happen?

*What are the biggest obstacles to performing this position well?

*What would represent success for a person in this position in six months? In 12 months?

*What are the major challenges this position will present over the next six months?

*Do you foresee any major changes in this position over the next six months? The next 12 months?

*What are the challenges I would face in this position over the next three months?

*What is the first assignment you intend to give the person you hire?

*What are the three accomplishments that I will need to have "checked off" at three, six, and twelve months from starting this role? How do these support the department, division, and corporate strategic objectives? What resources are already allocated to accomplish these?

*What are the two or three things I would need to do to make sure the major goals of the job were accomplished?

Organizational Questions

*To whom does this position report?

*Tell me about some of the people this position interacts with on a regular basis.

*Is this a new position? If it is new, why are you adding it at this time?

*What types of people tend to excel in this company?

You can find answers to these questions from the following sources:

*Position advertisement

*Information on the company's website

*An initial screening interview (typically with a recruiter from human resources or a third party)

*First round of interviews

*A pre-interview conversation with the hiring manager

*Current or former employees of the company

*Hiring managers in similar positions at other companies

Position Title

_____

Position Requirement #1

_____

_____

Your Match with Requirement #1

Match #1

_____

_____

_____

Match #2

_____

_____

_____

Match #3

_____

_____

_____

Position Requirement #2

_____

_____

Your Match with Requirement #2

Match #1

_____

_____

_____

Match #2

_____

_____

Match #3

_____

_____

_____

Position Requirement #3

_____

_____

Your Match with Requirement #3

Match #1

_____

_____

_____

Match #2

_____

_____

_____

Match #3

_____

_____

_____

Position Requirement #4

_____

_____

Your Match with Requirement #4

Match #1

_____

_____

_____

Match #2

_____

_____

_____

Match #3

_____

_____

_____

Position Requirement #5

_____

_____

Your Match with Requirement #5

Match #1

_____

_____

_____

Match #2

_____

_____

_____

Match #3

_____

_____

_____

Position Requirement #6

_____

_____

Your Match with Requirement #6

Match #1

_____

_____

_____

Match #2

_____

_____

_____

Match #3

_____

_____

_____

Excellent References

_____

_____

_____

_____

_____

Interview Presentation Section 4: Additional Areas of Expertise

This page lists the additional areas of expertise you will bring to the job that are beyond the basic job requirements. The statement this page makes is:

> "In the first section of my presentation, I communicated how I match the basic job requirements. These additional areas of expertise are other skills and experiences I bring to the position that will contribute to my performance and differentiate me from other candidates."

These areas of expertise may differentiate you from other candidates. They might include knowledge of computer programs, special sales training, fundraising background, organizational expertise, and so on.

When choosing additional areas of expertise, consider these questions:

*How would this additional area of expertise relate to your performance on the job?

*How would you see using this additional area of expertise on the job?

*How do you think this additional area of expertise differentiates you from other candidates?

*How did you develop this additional area of expertise?

*Do you have licensure or certification in this additional area of expertise?

.... Additional Areas of Expertise

1) _____

2) _____

3) _____

4) _____

5) _____

6) _____

7) _____

Interview Presentation Section 5: Outstanding Accomplishments

Your career and life are filled with accomplishments—times when you went above and beyond the scope of your job responsibilities or your own expectations of yourself (on the job or off the job). Accomplishment stories state very specifically what positive things you have done for your previous or current employer and in your personal life, and therefore they clearly indicate what you will be able to achieve for your new employer!

Accomplishments Memory Jogger

Use the following list of situations to remind yourself of your accomplishments. Remember, your accomplishments can be either work-related or non-work-related. In addition to work situations, think about volunteer work, work for a religious organization, family activities, and so on.

*Accomplished more with the same/fewer resources? (How? Results?)

*Accomplished something for the first time? (What? Results?)

*Been promoted or upgraded? (When? Why important?)

*Contribution to a charity or civic group? (What did you contribute, and what was the value?)

*Developed or implemented new system or procedure? (What? Benefit to the organization?)

*Developed, created, designed, or invented something? (What? Why important?)

*Established safety record? (What? Result?)

*Identified problem(s) others did not see? (What? Results?)

*Increased production? (How? Results?)

*Increased sales? (How? By how much?)

*Made a task or a process more efficient? (How? Results?)

*Managed budget? (How much? Result?)

*Managed work group department? (Who? How many? Results?)

*Met company standards under unusual/difficult circumstances? (What? How?)

*Prepared original papers, reports, articles? (What? Why important?)

*Provided special customer service? (What? How?)

*Received recognition/special awards? (What? Why?)

*Reduced downtime? (How? How much? Result?)

*Repaired equipment? (Which? Result?)

*Responded in a crisis? (How? Result?)

*Saved the company money? (How? How much?)

*Solved difficult problems? (How? Results?)

*Supervised, managed, trained employees? (Where? How many? Results?)

For each accomplishment, think about:

*The situation

*Barriers/obstacles you were faced with

*Specific actions you took

*The results

*Skills you used

Accomplishment Stories

(Be specific and use numbers where appropriate)

Title (1): _____

Situation: _____

_____

Barriers: _____

_____

Actions: _____

_____

Results: _____

_____

Skills Used: _____

_____

Title (2): _____

Situation: _____

_____

Barriers: _____

_____

Actions: _____

_____

Results: _____

Skills Used: _____

_____

Title (3): _____

Situation: _____

_____

Barriers: _____

_____

Actions: _____

_____

Results: _____

_____

Skills Used: _____

_____

Title (4): _____

Situation: _____

_____

Barriers: _____

_____

Actions: _____

_____

Results: _____

_____

Skills Used: _____

_____

Title (5): _____

Situation: _____

_____

Barriers: _____

Actions: _____

_____

Results: _____

_____

Skills Used: _____

_____

Title (6): _____

Situation: _____

_____

Barriers: _____

_____

Actions: _____

_____

Results: _____

_____

Skills Used: _____

_____

Title (7): _____

Situation: _____

_____

Barriers: _____

_____

Actions: _____

_____

Results: _____

_____

Skills Used: _____

_____

In addition, consider the following:

*Were you recognized for this accomplishment? If so, how?

*How do you think this accomplishment relates to the requirements of this position?

*What company did you work for when you achieved this accomplishment, and what did the company do?

*How long ago did this accomplishment take place?

*What was the importance of this accomplishment to your company?

*Why were you were chosen for this project?

*What were the most critical decisions you made?

*What were the most important skills required for success?

*What were some of the mistakes you made? What would you do differently?

*How did this accomplishment influence you as a person?

*What were the greatest lessons learned from this accomplishment?

*What would you do differently if you could do it again?

*What was the most enjoyable aspect of this accomplishment?

*What were other people's responsibilities in this accomplishment?

*Can you identify an action or decision that was most critical to the success of this accomplishment?

Interview Presentation Section 6: Personal Success Factors

Organizations want honest, smart, friendly, motivated, and responsible employees. Personal success factors are personal characteristics that contribute to your success on the job. They are distinct from skills and knowledge that you have acquired and relate more to personality characteristics.

Select personal success factors that you think best represent those parts of your personality that contribute to you career success. Your choice of personal success factors is very revealing of what you believe to be the most important personal contributions you make to a job and what will make you successful in this position. Your choice of personal success factors will give the hiring manager a great deal of information about how you will fit into the organization's culture.

(See of the "Personal Success Factors" section later in this appendix.)

.... Personal Success Factors

1) _____

2) _____

3) _____

4) _____

5) _____

6) _____

7) _____

Interview Presentation Section 7: Strategic Action Plan

Your 30/60-day strategic action plan communicates to the hiring manager that you are proactive, action-oriented, and a self-starter. In addition, it communicates that you have thought about being in the position for which you are interviewing and have begun to establish success-oriented goals. These are all very powerful positive messages to a hiring manager.

As you think about goals for the position, use the following guidelines for establishing good goals. Your goals should be S.M.A.R.T. That is:

*<u>**Specific.**</u> Your goals should be easy to understand and precise. They should communicate exactly what you will do and how you will do it.

*<u>**Measurable.**</u> Lay out how your goal will be measured or recorded. It may include length of time to complete something or it might be a target numerical goal.

*<u>**Attainable.**</u> Can your goals be met in the first 30 or 60 days, or is initiation of the goals the best that can be expected? If it is starting a process, say so; if it is completing a process. say that as well.

*<u>**Relevant.**</u> Set appropriate goals that are specific and relevant to the position for which you are applying.

*<u>**Timely.**</u> When will the goal start and when will it end, and it is a realistic goal given the timeframe?

(See the "Strategic Action Plan" section later in this chapter.)

.... 30-Day Goals

1) _____

_____

2) _____

_____

3) _____

_____

4) _____

_____

5) _____

_____

6) _____

_____

7) _____

_____

.... 60-Day Goals

1) _____

_____

2) _____

_____

3) _____

_____

4) _____

_____

5) _____

_____

6) _____

_____

7) _____

_____

Consider the following questions:

*How did you decide on this goal?

*What do you think might be barriers to achieving this goal?

*Did you achieve this goal in a prior position? How and at what point in your employment?

*Of the goals listed, which do you think will be the most achievable?

*Of the goals listed, which do you think will be the most challenging?

*Specifically how will you achieve this goal?

*How will you measure success for this goal?

Interview Presentation Section 8: Why Hire Me?

This page contains information that you have already presented. It is an opportunity for you to restate the most important experiences, skills, or accomplishments that you think make you the best person for this position. It is a "why hire me" statement based on all the important material you have already shared. This page gives the hiring manager the opportunity to hear your strongest selling points. The hiring manager will also have an opportunity to observe you making a summary statement highlighting the key elements of a detailed presentation. This is a critical skill for most workers in our knowledge economy.

.... Hire Me Because…

1) _____

_____

2) _____

_____

3) _____

_____

4) _____

_____

5) _____

_____

6) _____

_____

7) _____

_____

Interview Presentation Section 9: Closing Questions

Asking good questions displays knowledge of the position, company, or industry. It also indicates having prepared for the interview and being motivated and interested in the job.

Use these questions as an opportunity to ask a question that displays your knowledge of the company and/or the industry. For example, "You just launched the new product_____; how do you see it complementing the other products in your product line?" or "You just acquired_____; how do you envision the merger taking place?" or "This position reports to the director of manufacturing, who is located overseas—how much access will I have to the director?"

.... Closing Questions

1) _____

_____

2) _____

_____

3) _____

_____

4) _____

_____

5) _____

_____

6) _____

_____

7) _____

_____

Suggested Standard Questions

These are questions that are important to ask in every interview.

Based on My Background and Experience, What Do You Think Would Be the Greatest Challenges for Me in This Position?

This is perhaps the all-time best interview question. It gives hiring managers an opportunity to express in a positive way any reservations or concerns they may have about you. Correspondingly, it gives you important information about how strong a candidate you are based on the magnitude of the challenge(s).

If an interviewer uses this question to express any hesitations or concerns she may have, you can react to the concern. For example, the hiring manager might say, "Your greatest challenge may be your lack of experience in…" or, "Your greatest challenge may be not having worked in this specific industry," or, "Your greatest challenge may be getting comfortable with our culture." After the hiring manager expresses a "challenge," you have an opportunity to respond to the challenge by offering additional information relative to it or by offering a strategy for overcoming the challenge. Your responses may eliminate or significantly reduce the hiring manager's concerns.

How and When Would You Like Me to Follow Up with You?

The answer will tell you exactly how to follow up. A good answer would be, "We are interviewing through the rest of the week, so give me a call early next week to follow up," or, "We are interviewing through the rest of the week, and we will contact you early next week to let you know our decision." Once the hiring manager tells you how to follow up, you will know exactly how and when to contact her or when you should expect to hear from her